Building Intelligent Apps with .NET and Azure AI Services

Start Your Journey in Building Intelligent Solutions

Ashirwad Satapathi

Apress®

Building Intelligent Apps with .NET and Azure AI Services: Start Your Journey in Building Intelligent Solutions

Ashirwad Satapathi
Gajapati, Odisha, India

ISBN-13 (pbk): 979-8-8688-0434-2   ISBN-13 (electronic): 979-8-8688-0435-9
https://doi.org/10.1007/979-8-8688-0435-9

Copyright © 2024 by Ashirwad Satapathi

This work is subject to copyright. All rights are reserved by the Publisher, whether the whole or part of the material is concerned, specifically the rights of translation, reprinting, reuse of illustrations, recitation, broadcasting, reproduction on microfilms or in any other physical way, and transmission or information storage and retrieval, electronic adaptation, computer software, or by similar or dissimilar methodology now known or hereafter developed.

Trademarked names, logos, and images may appear in this book. Rather than use a trademark symbol with every occurrence of a trademarked name, logo, or image we use the names, logos, and images only in an editorial fashion and to the benefit of the trademark owner, with no intention of infringement of the trademark.

The use in this publication of trade names, trademarks, service marks, and similar terms, even if they are not identified as such, is not to be taken as an expression of opinion as to whether or not they are subject to proprietary rights.

While the advice and information in this book are believed to be true and accurate at the date of publication, neither the authors nor the editors nor the publisher can accept any legal responsibility for any errors or omissions that may be made. The publisher makes no warranty, express or implied, with respect to the material contained herein.

> Managing Director, Apress Media LLC: Welmoed Spahr
> Acquisitions Editor: Smriti Srivastava
> Development Editor: Laura Berendson
> Editorial Assistant: Kripa Joseph

Cover designed by eStudioCalamar
Cover image designed by Freepik (www.freepik.com)

Distributed to the book trade worldwide by Springer Science+Business Media New York, 1 New York Plaza, Suite 4600, New York, NY 10004-1562, USA. Phone 1-800-SPRINGER, fax (201) 348-4505, e-mail orders-ny@springer-sbm.com, or visit www.springeronline.com. Apress Media, LLC is a California LLC and the sole member (owner) is Springer Science + Business Media Finance Inc (SSBM Finance Inc). SSBM Finance Inc is a **Delaware** corporation.

For information on translations, please e-mail booktranslations@springernature.com; for reprint, paperback, or audio rights, please e-mail bookpermissions@springernature.com.

Apress titles may be purchased in bulk for academic, corporate, or promotional use. eBook versions and licenses are also available for most titles. For more information, reference our Print and eBook Bulk Sales web page at http://www.apress.com/bulk-sales.

Any source code or other supplementary material referenced by the author in this book is available to readers on GitHub. For more detailed information, please visit https://www.apress.com/gp/services/source-code.

If disposing of this product, please recycle the paper

This book is dedicated to my father, Mr. Upendra Satapathi, and mother, Mrs. Sabita Panigrahi, for supporting me through each and every phase of my life.

Table of Contents

About the Author ix

About the Technical Reviewer xi

Chapter 1: Introduction 1
    Structure 1
    Objectives 2
    What Is Artificial Intelligence? 2
    Introduction to Azure AI Services 3
    A Quick Tour of Azure AI Services 4
        Azure AI Search 4
        Azure OpenAI 4
        Language 5
        Speech 5
        Translator 6
        Bot Service 6
        Content Safety 6
        Document Intelligence 7
        Immersive Reader 7
        Video Indexer 8
        Vision 8
        Custom Vision 8
        Face 9
    Summary 9

Table of Contents

Chapter 2: Build a Language-Based Document Classifier with Azure Functions 11

Structure 12

Objectives 12

Introduction to Azure AI Language Service 12

Problem Statement 14

Proposed Solution 14

Create an Azure AI Language Service 15

Create an Azure Storage Account 22

Create a Language-Based Document Classifier with Azure Functions ... 30

Test the Language-Based Document Classifier Function 38

Summary 42

Chapter 3: Build a Multi-language Text Translator App with Azure Functions 43

Structure 44

Objectives 44

Introduction to Azure AI Translator Service 44

Problem Statement 46

Proposed Solution 47

Create an Azure AI Translator Service 47

Create a Multi-language Text Translator App 53

Test the Multi-language Text Translator Function with Postman 64

Summary 65

Chapter 4: Build a Desktop App with .NET MAUI to Generate Texts from Audio Files 67

Structure 67

Objectives 68

Introduction to Azure AI Speech Service 68

Problem Statement 70

Proposed Solution 70

Create an Azure AI Speech Service 71

Create a Desktop App with .NET MAUI to Generate Texts from Audio Files	77
Test the .NET MAUI App	85
Summary	87

Chapter 5: Build a Desktop App with .NET MAUI to Extract Text from Images 89

Structure	89
Objectives	90
Introduction to Azure AI Vision Service	90
Problem Statement	92
Proposed Solution	92
Create an Azure AI Computer Vision Service	93
Create a Desktop App with .NET MAUI to Extract Text from Images	99
Test the .NET MAUI App	107
Summary	110

Chapter 6: Build a Web App to Extract Data from Invoices Using Azure AI Document Intelligence 111

Structure	111
Objectives	112
Introduction to Azure AI Document Intelligence Service	112
Problem Statement	114
Proposed Solution	114
Create an Azure AI Document Intelligence Service	115
Build a Web App to Extract Data from Receipts Using Azure AI Document Intelligence	120
Test the Web App	141
Summary	143

Chapter 7: Build a Content-Flagging App with Azure AI Content Safety 145

Structure	145
Objectives	146
Introduction to Azure AI Content Safety Service	146
Problem Statement	147

Proposed Solution	148
Create an Azure AI Content Safety Service	148
Build a Content-Flagging App with Azure AI Content Safety Service	155
Test the Content-Flagging App	166
Summary	167

Chapter 8: Build a Text Summarizer with Azure OpenAI 169

Structure	169
Objectives	170
Introduction to Azure OpenAI Service	170
Problem Statement	172
Proposed Solution	172
Create an Azure OpenAI Service	173
Build a Text Summarizer with Azure OpenAI	184
Test the Text Summarizer App	195
Summary	197

Index 199

About the Author

Ashirwad Satapathi works as a software engineer at Microsoft and has expertise in building scalable applications with .NET Core. He has a deep understanding of building full-stack applications using .NET and Azure PaaS and serverless offerings. He is also an active blogger in the C# developer community. He has been awarded the C# Corner Most Valuable Professional (MVP) in September 2020 and September 2021 for his remarkable contributions to the developer community.

Ashirwad is an active speaker and delivers sessions on Blazor and Microsoft Azure. He has spoken for multiple communities such as Microsoft Reactor Bangalore, UTF, KonfHub Tech Conferences, and ServerlessDays Amsterdam. He is also an active community organizer and member of Utkal Techies Forum (UTF), a developer community based out of Odisha, India, and helps organize events for the community. He is a member of the Outreach Committee of the .NET Foundation. In addition, he has started ServerlessDays Bhubaneswar and hosts virtual sessions to build awareness among the developer community in the region about serverless technologies and make them proficient enough to build highly scalable and efficient serverless applications.

About the Technical Reviewer

 **Viktoria** is an experienced team leader of blockchain projects. An expert in .NET and NestJS, she designs architecture and develops projects from scratch to finish. She has authored several articles and books as well as is a frequent speaker at online conferences.

CHAPTER 1

Introduction

With the rapid development in the technology world, AI has become an integral part of our lives. Starting from unlocking your smartphones with facial recognition to getting personalized product recommendations while shopping on ecommerce websites, the impact of AI can be felt everywhere. Nowadays, most of the applications have become AI powered in one way or the other. Instead of just being a good feature, it has become one of the core functionalities of modern apps to provide better user experience.

Building AI-powered intelligent applications comes with its own fair set of challenges. To add the AI capabilities, you require a team of AI researchers and domain experts to build AI models which can be leveraged by the application. Training and developing such models require a large amount of data and computational power. This requires up-front investments in setting up infrastructure and collection and preparation of data, which are both capital and time intensive.

A potential solution to overcome these hurdles is to leverage the AI models offered as cloud services by different cloud vendors. Azure AI Service is one such cloud service offered by Microsoft Azure. It enables organizations and developers to leverage prebuilt AI models created by a team of researchers at Microsoft to build intelligent solutions without worrying about the overhead of managing the underlying infrastructure.

The focus of this chapter will be to get a brief understanding about the various services which are part of the Azure AI Services. In the subsequent chapters, we will learn about ways to integrate these services in our applications to build intelligent solutions.

Structure

In this chapter, we will explore the following aspects of Azure:

- What is artificial intelligence?
- Introduction to Azure AI Services
- A Quick tour of Azure AI Services

CHAPTER 1   INTRODUCTION

Objectives

After studying this chapter, you should be able to

- Grasp the essentials of Azure AI Services
- Identify applicable scenarios for Azure AI Services

What Is Artificial Intelligence?

Artificial intelligence is a field of computer science which works toward building computational systems which can perform tasks that require human intelligence. The term AI was first coined by John McCarthy in 1956 during the Dartmouth summer research project. As an outcome of this project, AI came out as a field of study to do collaborative research aimed at building computational machines that can simulate human intelligence to solve complex problems.

Early progress in the field led to the birth of expert systems which focused on leveraging rules and symbols for knowledge and reasoning processing. With dwindling research funding and technological limitations, the field saw a period of stagnation during the 1970s and 1980s. This period is referred to as the AI winter. With the affordability of computational power and the advent of big data, the field has seen substantial growth over a period of time.

The field of AI encompasses various subfields like machine learning, natural language processing, computer vision, speech analysis, expert systems, reinforcement learning, and robotics. Often, these subfields overlap, and advancement in one greatly contributes to the progress of the other.

Today, AI has transformed from a futuristic concept to being an integral part of our day-to-day lives. It helps in performing various tasks ranging from predicting the weather forecast for a location to analyzing videos and generating insights. Some popular use cases of AI that are part of our daily lives are as follows:

1. Voice assistants are a common use case of AI. For example, using Siri on your iPhone to set a timer involves simply saying, "Hey Siri, set a timer for ten minutes." Siri understands your voice instructions and sets the timer accordingly.

2. Product recommendations in ecommerce are a prominent use case of AI. For example, after purchasing a book on Amazon, the platform suggests other books that you may like based on your purchase history and buying patterns of similar users.

3. Content moderation in social networking sites is a key use case of AI. Social media platforms like Facebook and Instagram utilize AI to identify and remove inappropriate content which in turn enhances user safety.

In this book, we will explore ways to add AI to our application by leveraging the power of Azure AI Services.

Introduction to Azure AI Services

The demand for building AI-powered solutions is at an all-time high. But creating AI models from scratch comes with its own set of challenges. Developing and optimizing AI models from scratch require deep technical and domain expertise in the field and a considerable amount of time and resources. This is a capital- and time-intensive process. For many developers, it was a big obstacle as learning and gaining AI had a steep learning curve which restricted their ability to integrate AI into their application. To address this issue, we can use services offered by third-party cloud vendors that enable developers to use their prebuilt AI models via REST API calls or through client libraries instead of building one from scratch. Azure AI Service is one such offering of Microsoft Azure which enables developers and organizations to add AI to their applications with ease.

Utilizing Azure AI Services enables the development of solutions characterized by reliability, strong security measures, high availability, and fault tolerance, enriched with intelligent functionalities spanning areas such as vision, speech, language understanding, and search. It comes with an easy-to-use UI interface, with readily accessible solutions combined with responsible AI principles, empowering organizations to overcome the challenges of integrating AI in their applications. Organizations, regardless of size, can utilize them to create intelligent, responsible, and market-ready applications, delivering not only business value but also addressing real-world challenges.

CHAPTER 1 INTRODUCTION

A Quick Tour of Azure AI Services

In this section, we are going to explore the suite of services available through Azure AI Services.

Azure AI Search

Azure AI Search, formerly known as Azure Cognitive Search, is a fully managed enterprise-grade, search-as-a-service offering by Microsoft Azure. With Azure AI Search, organizations and developers are empowered to build information retrieval systems which can find relevant data for queries from their data sources without going through the hassles of building a search engine of their own. Apart from supporting full text search, it is also able to find semantically similar information by performing vector search throughout the vector representations of your data.

Azure AI Search has various applications across industries like ecommerce and healthcare, to name a few. We leverage its power to build solutions for enterprise search, knowledge mining, or geospatial search. By integrating Azure AI Search, we reduce the time to market of our solutions and provide a rich search experience for our end users.

Azure OpenAI

Azure OpenAI is a managed service offered by Microsoft Azure which enables enterprises and developers to use the AI models offered by OpenAI. With Azure OpenAI, we can integrate various pretrained models like GPT 4, GPT 3.5, Embedding, and DALL-E in our applications with minimal effort. With GPT 4 and GPT 3.5 series of models, you can create a conversational experience like ChatGPT in your applications. Developers can also fine-tune the foundational models to train with their own data to retrieve answers based on their data. In the entire process, the data you use to train the models stays within the boundary of your tenant and is not used to train any of the foundational models.

Azure OpenAI has various applications and is one of the most popular cloud services in Microsoft Azure. With most of the models, we can integrate various capabilities into our application, such as text generation, summarization, and language translation, to name a few. With the DALL-E model, we can also generate visual content by providing prompts. Prompts are textual queries that we pass to the models as input. With models like GPT 4 with Vision, we can pass visual content, and it can generate answers for our prompts by analyzing the visual content. At the time of writing this book, GPT 4 with Vision was in public preview. We will explore more about Azure OpenAI in Chapter 8.

Language

The Azure AI Language service is an enterprise-grade managed cloud service offered by Microsoft Azure to process and gather insights from unstructured textual data. With the help of the Azure AI Language service, organizations and developers can enable natural language processing capabilities such as sentiment analysis, named entity recognition, personally identifiable information extraction, language detection, and text summarization in their applications. It also enables them to customize AI models to generate insights specific for our use cases. A potential use case for this could be a scenario where we want to categorize documents into user-defined categories.

One of the most common use cases of Azure AI Language that can be applied across industries is analyzing customer sentiments from the feedback received for the service or product offered by the companies. We are going to explore more about the Azure AI Language service in Chapters 2 and 3 where we build solutions to perform sentiment analysis and language detection.

Speech

The Azure AI Speech service is a fully managed cloud service offered by Microsoft Azure which enables developers to add speech capabilities to their applications. Speech to text, text to speech, speech translation, and speaker recognition are some of the key functionalities of the Speech service. At the time of writing this book, it can accurately analyze audios from 100 languages and generate their transcripts. With functionality like custom neural voice, you can train a custom model on your voice and generate audio in multiple languages.

The Azure AI Speech service can be leveraged for industry use cases such as caption generation, audio content creation, and adding voice capabilities to bots. A key use case for the Azure AI Speech service would be to build accessible solutions for individuals with visual or hearing impairments. With the help of the speech-to-text and text-to-speech capabilities, we can make our apps more accessible. In Chapter 4, we are going to explore ways to integrate the speech-to-text feature of the Speech service in our application.

Translator

The Azure AI Translator service is a fully managed cloud-based machine translation service of Microsoft Azure. With the Translator service, developers can easily integrate machine translation capabilities like text translation, transliteration, and language detection to their applications with minimal development efforts. We can also create custom models with the custom translator feature to build systems which can handle domain- or industry-specific terminologies.

The Azure AI Translator service has various use cases across industries. A potential use case can be content localization in ecommerce websites. With the help of the Translator service, we can translate product descriptions, reviews, and other information in the local language of the customers. In Chapter 3, we are going to explore ways to integrate the language translation feature of Translator services in our application.

Bot Service

Azure Bot Service provides a development platform to build, test, manage, and deploy chatbots to enable conversational experience for business. The platform comes up with tools like Bot Framework SDK and Bot Framework Composer. We can build, test, and maintain bots by leveraging these tools. Azure Bot Services enable developers and organizations to deploy their bots to multiple channels such as web apps, Microsoft Teams, Skype, or Slack. It easily integrates with other Azure AI Services. This enables us to build intelligent bots which can understand natural language, interpret speech, and address queries. Azure Bot Service provides metrics like latency and traffic to monitor the health of the bots.

Azure Bot Service enables organizations and developers to build chatbots which can cater to various use cases, including but not limited to bots which can automate internal processes like IT support or handle common scenarios like answering commonly asked customer queries.

Content Safety

The Azure AI Content Safety service is a fully managed cloud-based solution for content moderation. It can moderate text and image content to detect the presence of any harmful content. With the help of the Content Safety service, developers can build systems which can analyze user-generated content to detect the presence of potentially inappropriate or unsafe material. If detected, it provides the ability to filter them out. It classifies objectionable content into four main categories which are hate and fairness, sexual, violence, and self-harm with a severity score.

Content monitoring in social media platforms like Facebook and Twitter and educational platforms to prevent the spread of hate messages and inappropriate content is a potential use case of the Content Safety service. In Chapter 7, we are going to explore ways to integrate the Content Safety service in our solutions.

Document Intelligence

Azure AI Document Intelligence, formerly known as Form Recognizer, is a fully managed cloud service for text extraction from documents by using advanced machine learning algorithms. With the help of document intelligence, developers can build a document processing system which can process documents to extract data from documents like invoices, receipts, and forms irrespective of the layouts. It is capable of extracting printed as well as handwritten texts from documents. With the custom model features, we can train custom models on our documents to learn the structure of the document to extract data efficiently.

Invoice and claims processing systems are classic examples where we can leverage the power of document intelligence to process documents and extract key information. In Chapter 6, we are going to explore ways to integrate the Document Intelligence service in our solutions.

Immersive Reader

Azure AI Immersive Reader is an AI service of Microsoft Azure which is designed to enhance the reading experience for users with different abilities. With features like reading aloud, isolating content for improved readability, and translating content in real time, the Immersive Reader aims at making lives easier for individuals who are new to reading, people who are in the process of learning a new language, or people who are diagnosed with dyslexia. Developers can build accessible solutions by leveraging the Immersive Reader library.

CHAPTER 1   INTRODUCTION

Video Indexer

Azure AI Video Indexer is a cloud-based video analytics service of Microsoft Azure. Video Indexers leverage more than 30+ AI models to extract insights from videos. Developers can leverage the power of the Video Indexer service to build applications which can perform operations such as face detection and recognition, content creation, transcript generation, or textual logo detection over stored video files. One of the popular use cases of Video Indexers is to generate content like trailers and highlight reels from stored videos. It can also be used to build monitoring systems which can detect if a particular object or face was identified in a particular video.

Vision

The Azure AI Vision service is a cloud-based service provided by Microsoft Azure to perform image processing and analysis. It leverages advanced machine learning models to extract key insights from visual content. With the help of the Vision service, we can add a range of computer vision capabilities like image analysis, spatial analysis, Optical Character Recognition (OCR), and image classification in our application. The Vision service can understand and extract information from images in many different languages. It comes with a vision studio where you can explore the various features of the Vision service. Apart from that, we can leverage the client SDKs to interact with the AI models of the Vision service.

The Vision service has wide application across industries like healthcare, manufacturing, media, and retail. Facial detection and image captioning are some of the popular use cases of the Vision service. In Chapter 5, we are going to explore ways to integrate the text extraction feature of the Azure AI Vision service in our solutions.

Custom Vision

Azure Custom Vision is a cloud offering of Microsoft Azure which enables teams to build, train, test, and deploy their own custom image classification models. It provides an interactive UI interface to build and test our own custom vision models in the browser itself. We can leverage the prebuilt vision models to create our custom vision models. This feature is a lifesaver when we don't have a large corpus of labeled data to train our models. By leveraging the existing models, we can accelerate the training process of our custom models, resulting in shorter time to market.

Product recognition can be one of the many use cases of Azure Custom Vision. With the Custom Vision service, we can train prebuilt models with the labeled data of our products. This can enable teams in the retail industry to identify the product Stock-Keeping Units (SKUs) present on the shelf and get their counts. The possibilities are endless.

Face

The Azure AI Face service is a fully managed cloud service offered by Microsoft Azure which enables teams to build cloud-native solutions with facial recognition features. We can add capabilities like face verification for touchless access control and emotion detection in our application with the help of the Face service. It is also able to detect the gender and age of the person present in the image. A popular use case for the Face service is to perform liveness checks while performing authentication with facial recognition. With the liveness check features, we can validate if a user is actually present in front of the camera or someone is trying to impersonate the person's identity by using a picture or video of theirs. We use the REST APIs or client libraries of the Face service to integrate them in our application with minimal coding efforts.

Summary

Azure AI Service is one of the fastest-growing cloud services within the Microsoft Azure ecosystem. It enables enterprises and developers to build intelligent applications with a shorter time to market. With the help of Azure AI Services, we leverage prebuilt AI models offered by Microsoft Azure to solve complex problems which require applications to comprehend visual, audio, and textual context from structured or unstructured data. In this chapter, we gained a brief understanding about all the services falling under the umbrella of Azure AI Service. In the subsequent chapters, we are going to take a deep dive and learn ways to add cognitive capabilities to our applications by leveraging these services.

CHAPTER 2

Build a Language-Based Document Classifier with Azure Functions

Language serves as a crucial means of communication for individuals across the world to express their thoughts and enable information exchange. For applications to be truly intelligent, they must possess the ability to understand and comprehend human language. Much of the data generated over the past few decades have been in textual, audio, or video formats which are unstructured by nature. A lot of insights can be derived from these data. Natural language processing (NLP) is a subfield of AI which focuses on enabling computational systems to interpret data, extract insights, understand context, and generate content. With NLP, applications can perform various tasks ranging from sentiment analysis to machine translations.

Some of the popular industry use cases of NLP are Google Translate, ChatGPT, and Grammarly. Google Translate leverages the power of the NLP to translate texts from one language to another on a real-time basis. Grammarly uses NLP algorithms to analyze written text and provide recommendations to improve the textual content. ChatGPT leverages NLP-based large language models (LLMs) to understand, interpret, and generate human-like response for queries. The use cases are many but to build an NLP system from scratch require intensive investments on hiring domain experts and setting up the computational infrastructure to build, train, and deploy models. It can take years to design and build such systems. To overcome these challenges, we can leverage the powers of the Azure AI Language service. It is a specialized AI service offered by Microsoft Azure to build solutions which can understand and extract insights from textual data.

In this chapter, we are going to briefly discuss about the Azure AI Language service and its use cases and build a language-based document classifier by leveraging its client SDK.

Structure

In this chapter, we will explore the following aspects of Azure:

- Introduction to the Azure AI Language service
- Create your first Azure AI Language service in the Azure Portal
- Create a language-based document classifier

Objectives

After studying this chapter, you should be able to

- Grasp the essentials of the Azure AI Language service
- Add the capabilities of the Azure AI Language service to your applications

Introduction to Azure AI Language Service

In a world where millions of research papers, articles, and books are published every year, it is difficult to analyze and extract data out from them. This is an area where NLP systems have proven to be effective. By leveraging different kinds of NLP algorithms, we can parse through a large amount of textual data and extract meaningful insights from them. This can help us in taking data-backed decisions. Although there are well-established algorithms in the field of natural language processing, building them from scratch to solve industrial use cases is often time-consuming and resource intensive. This in turn increases the time to market for your solutions. An alternative and popular choice to integrate the NLP powers to your application can be to use prebuilt AI models offered by vendors as AI services. One such offering by Microsoft Azure is the Azure AI Language service.

The Azure AI Language service is a fully managed AI service of Microsoft Azure which enables developers to add NLP capabilities to their applications. It is a unified solution which combined the erstwhile Azure AI Services – Text Analytics, LUIS, and QnA Maker. The AI Language service provides an abstraction on top of prebuilt AI models by Microsoft which can analyze a large amount of textual data. With the help of this service, developers can build systems which can analyze a large amount of unstructured data and gain insights from them without worrying about gaining expertise in the field or about the underlying algorithms. It also provides the ability to create custom models which are trained on their own data.

Some of the key features of the Azure AI Language service are as follows:

1. **Named Entity Recognition** – With the named entity recognition (NER) features, you can build systems which can automatically identify entities such as people, organizations, locations, and dates from unstructured data. For example, you can use this feature to extract names of companies or of famous celebrities from articles or social media posts.

2. **PII and PHI Detection** – With this feature, you can build systems which can detect personally identifiable information (PII) and personal health information from text documents. Protecting sensitive data is crucial for organizations, and by leveraging this feature, you can build systems that can mask such information.

3. **Sentiment Analysis** – With this feature, you can build systems which can analyze the sentiment of a given text. This can be used by organizations to understand customer sentiments by analyzing customer reviews and feedback.

4. **Language Detection** – With this feature, you can build systems that can identify language in which a document is written in. In this chapter, we are going to explore the language detection feature by building a language-based document classifier.

5. **Text Summarization** – With this feature, you can build systems that can process large documents or texts and generate concise summaries from them.

6. **Key Phrase Extraction** – With this feature, you can extract key insights like most important phrases or key insights from a given textual content.

As we have explored what Azure AI Language service is and what its key features are, let's explore ways to integrate it in our solutions by building a language-based document classifier.

CHAPTER 2   BUILD A LANGUAGE-BASED DOCUMENT CLASSIFIER WITH AZURE FUNCTIONS

Problem Statement

Consider you are working at a startup which has a task of collecting people's views on various government schemes and social welfare programs. You have a fleet of employees who have been gathering information from people and are making reports on the same. Your team used to store all the reports in the Azure Blob Storage. Of late, you came to know that the reports are written in different languages. Now the problem is we cannot dump all the existing reports. That's too much data to miss out on. As a mitigation, your team has hired a few people to rewrite the reports in English. But prior to assigning the reports, we need to classify the reports in the language they are written in, which will help us assign the reports to the right resource to rewrite them. You are assigned with a task to build a proof of concept which can classify documents on the basis of the language they are written in.

Proposed Solution

After going through the requirement, you have broken down the problem into two tasks:

1. Identify the language a report is written in
2. Upload the report to the folder in which the language was written in

To solve both of these problems, you have decided to leverage the power to blob storage containers, Azure Functions, and the Azure AI Language service. Blob storage containers will be used to store the report post classifications; we will use a blob-triggered Azure Function to process the document and integrate the Azure AI Language service to detect the language in which the report is written in and upload it inside the folder in the blob container with the name depicting the language in which the report was written in.

Before we start building the blob-triggered Azure Function, we need a couple of things in place. The following are the prerequisites to start the development activities:

1. Create an Azure AI Language service
2. Create an Azure storage account with the required container

Once we have these two things in place, we can start building our solution using Visual Studio 2022. Let's get started.

Create an Azure AI Language Service

To create an Azure AI Language service, go to the Azure Portal and type Language in the search box. Click the **Language** in the search results as shown in Figure 2-1.

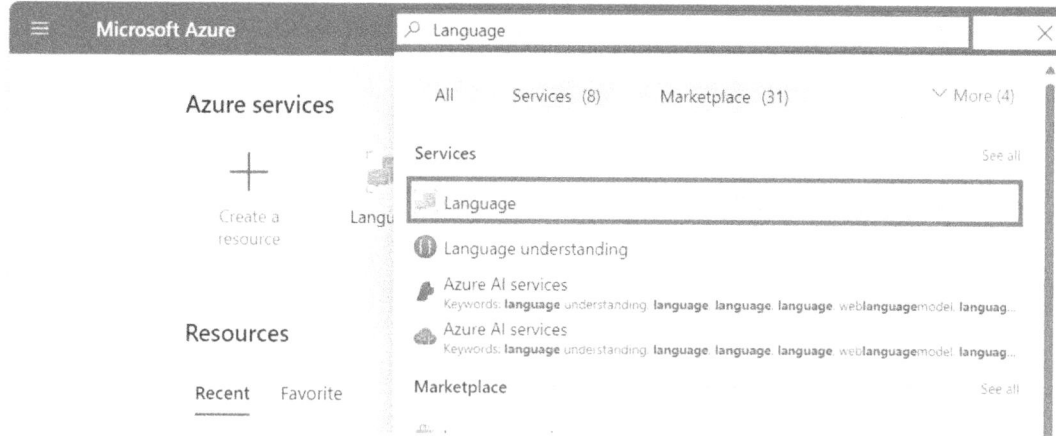

Figure 2-1. *Search for Language*

On the screen shown in Figure 2-2, you can view the list of Language services that you have provisioned. Click **Create** to provision our Language service in Azure.

CHAPTER 2 BUILD A LANGUAGE-BASED DOCUMENT CLASSIFIER WITH AZURE FUNCTIONS

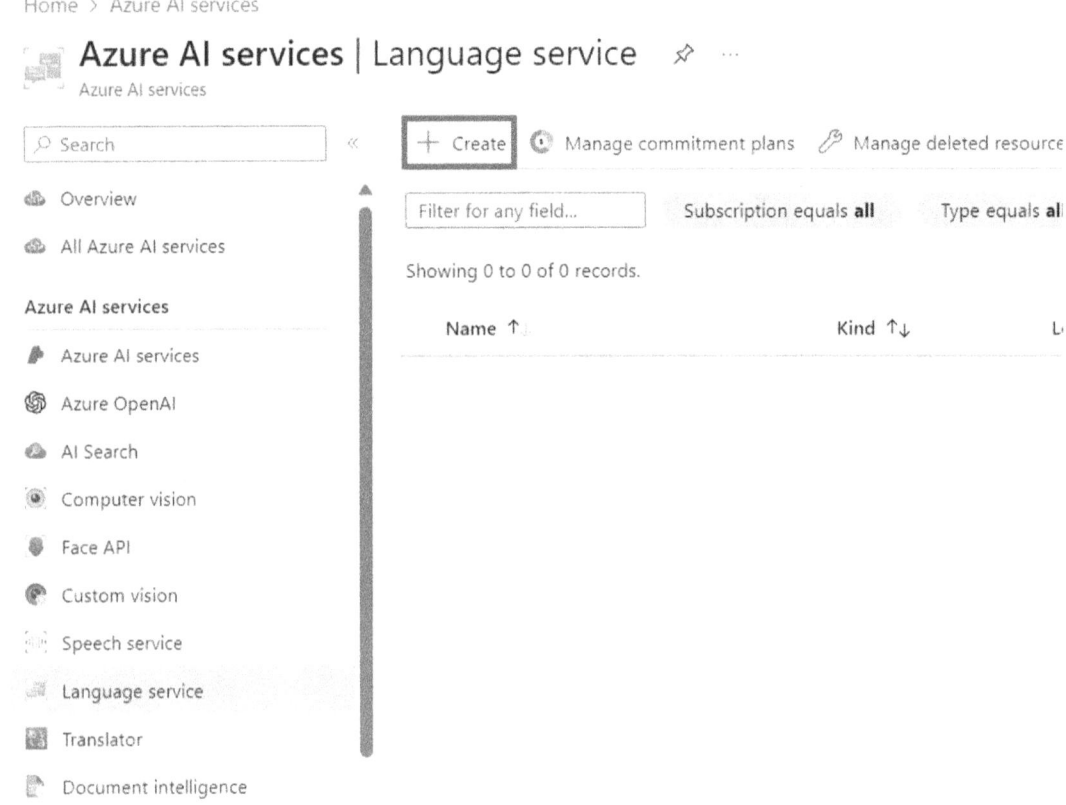

Figure 2-2. Click Create

For the purpose of this solution, we are going to opt for the default features. Let's click Continue to create your resource as shown in Figure 2-3.

CHAPTER 2   BUILD A LANGUAGE-BASED DOCUMENT CLASSIFIER WITH AZURE FUNCTIONS

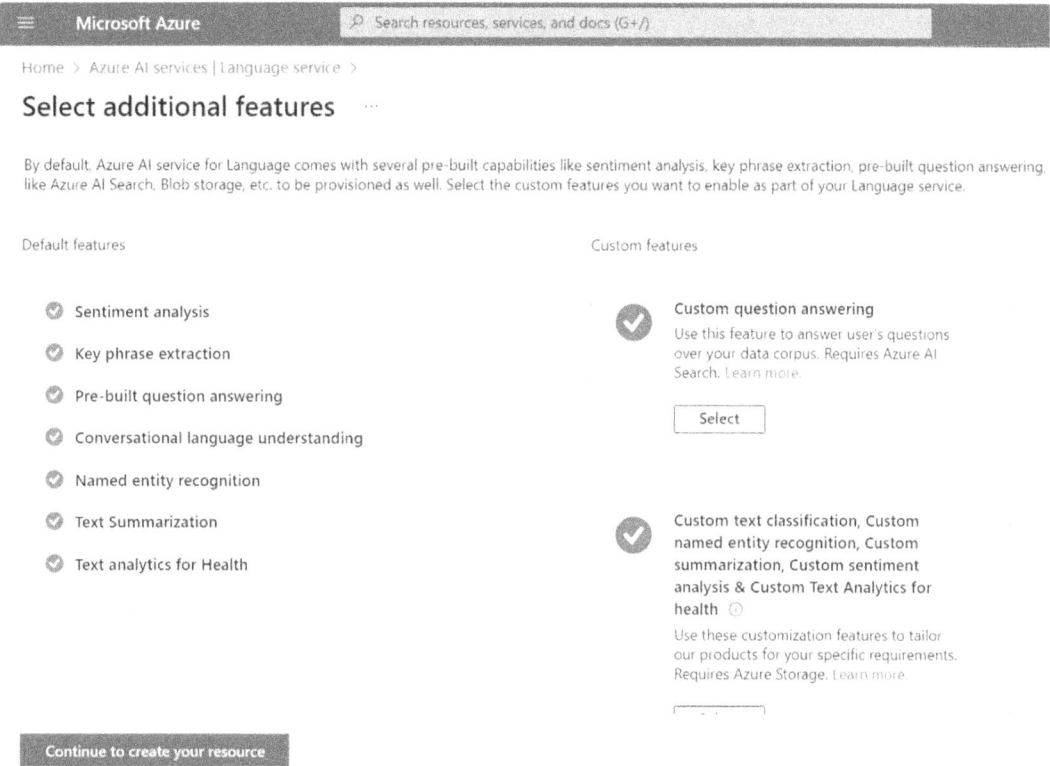

Figure 2-3. *Click Continue to create your resource*

Next, select your subscription and resource group from the drop-downs available on the screen as can be seen in Figure 2-4. If you don't have a resource group, you can create a new one on this screen. After that, select the region, provide the resource name, and select the pricing tier. The resource name needs to be a unique one. For the purpose of building this solution, we are going to the **Free F0** tier. This tier provides us with the capability to perform 5K transactions per 30 days, which should be enough to build and test our proof of concept (PoC). For workloads running in a production environment, it is advised to use higher tiers. Once you have entered the preceding details, you will have to check the tick box stating that you have reviewed and acknowledge the terms in the Responsible AI Notice. Once done, click **Review + create**.

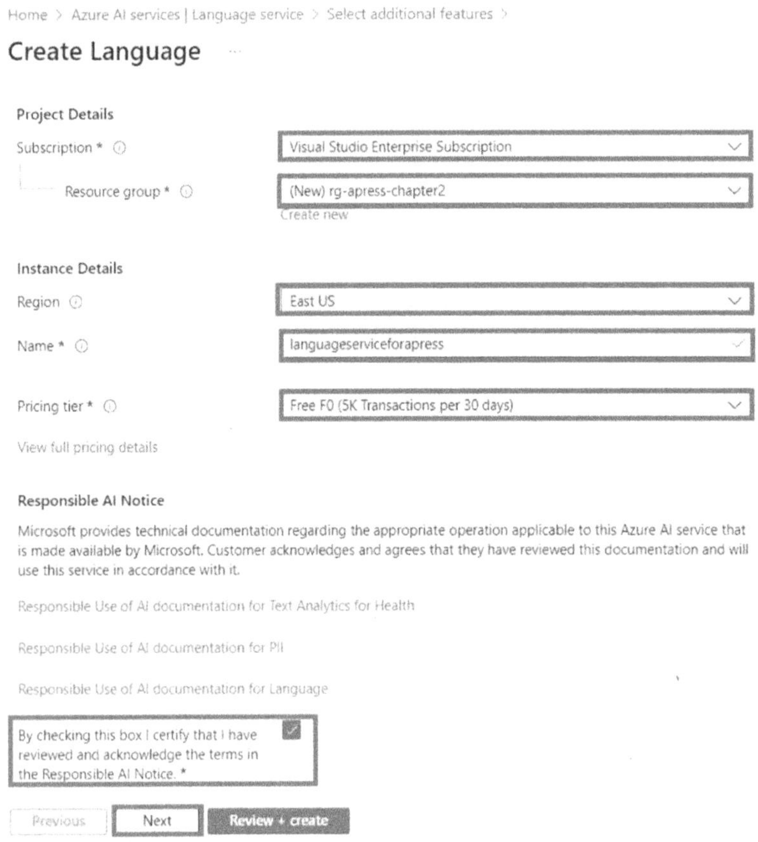

CHAPTER 2   BUILD A LANGUAGE-BASED DOCUMENT CLASSIFIER WITH AZURE FUNCTIONS

Figure 2-4.   Click Review + creategroup

Now you will see a summary of the configuration for the language resource that you had entered on the previous screen as shown in Figure 2-5. A validation check will be done on the configurations. Once the validation of the configuration is done, click **Create** to provision the resource. If you wanted to make any changes, you could click **Previous** and make the necessary changes for the resource.

CHAPTER 2 BUILD A LANGUAGE-BASED DOCUMENT CLASSIFIER WITH AZURE FUNCTIONS

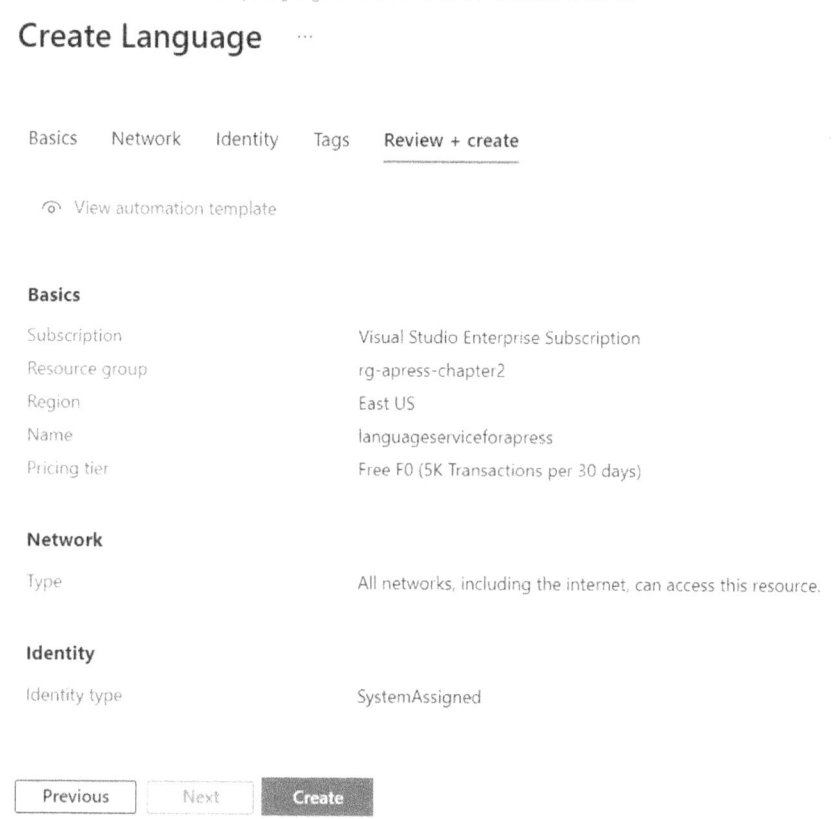

Figure 2-5. *Click Create*

Once the resource has been created successfully, you will see the message "Your deployment is complete," as shown in Figure 2-6. Once you see that message, click **Go to resource group** to view the newly provisioned language resource.

19

CHAPTER 2 BUILD A LANGUAGE-BASED DOCUMENT CLASSIFIER WITH AZURE FUNCTIONS

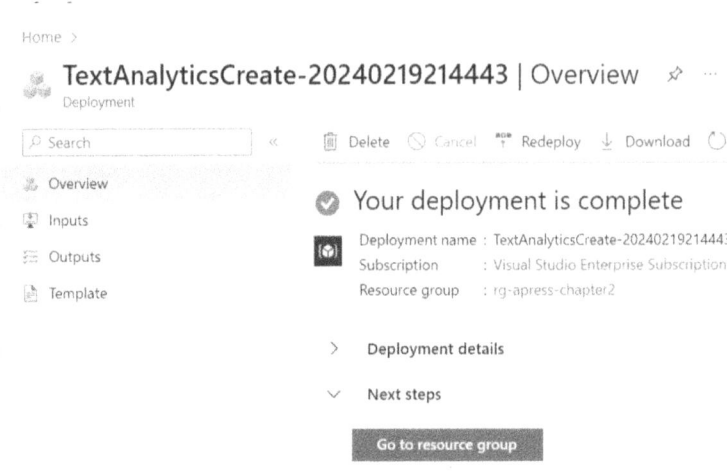

Figure 2-6. *Click Go to resource group*

Now that we have provisioned our AI Language service in the Azure Portal, we will need to fetch the access key and endpoint to interact with it from our solution. Access keys are just one way of authenticating our calls to the Language service. We can use other methods like Managed Identity–based authentication which is recommended for production workloads. For the purpose of our PoC, we are going to use key-based authentication.

To fetch the key and endpoint for our language, click Keys and Endpoint as shown in Figure 2-7.

CHAPTER 2   BUILD A LANGUAGE-BASED DOCUMENT CLASSIFIER WITH AZURE FUNCTIONS

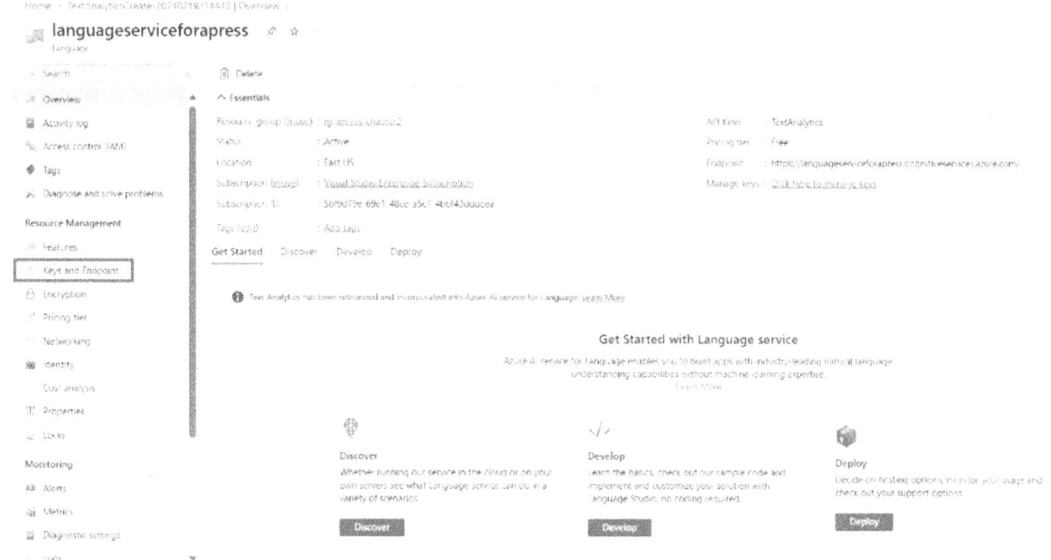

Figure 2-7. *Click Keys and Endpoint*

We will have to fetch either one of the primary or secondary key, the resource endpoint, and the region from the screen shown in Figure 2-8. We will use these values later in our application for authentication purposes.

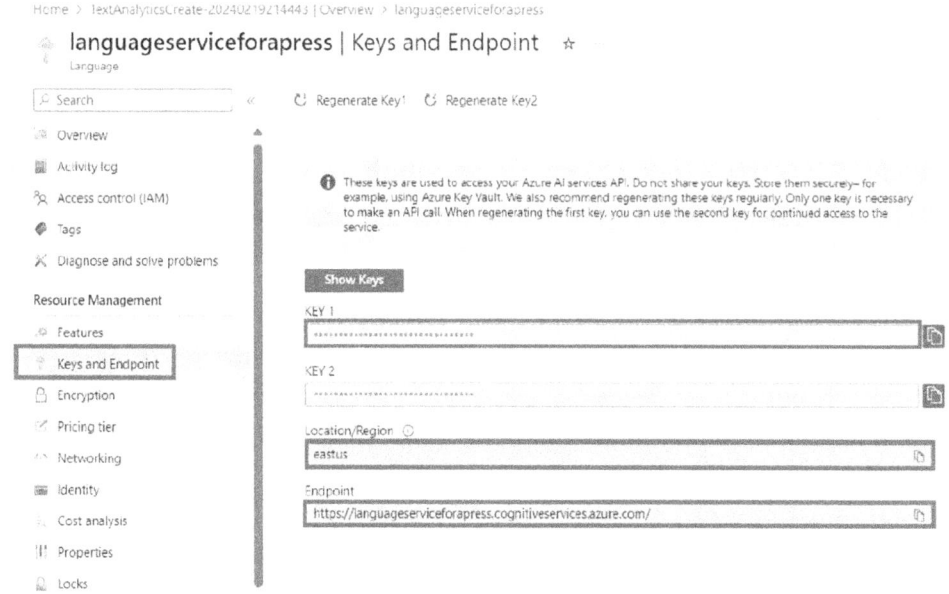

Figure 2-8. *Get the key, endpoint, and region*

CHAPTER 2 BUILD A LANGUAGE-BASED DOCUMENT CLASSIFIER WITH AZURE FUNCTIONS

Now that we have provisioned the language resource and have the required information to authenticate requests from our application to the Language service, we have completed one of the prerequisites. In the next section, we will provision a storage account.

Create an Azure Storage Account

To create blob containers, we will have to provision an Azure storage account. Let's go to the Azure Portal, type Storage accounts in the search box, and click **Storage accounts** from the search results as shown in Figure 2-9.

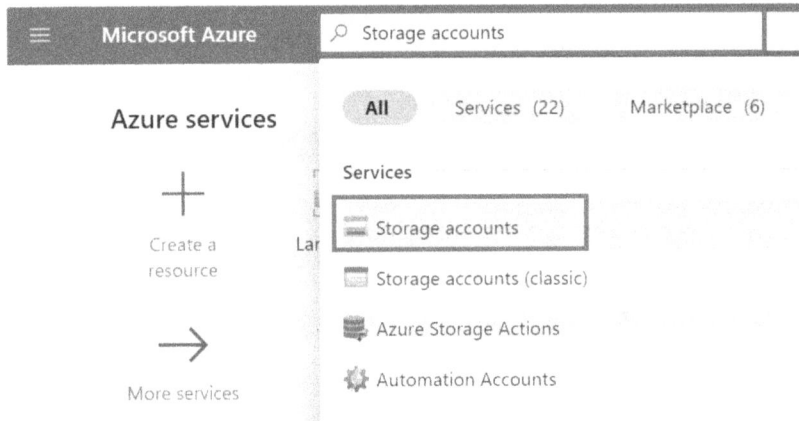

Figure 2-9. *Click Storage accounts*

On the screen shown in Figure 2-10, you can view the list of storage accounts that you have provisioned. Click **Create** to provision our storage account in Azure.

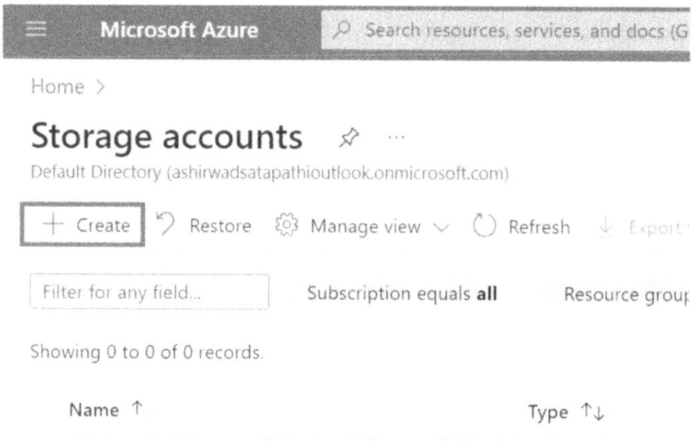

CHAPTER 2 BUILD A LANGUAGE-BASED DOCUMENT CLASSIFIER WITH AZURE FUNCTIONS

Figure 2-10. *Click Create*

Next, select your subscription and resource group from the drop-downs available on the screen as can be seen in Figure 2-11. If you don't have a resource group, you can create a new one on this screen. After that, select the region, provide the resource name, and select the performance and redundancy type. The resource name needs to be a unique one. For the purpose of building this solution, we are going to the **Standard** tier for performance and **GRS** for redundancy. For workloads running in the production environment, it is advised to use higher tiers. Once you have entered the preceding details, click **Review**.

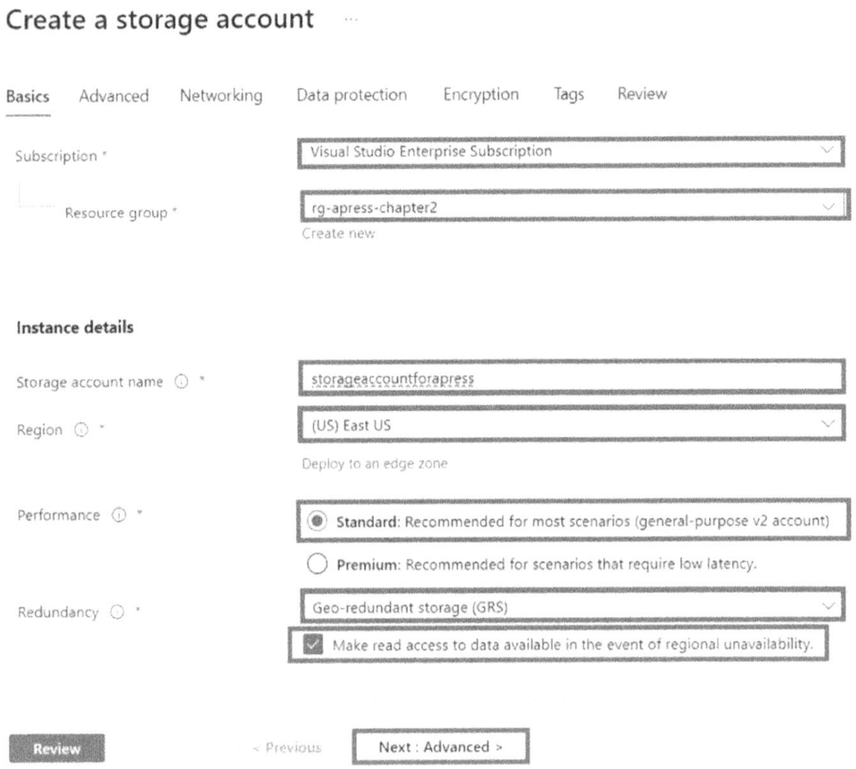

CHAPTER 2   BUILD A LANGUAGE-BASED DOCUMENT CLASSIFIER WITH AZURE FUNCTIONS

Figure 2-11. *Click Review*

Now you will see a summary of the configuration for the language resource that you had entered on the previous screen as shown in Figure 2-12. A validation check will be done on the configurations. Once the validation of the configuration is done, click **Create** to provision the resource. If you wanted to make any changes, you could click **Previous** and make the necessary changes for the resource.

CHAPTER 2 BUILD A LANGUAGE-BASED DOCUMENT CLASSIFIER WITH AZURE FUNCTIONS

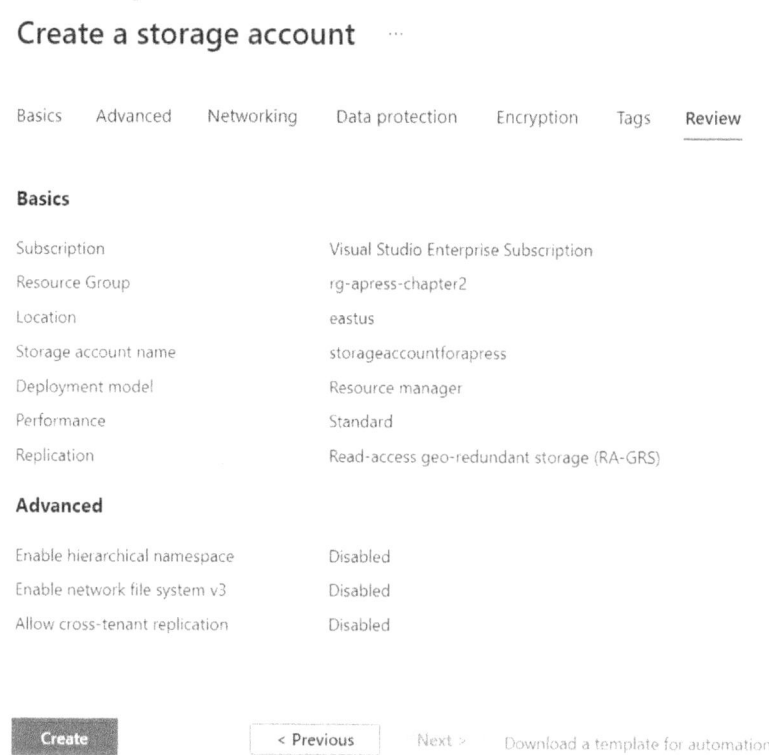

Figure 2-12. Click Create

Once the resource has been created successfully, you will see the message "Your deployment is complete," as shown in Figure 2-13. Once you see that message, click **Go to resource** to view the newly provisioned language resource.

CHAPTER 2 BUILD A LANGUAGE-BASED DOCUMENT CLASSIFIER WITH AZURE FUNCTIONS

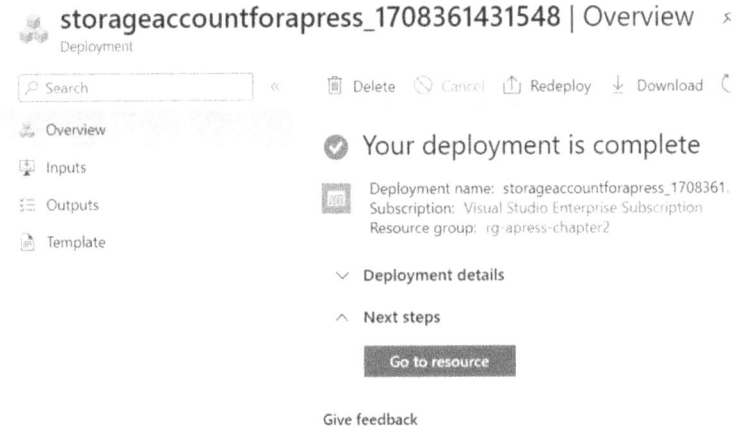

Figure 2-13. Click Go to resource

Now let's click the container section to create our first blob container as shown in Figure 2-14.

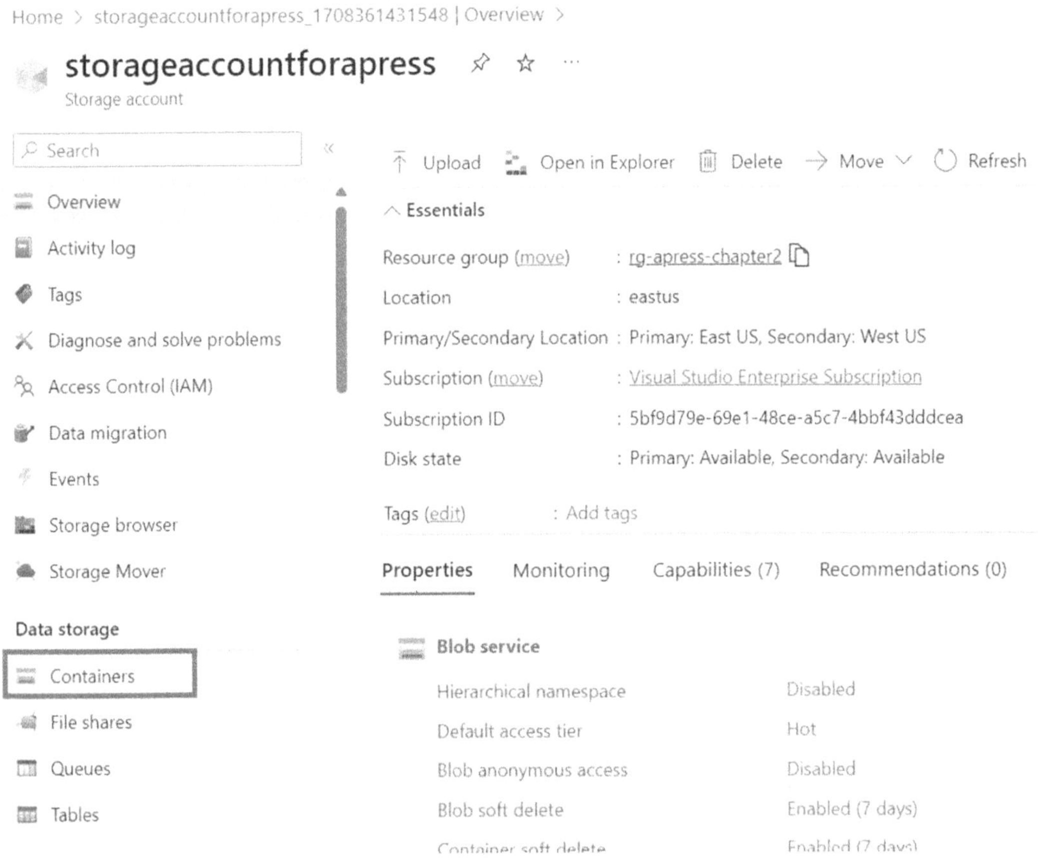

Figure 2-14. Click Containers

26

CHAPTER 2 BUILD A LANGUAGE-BASED DOCUMENT CLASSIFIER WITH AZURE FUNCTIONS

On the screen shown in Figure 2-15, we can view the list of containers that we have as part of the storage account. To create a new container, click **+ Container**.

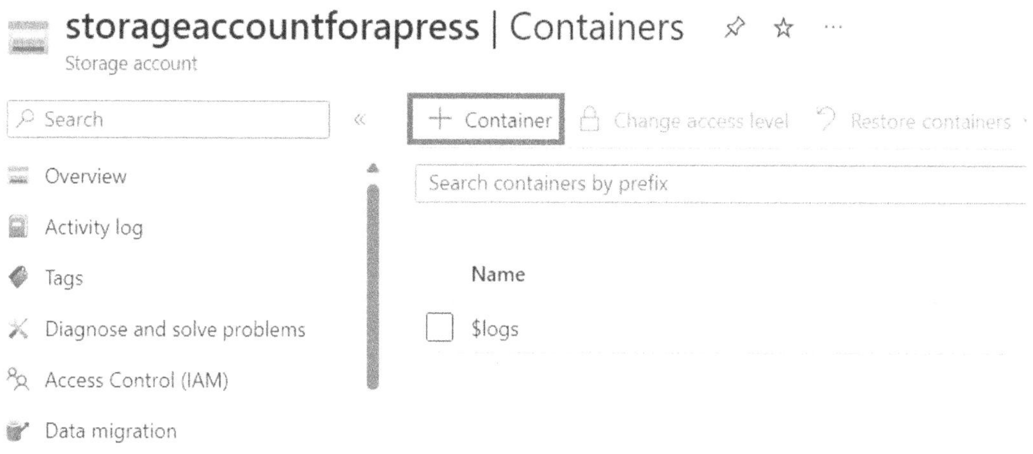

Figure 2-15. Click + Container

Now, we will see a pop-up to fill in the details of the container. Let's fill in the details as follows: container name as **source** and anonymous access level as **Private**. Once we filled in the details, we need to click **Create** to provision the container as shown in Figure 2-16.

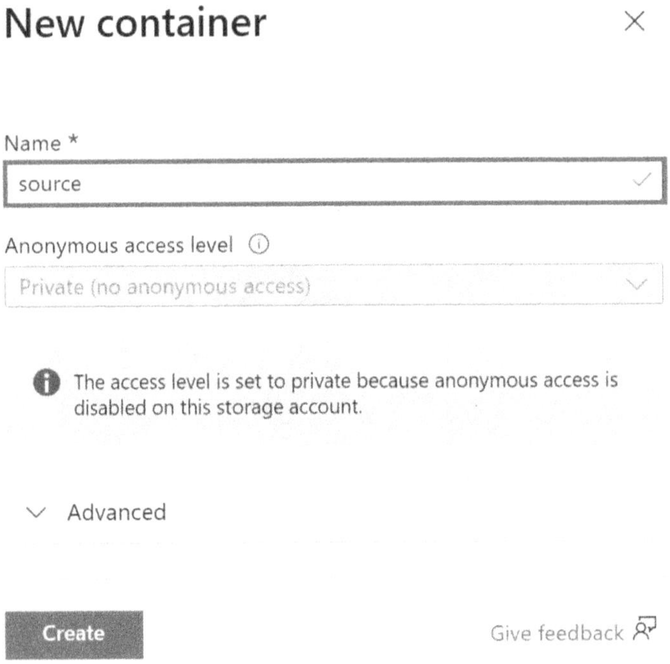

CHAPTER 2   BUILD A LANGUAGE-BASED DOCUMENT CLASSIFIER WITH AZURE FUNCTIONS

Figure 2-16. Click Create

For the purpose of our solution, we need to create one more container. Let's repeat the preceding process and create one more container called **Destination**. After both containers have been created, they should appear in the containers section, as shown in Figure 2-17.

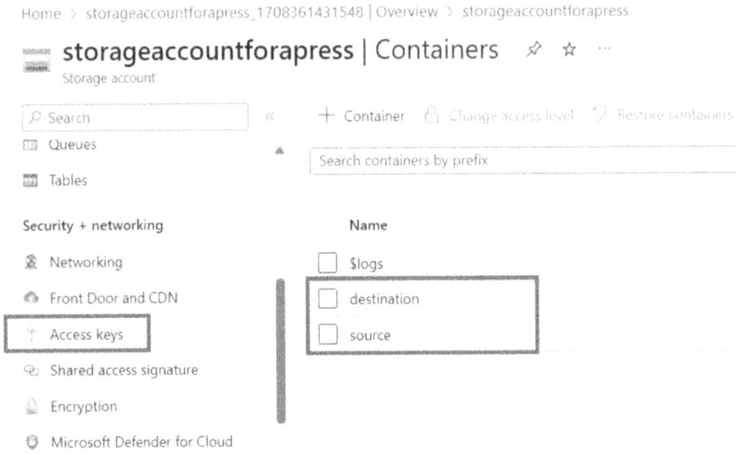

Figure 2-17. Two blob containers are created

CHAPTER 2 BUILD A LANGUAGE-BASED DOCUMENT CLASSIFIER WITH AZURE FUNCTIONS

Now that we have created the storage account and the two blob containers, the next step is to get the **connection string** of the storage account to authenticate requests to it from our application. To fetch the connection string, click **Access keys** as highlighted in Figure 2-18 and copy the connection string generated from key1 or key2.

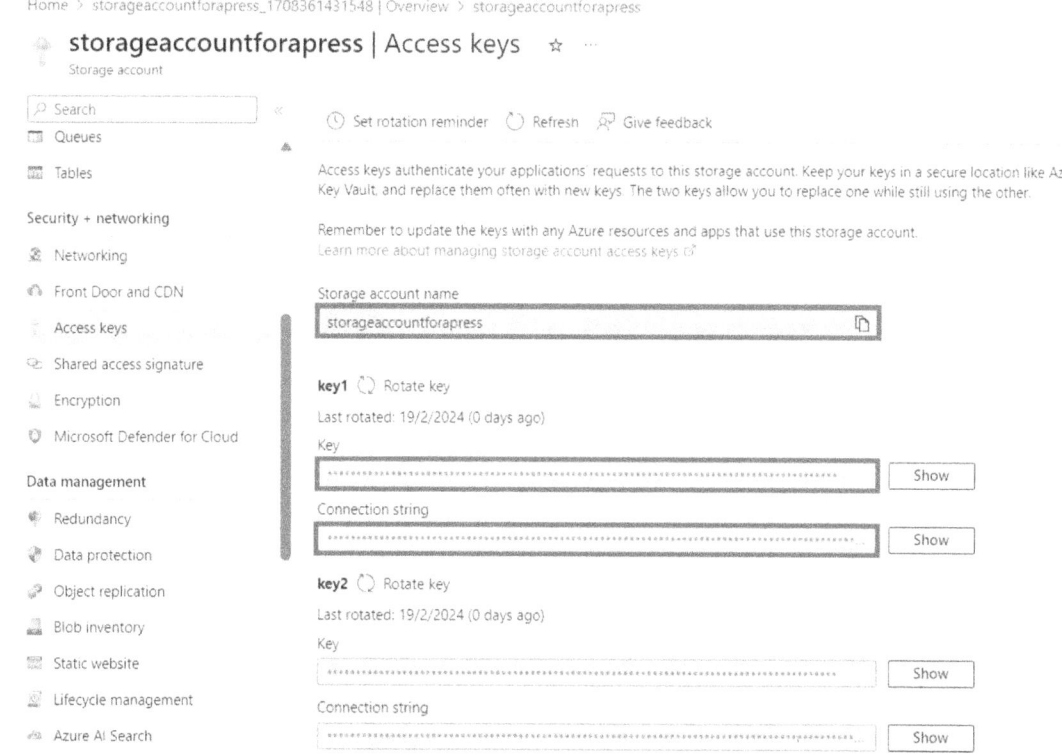

Figure 2-18. *Fetch the connection string*

Now that we have provisioned the storage account and Language service and fetched the connection string of the storage account as well as the key and endpoint of the Language service, we are well equipped to start developing our applications. In the next section, we will use the Visual Studio 2022 to build our language-based document classifier using a blob-triggered Azure Function.

29

CHAPTER 2   BUILD A LANGUAGE-BASED DOCUMENT CLASSIFIER WITH AZURE FUNCTIONS

Create a Language-Based Document Classifier with Azure Functions

In this section, we are going to complete the proof of concept for our fictional company to build a feature for our product as briefly discussed in the "Proposed Solution" section.

As we have already discussed the business requirement and provisioned the required resources, let's start building our language-based document classifier app using the Azure Function template. Open Visual Studio 2022 and click **Create a new project** as shown in Figure 2-19.

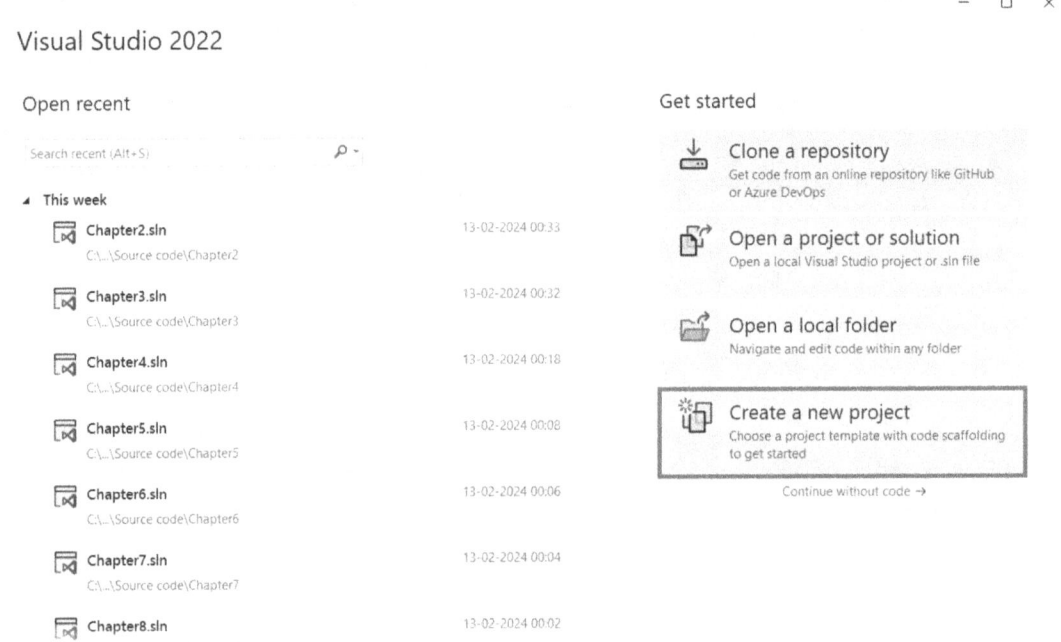

Figure 2-19. *Create a new project*

Select the **Azure Functions** project template as shown in Figure 2-20 and click **Next**.

CHAPTER 2   BUILD A LANGUAGE-BASED DOCUMENT CLASSIFIER WITH AZURE FUNCTIONS

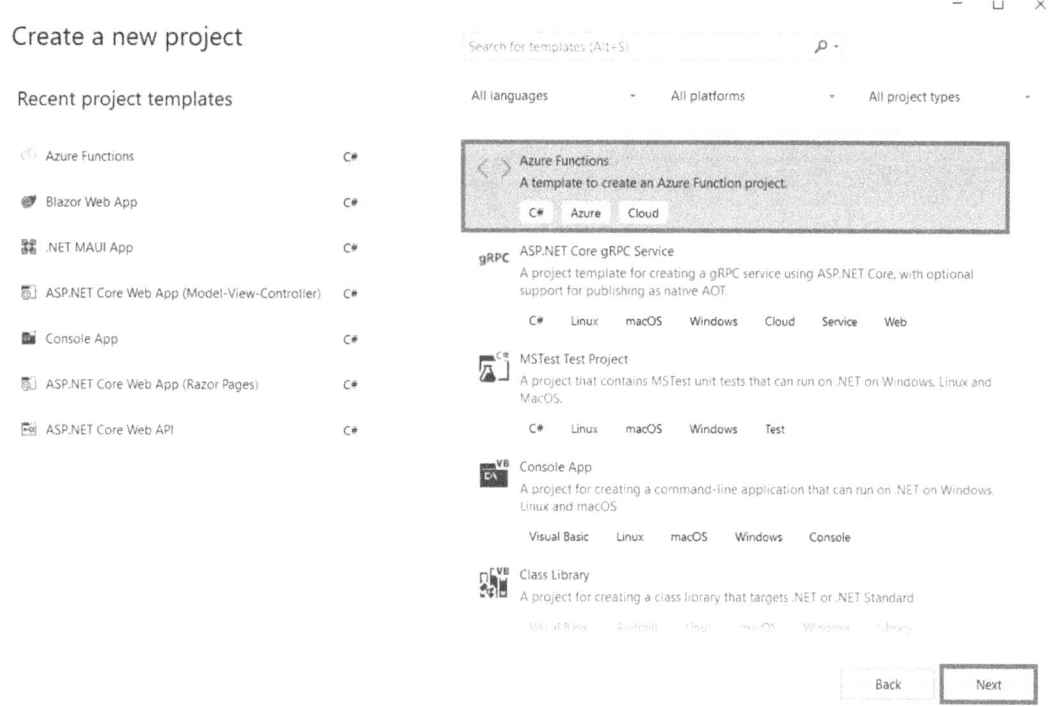

Figure 2-20. *Click Next*

Enter the **project name**, **location**, and **solution name** as shown in Figure 2-21 and click **Next**.

31

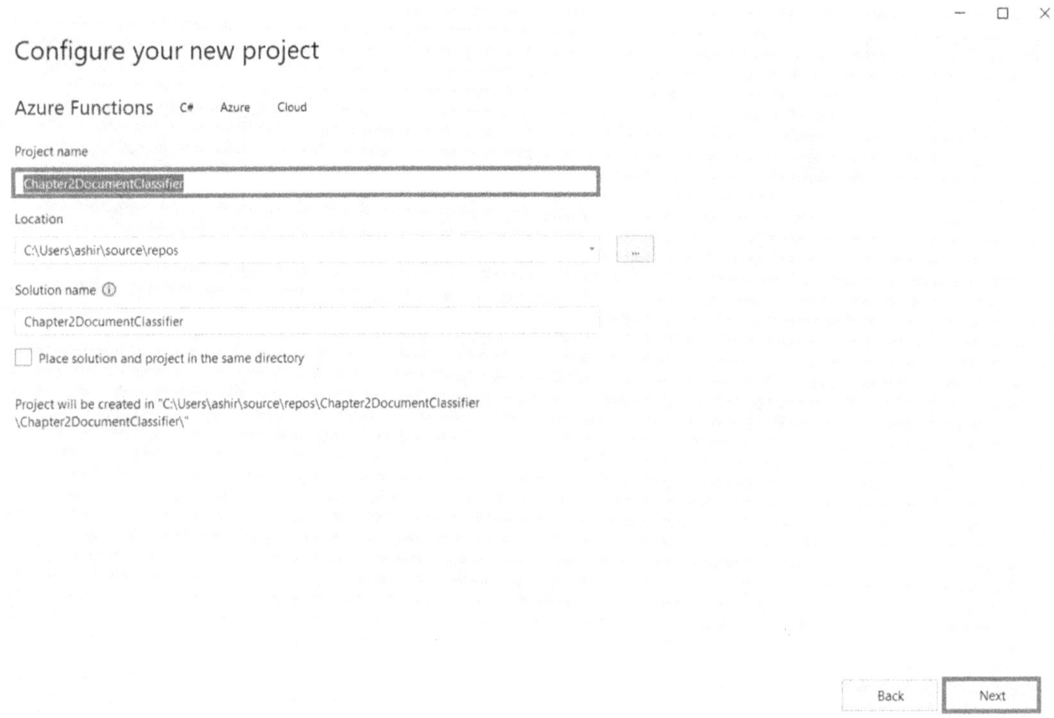

CHAPTER 2   BUILD A LANGUAGE-BASED DOCUMENT CLASSIFIER WITH AZURE FUNCTIONS

Figure 2-21. Enter the project name, location, and solution name

Now, select **.NET 8.0 Isolated** as the Functions worker and **Blob Trigger (using Event Grid)** as the Function trigger type. Check the option to **Use Azurite for runtime storage account** and set the authorization level to **Function**. Specify **blobConn** as the connection string setting name and **source** as the value for the path. The connection string setting name (**blobConn**) is the key where the storage account connection string will be stored. We will add the value of **blobConn** to the **local.settings.json** file later in this section. The path (**source**) refers to the container and folder that our function will monitor and trigger whenever a new file is uploaded. Once you have completed these steps, click **Create** as shown in Figure 2-22.

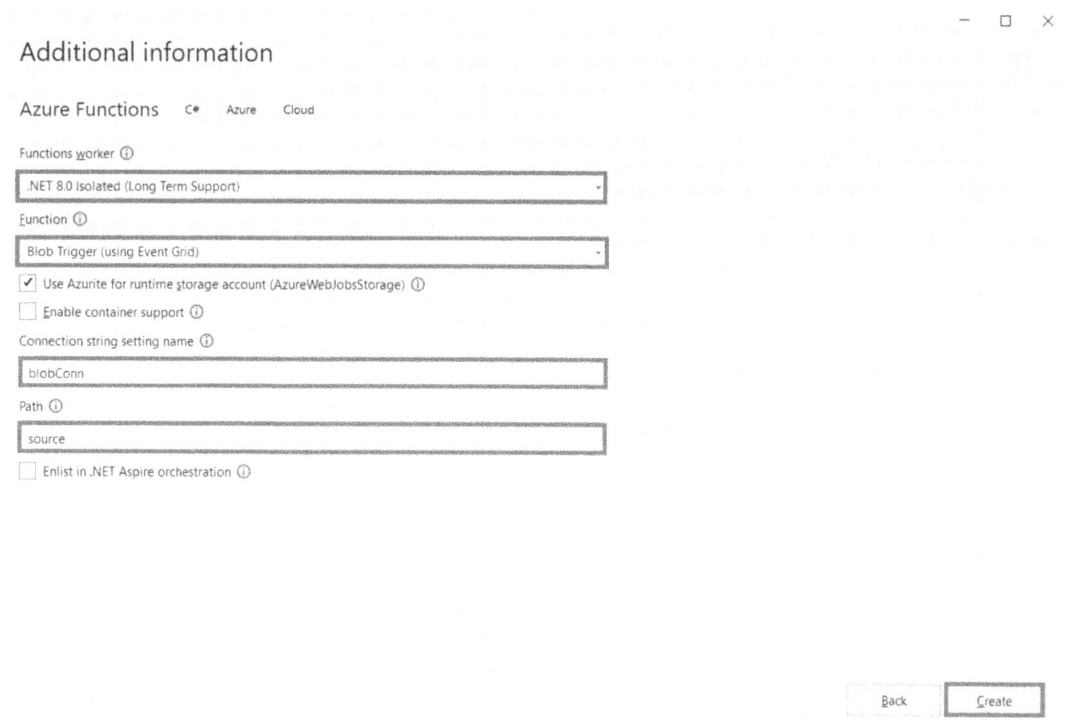

Figure 2-22. Click Create

Now Visual Studio will generate a blob-triggered Azure Function named **Function1** out of the box. Let's rename the function as **DocumentClassifier** and update the function attribute with the same. As a next step, let's add all the packages that we would need to build our solutions. To do so, open the NuGet package manager and install the following packages:

1. Azure.AI.TextAnalytics

2. Azure.Storage.Blobs

3. Microsoft.Extensions.Azure

Azure.AI.TextAnalytics is the official SDK for the Azure AI Language service. We will leverage its capabilities to perform language detection in our application.

Azure.Storage.Blobs is the official SDK for Azure Blob Storage. We will use its capabilities to perform operations such as moving files from one container to another and deleting files from a blob container.

Microsoft.Extensions.Azure is a set of extension libraries of Azure services which enables an easier life cycle management for resources. We will leverage it to inject Azure clients into our Dependency Injection (DI) container.

After installing all the abovementioned NuGet packages, let's open the local.settings. json and then add the **sourceContainerName**, **targetContainerName**, **blobConn**, **textAnalyticsEndpoint**, **textAnalyticsLocation**, and **textAnalyticsKey** keys along with their values. These values are required to authenticate our requests to the Blob Storage and Azure AI Language service. We had fetched these values in the previous section. Let's add these keys and their values, as demonstrated in Listing 2-1.

Listing 2-1. Add the key-value pairs in local.settings.json

```
{
    "IsEncrypted": false,
  "Values": {
    "AzureWebJobsStorage": "UseDevelopmentStorage=true",
    "FUNCTIONS_WORKER_RUNTIME": "dotnet-isolated",
    "sourceContainerName": "source",
    "targetContainerName": "destination",
    "blobConn": "enter the connection string of your storage account",
    "textAnalyticsEndpoint": "enter the endpoint of your Azure AI Language Service",
    "textAnalyticsLocation": "enter the location of your Azure AI Language Service",
    "textAnalyticsKey": "enter the key of your Azure AI Language Service"
  }
}
```

Please do note that storing function secrets or sensitive information in the local. settings.json file or hard-coding such information in a variable is not advisable. We recommend using a key vault to store function secrets.

Now that we have added the required key-value pairs in the local.settings.json file, let's open the Program.cs file and update it with the lines shown in Listing 2-2.

Listing 2-2. Inject instances of BlobServiceClient and TextAnalyticsClient in the DI container

```
using Microsoft.Azure.Functions.Worker;
using Microsoft.Extensions.DependencyInjection;
using Microsoft.Extensions.Hosting;
using Microsoft.Extensions.Azure;
using Azure;

var host = new HostBuilder()
    .ConfigureFunctionsWebApplication()
    .ConfigureServices(services =>
    {
        services.AddApplicationInsightsTelemetryWorkerService();
        services.ConfigureFunctionsApplicationInsights();
        services.AddAzureClients( builder =>
        {
            builder.AddBlobServiceClient(Environment.GetEnvironmentVariable
            ("blobConn"));
            builder.AddTextAnalyticsClient(new Uri(Environment.Get
            EnvironmentVariable("textAnalyticsEndpoint")),
                new AzureKeyCredential(Environment.GetEnvironmentVariable
                ("textAnalyticsKey"))
                );
        });
    })
    .Build();

host.Run();
```

In Listing 2-2, we inject instances of the **Text Analytics** client and **Blob Service** client into the DI container by retrieving credentials from **local.settings.json**. We utilize the **AddAzureClients** method from the **Microsoft.Extensions.Azure** SDK to configure these clients, enabling interaction with Azure AI for Language and Blob Storage resources that have been provisioned.

CHAPTER 2   BUILD A LANGUAGE-BASED DOCUMENT CLASSIFIER WITH AZURE FUNCTIONS

Now that we've configured the required client instances in our DI container, let's proceed to our blob-triggered function, DocumentClassifier.cs, where we'll implement the logic to classify documents based on their language. To accomplish this, update the code in DocumentClassifier.cs with the code provided in Listing 2-3.

Listing 2-3. Code for DocumentClassifier.cs

```
using System.IO;
using System.Threading.Tasks;
using Azure.AI.TextAnalytics;
using Microsoft.Azure.Functions.Worker;
using Microsoft.Extensions.Logging;
using Azure.Storage.Blobs;
using System.Text;
namespace Chapter2DocumentClassifier
{
    public class DocumentClassifier
    {
        private readonly ILogger<DocumentClassifier> _logger;
        private readonly TextAnalyticsClient _textAnalyticsClient;
        private readonly BlobServiceClient _blobServiceClient;
        private readonly BlobContainerClient _blobSourceContainerClient;
        private readonly BlobContainerClient _blobDestination
        ContainerClient;
        public DocumentClassifier(ILogger<DocumentClassifier> logger,
        TextAnalyticsClient textAnalyticsClient, BlobServiceClient
        blobServiceClient)
        {
            _logger = logger;
            _textAnalyticsClient = textAnalyticsClient;
            _blobServiceClient = blobServiceClient;
            _blobSourceContainerClient = _blobServiceClient.GetBlobContainer
            Client(Environment.GetEnvironmentVariable("sourceContainerName"));
            _blobDestinationContainerClient = _blobServiceClient.GetBlob
            ContainerClient(Environment.GetEnvironmentVariable("target
            ContainerName"));
        }
```

```csharp
[Function(nameof(DocumentClassifier))]
public async Task Run([BlobTrigger("source/{name}", Source =
BlobTriggerSource.LogsAndContainerScan, Connection = "blobConn")]
Stream stream, string name)
{
    using var blobStreamReader = new StreamReader(stream);
    var content = await blobStreamReader.ReadToEndAsync();
    _logger.LogInformation($"C# Blob Trigger processed blob\n Name:
    {name} \n Data: {content}");

    var result = await _textAnalyticsClient.
    DetectLanguageAsync(content);

    string detectedLanguage = result.Value.Name;

    _logger.LogInformation($"Detected language:
    {detectedLanguage}");

    string targetBlobName = $"{detectedLanguage}/{name}";

    BlobClient blobClient = _blobDestinationContainerClient.
    GetBlobClient(targetBlobName);
    byte[] byteArray = Encoding.UTF8.GetBytes(content);
    await blobClient.UploadAsync(new MemoryStream(byteArray));

    _logger.LogInformation($"Upload blob - {targetBlobName} in the
    {Environment.GetEnvironmentVariable("targetContainerName")}
    container.");

    await _blobSourceContainerClient.DeleteBlobIfExistsAsync(name);

    _logger.LogInformation($"Deleted blob - {name} from
    {Environment.GetEnvironmentVariable("sourceContainerName")}
    container.");
    }
  }
}
```

In Listing 2-3, we initialize three essential components in the function's constructor – an instance of **ILogger**, **TextAnalyticsClient**, and **BlobServiceClient** – using constructor injection. Afterward, we use the **BlobServiceClient** instance to initialize **_blobSourceContainerClient** and **_blobDestinationContainerClient** to facilitate interaction with the source and destination containers. Now that we have initialized the required clients, let's focus on the **DocumentClassifier** function.

The **DocumentClassifier** function is triggered whenever a new blob is uploaded to the source container. It reads the blob's content and uses the TextAnalyticsClient's **DetectLanguageAsync** method to determine the language. Then, it creates a new blob in the destination container, named according to the detected language. Using the **blobClient** instance's **uploadAsync** method, it transfers a copy of the blob to the destination. The **blobClient** references the blob by utilizing the **GetBlobClient** method of the **_blobDestinationContainerClient** instance. Once the upload to the destination container is complete, the function removes the blob from the source container using the **_blobSourceContainerClient**'s **DeleteBlobIfExists** method.

Now that we have written the code for our solution, in the next section we will test it out by running our function.

Test the Language-Based Document Classifier Function

To test the **DocumentClassifier** function, we need to run it. However, before doing so, let's examine the files in the source and destination containers. As shown in Figure 2-23, the source container contains four text files, each written in a different language. These are plain text files which I had uploaded to the source container to test our solution.

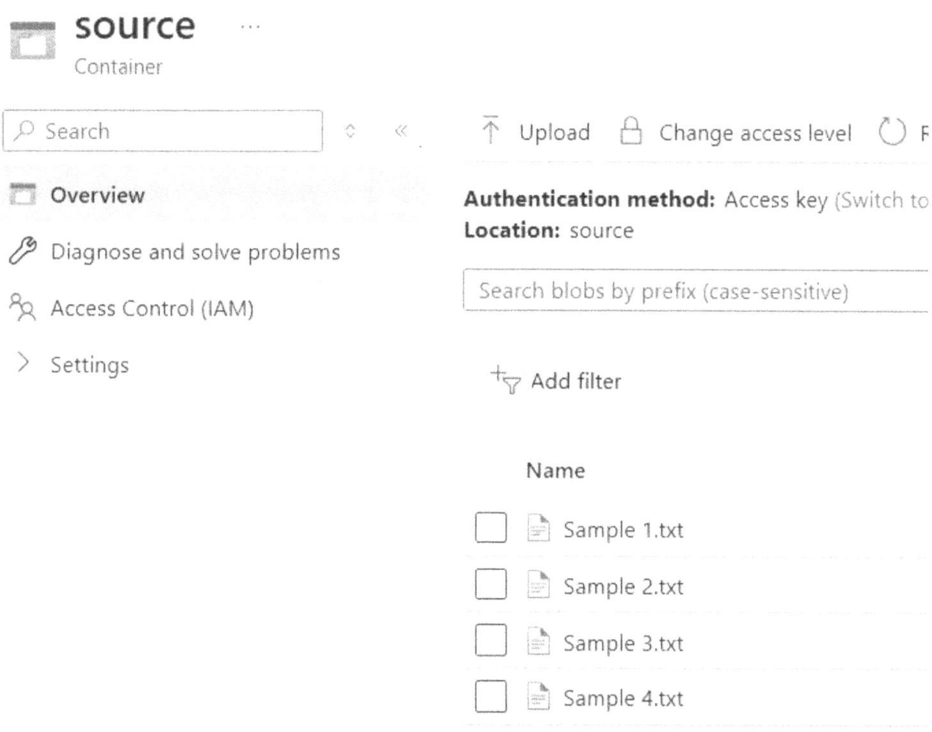
source
Container
Search
Upload
Change access level
Overview
Authentication method: Access key (Switch to
Location: source
Diagnose and solve problems
Search blobs by prefix (case-sensitive)
Access Control (IAM)
Settings
Add filter
Name
Sample 1.txt
Sample 2.txt
Sample 3.txt
Sample 4.txt

Figure 2-23. *Source container before function execution*

Now, let's examine the files in the destination container. As shown in Figure 2-24, the destination container is currently empty and contains no uploaded files. Once we run the **DocumentClassifier** function, it will populate the container with the files, organized within a folder hierarchy based on their respective languages.

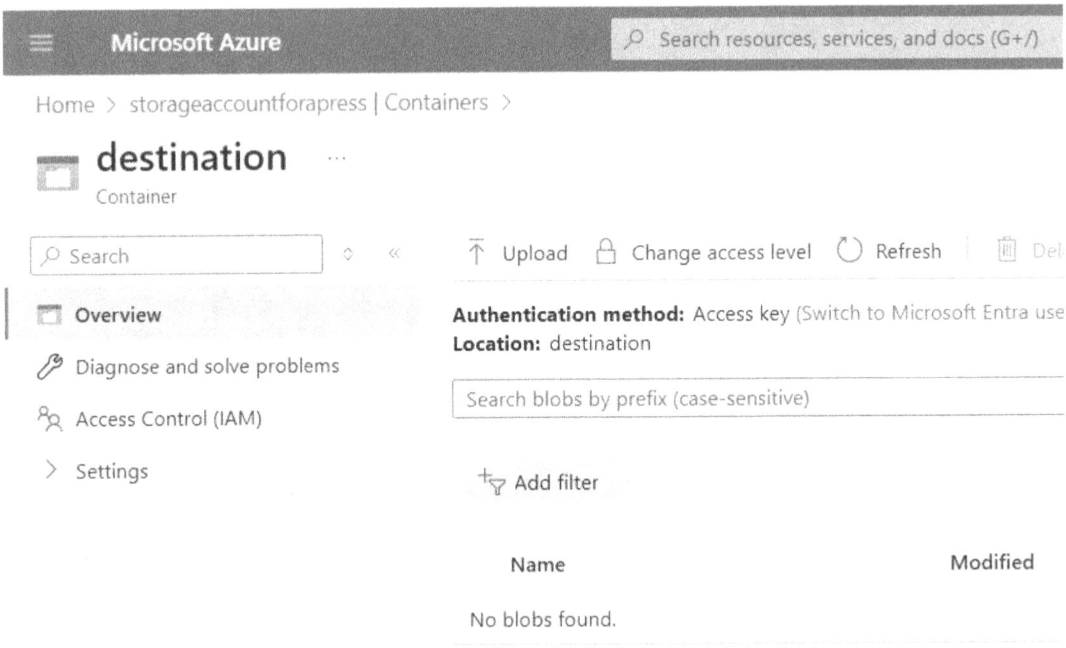

CHAPTER 2   BUILD A LANGUAGE-BASED DOCUMENT CLASSIFIER WITH AZURE FUNCTIONS

Figure 2-24. Destination container before function execution

Now that you've seen the files in both containers, let's run our **DocumentClassifier** function and check the containers again.

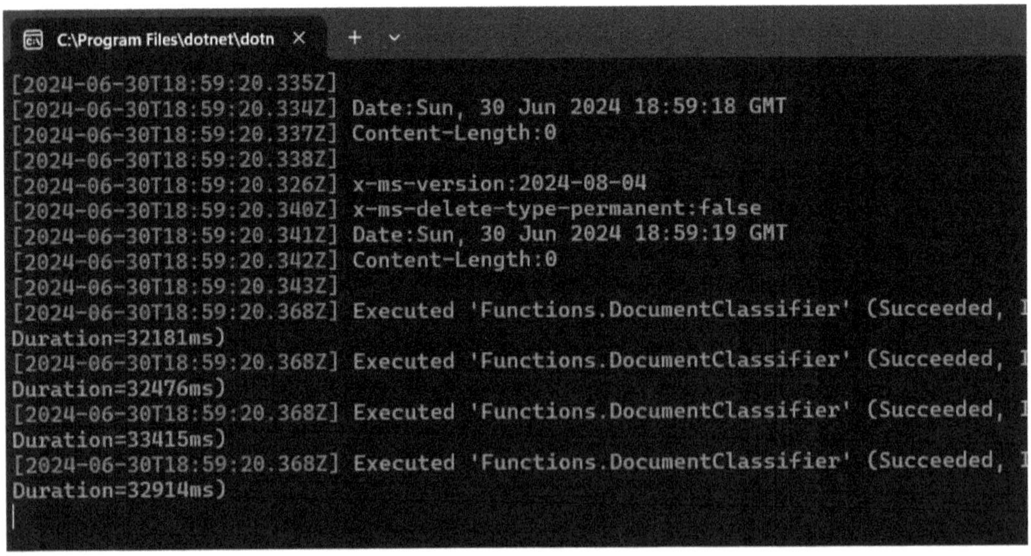

Figure 2-25. Logs of the DocumentClassifier function

CHAPTER 2   BUILD A LANGUAGE-BASED DOCUMENT CLASSIFIER WITH AZURE FUNCTIONS

The DocumentClassifier function successfully classified the documents by their respective languages and uploaded them to the destination container, as verified by the logs in the Azure Functions Core tool as illustrated in Figure 2-25.

Let's check the destination container again to verify this. As shown in Figure 2-26, the destination container now contains four folders: English, Hindi, Oriya, and French. Each folder contains the files written in the respective language indicated by the folder name.

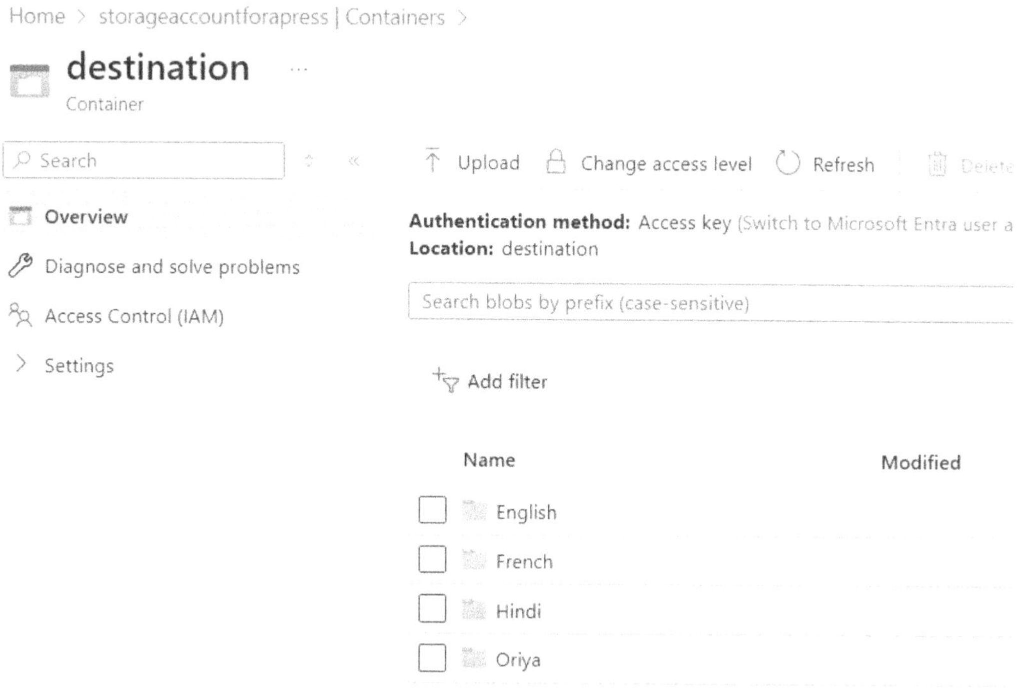

Figure 2-26. Destination container after function execution

The function also included functionality to remove files from the source container once they were successfully classified and uploaded to the destination container. Since the function execution was successful, the source container should now be empty. We can verify this by checking the source container again.

CHAPTER 2   BUILD A LANGUAGE-BASED DOCUMENT CLASSIFIER WITH AZURE FUNCTIONS

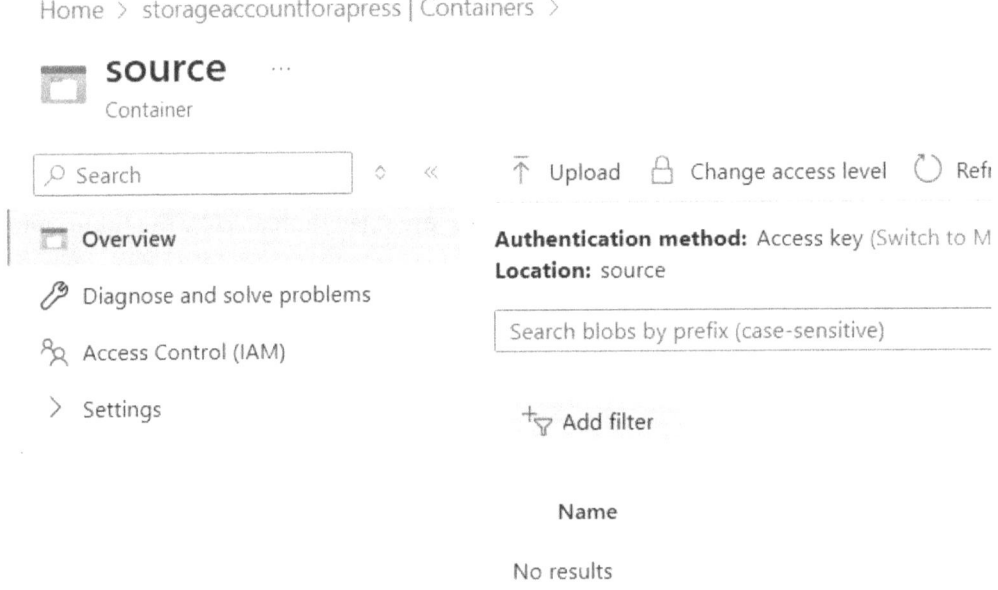

Figure 2-27. *Source container after function execution*

As shown in Figure 2-27, the source container is empty, indicating that our function worked as expected.

Summary

In this chapter, you've gained insights into creating intelligent solutions using Azure Functions and the Azure AI Language service through the development of a language-based document classifier. Our exploration delved into the Azure AI Language service, uncovering its features and applications. Additionally, we navigated through the steps of provisioning an Azure AI Language service within the Azure Portal. Throughout this process, we've acquired knowledge on constructing an intelligent, event-driven solution by harnessing the capabilities of the Azure AI Language service. The primary focus of this chapter centered around the language detection feature offered by the Azure AI Language service to build a document classifier on the basis of the language the content was written in. In the forthcoming chapter, our attention will shift toward exploring the text translation feature provided by the Azure AI Translator service.

CHAPTER 3

Build a Multi-language Text Translator App with Azure Functions

Language plays a vital role in facilitating knowledge transfer among humans. Throughout the history of mankind, different means have been employed to enable knowledge transfer. It can be through means of oral communication like storytelling to passing knowledge in written formats like manuscripts, inscriptions, or newspapers. With technological advancement, people have adopted newer means like websites, blogs, online forums, and social media to share knowledge and information. With the availability of all this information, we are empowered to take data-driven decisions by learning from these data sources. But the presence of data in different languages poses various challenges in effective knowledge transfer. Some of the common challenges are language barrier and accessibility to information for people. In a world where we have more than 7000 languages, this problem just gets bigger.

In a global economy, organizations collaborate across geographies, and often people operating from different regions may not speak or be proficient in the language spoken by the other. This language barrier can impact productivity as well as hinder collaboration opportunities, including efficient knowledge transfer. To overcome this, a lot of research has gone into the field of machine translation over the past few decades. Some of the popular machine translation systems out in the market are Google Translate and Microsoft Translator, to name a few. Designing such systems from scratch can be both resource and capital intensive. To build systems with machine translation capabilities without investing on building machine translation from scratch, we can leverage the power of Azure AI Translator. It is a specialized AI service offered by Microsoft Azure to build solutions which need the capability to translate text from one to another.

In this chapter, we are going to briefly discuss the Azure AI Translator service and its use cases and build a multi-language text translator by leveraging its client SDKs.

Structure

In this chapter, we will explore the following aspects of Azure:

- Introduction to the Azure AI Translator service
- Create your first Azure AI Translator service in the Azure Portal
- Create a multi-language text translator

Objectives

After studying this chapter, you should be able to

- Grasp the essentials of the Azure AI Translator service
- Add the capabilities of the Azure AI Translator service to your applications

Introduction to Azure AI Translator Service

Azure AI Translator is a fully managed cloud-based translation service of Microsoft Azure. It is designed to break down the language barrier and enable the flow of information across the globe, empowering people and organizations with information irrespective of language in which they were written in. It is a production-grade translation engine that comes up with an SLA of 99.9% for the paid tiers. It powers many Microsoft products like Word, PowerPoint, Teams, Edge, and Bing. Azure Translator leverages state-of-the-art machine learning algorithms, particularly neural machine translation (NMT), to perform language translation. It can translate words, phrases, and entire documents. Currently, the Azure AI Translator service supports more than 100 languages. It can perform language detection as well as language translation for the provided textual data. It comes up with a flexible pricing model where you can either opt for a pay-as-you-go model or avail any of the commitment tiers. You are priced as on the volume of characters that you have translated.

Some of the key features of the Azure AI Translator service are as follows:

1. **Text Translation** – It provides accurate translation of textual content in various languages. With the help of the Translator service, we can translate individual words, sentences, as well as an entire document in an instant.

2. **Multi-language Support** – With this service, we can translate text from more than 100 languages, and the list of supported languages is only going to grow in the coming times.

3. **Customizable Translations** – With this functionality, the Translator service enables users to fine-tune translation models for domain-specific needs which can increase the accuracy and relevance of translations.

4. **Security and Compliance** – The Azure AI Translator service is compliant with various industry standards like GDPR and HIPAA for data security and compliance.

5. **Automatic Language Detection** – With this functionality, the Translator service can automatically detect the language in which the input text was written. This eliminates the need for the user to specify the source language explicitly.

6. **Supports Client SDKS** – The service provides client SDKs in various languages like Python, Node.js, C#, and Java. It enables developers to easily integrate the Translator service in their applications. For the language for which the SDKs are not available, they can use the REST APIs to integrate the capabilities of the Azure AI Translator service in their application.

Now that we have explored some of the key features of the Azure AI Translator service, let's explore some of the potential use cases where it can come in handy:

1. **Education and E-Learning** – Consider a scenario where a university offers courses to students from a diverse linguistic background. The course materials, discussions, and lectures need to be accessible for students who may not be skilled in the language in which the course content is being delivered. In this scenario, we can leverage the power of the Azure AI Translator service to translate the course material, lectures, and discussion and enable students to access the content in the language of their preference.

2. **Global Business Communication** – Consider a scenario where you are working for a multinational company which operates from different regions across the globe. Employees often need to communicate and collaborate with colleagues, partners, and stakeholders who may or may not speak the same language. In this scenario, we can leverage the power of Azure AI Translator to translate documents, emails, and other business communications to facilitate effective communication by overcoming the language barrier.

As we have explored what Azure AI Translator service is and what its key features and use cases are, let's explore ways to integrate it in our solutions by building a multi-language text translator.

Problem Statement

You are working for a fictional company, AzTech Corp. The company has grown significantly and is now operating from different regions. In some of the regions, English is not a native language and is becoming a barrier for leveraging information like reports, documentations, etc., that the company has generated over a period of time. To assist the employees, your company is currently working toward building a product which can provide seamless content translation for the large amount of textual content that the company has generated over a period of time. You are part of the core team that is working on this product. Your dev lead and architect have decided to go ahead with the Azure AI Translator service to perform text translation. You are tasked with a proof of concept to build a multi-language text translator which can translate text from English to Spanish, Hindi, French, and German. Once the proof of concept is completed, your team members will leverage your work as a base for future development.

Proposed Solution

After going through the requirement, you have broken down the problem into two tasks:

1. Convert the textual content into the language of choice
2. Provide an interface to interact with the solution

To solve both of the abovementioned problems, you have decided to use Azure Functions and the Azure AI Translator service to develop the solution. With the help of Azure Functions, we are going to provide a REST endpoint to the end users to make requests and receive the desired responses. It is going to be an HTTP-triggered Azure Function which will take the textual content and the target language from the user's request, then leverage the power of the Azure AI Translator service to convert the textual content into the target language and return back the result as a response.

Before we start building the HTTP-triggered Azure Function, we need a couple of things in place. The following are the prerequisites to start the development activities:

1. Create an Azure AI Translator service
2. Fetch the endpoint and key of the Azure AI Translator service

Once we have these two things in place, we can start building our solution using Visual Studio 2022. Let's get started.

Create an Azure AI Translator Service

To create an Azure AI Translator service, go to the Azure Portal and type Language in the search box. Click **Translators** in the search results as shown in Figure 3-1.

CHAPTER 3   BUILD A MULTI-LANGUAGE TEXT TRANSLATOR APP WITH AZURE FUNCTIONS

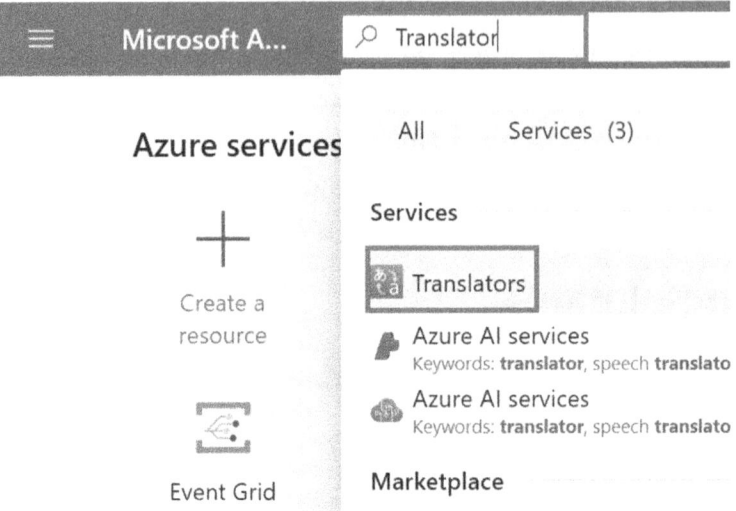

Figure 3-1. *Search for Translator*

On the screen shown in Figure 3-2, you can view the list of Translator services that you have provisioned. Click **Create** to provision our Translator service in Azure.

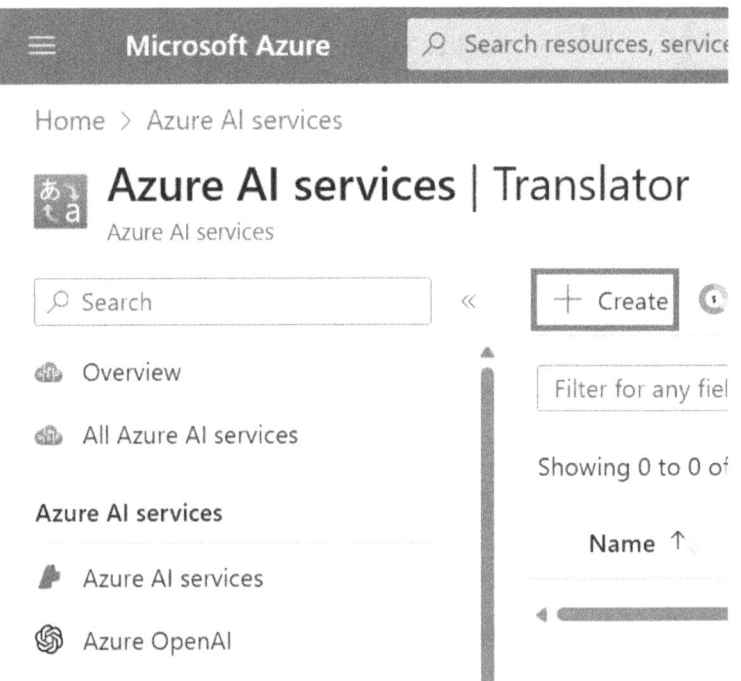

Figure 3-2. *Click Create*

Next, select your subscription and resource group from the drop-downs available on the screen as can be seen in Figure 3-3. If you don't have a resource group, you can create a new one on this screen. After that, select the region, provide the resource name, and select the pricing tier. The resource name needs to be a unique one. For the purpose of building this solution, we are going to the **Free F0** tier. This tier provides us with the capability to translate up to 2M characters per month which should be enough to build and test our proof of concept (PoC). For workloads running in a production environment, it is advised to use higher tiers. Once you have entered the preceding details, click **Review + create**.

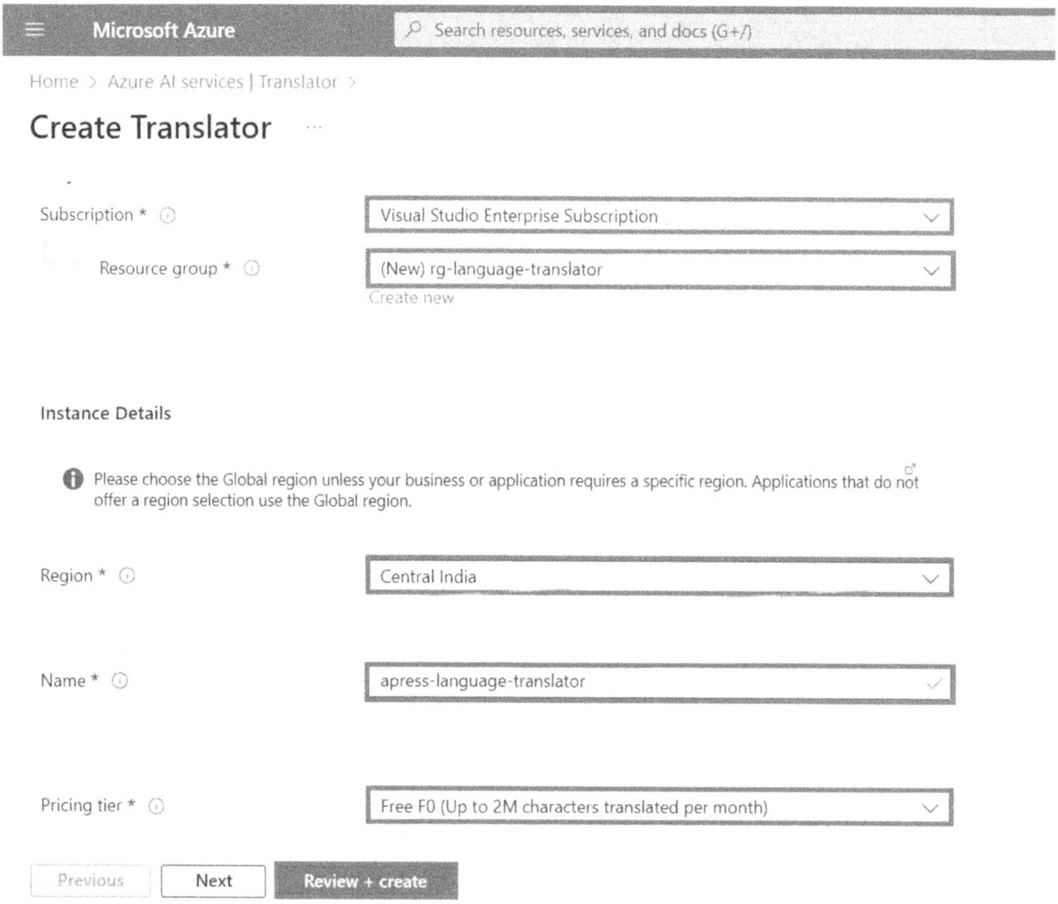

Figure 3-3. Click Review + create

CHAPTER 3   BUILD A MULTI-LANGUAGE TEXT TRANSLATOR APP WITH AZURE FUNCTIONS

Now you will see a summary of the configuration for the translator resource that you had entered on the previous screen. A validation check will be done on the configurations. Once the validation of the configuration is done, click **Create** to provision the resource as shown in Figure 3-4. If you wanted to make any changes, you could click **Previous** and make the necessary changes for the resource.

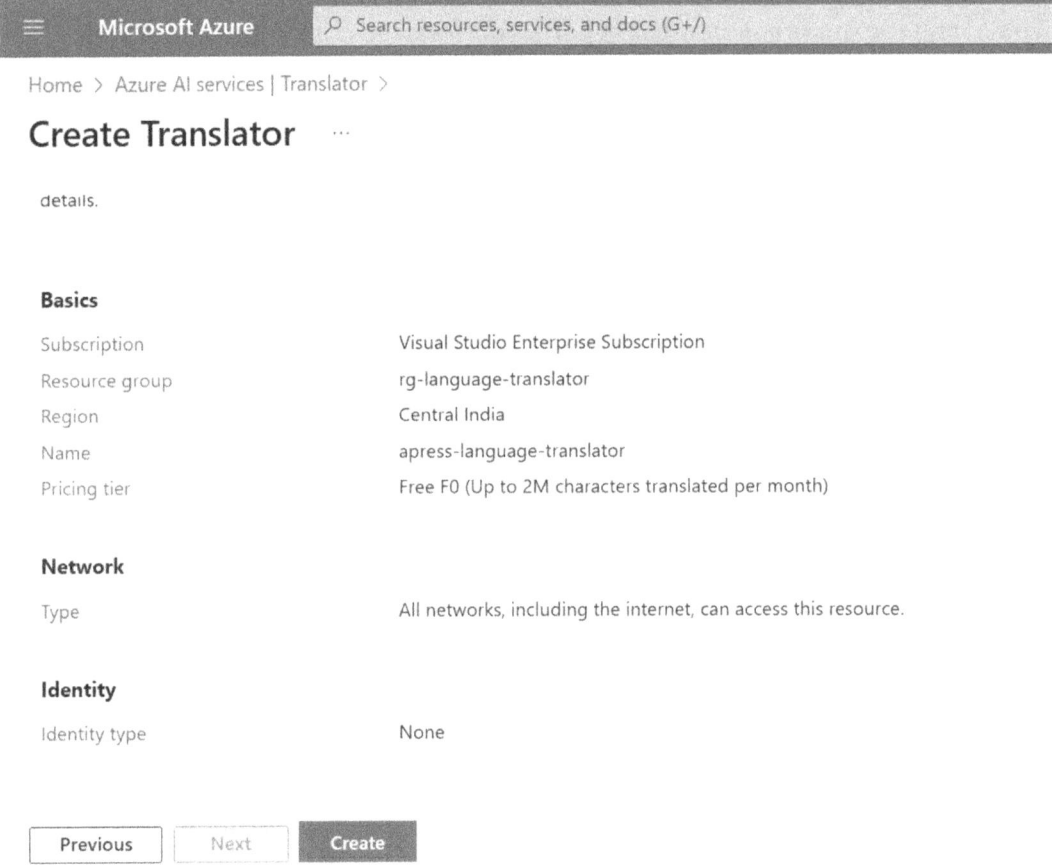

Figure 3-4. *Click Create*

Once the resource has been created successfully, you will see the message "Your deployment is complete," as shown in Figure 3-5. Once you see that message, click **Go to resource** to view the newly provisioned translator resource.

CHAPTER 3   BUILD A MULTI-LANGUAGE TEXT TRANSLATOR APP WITH AZURE FUNCTIONS

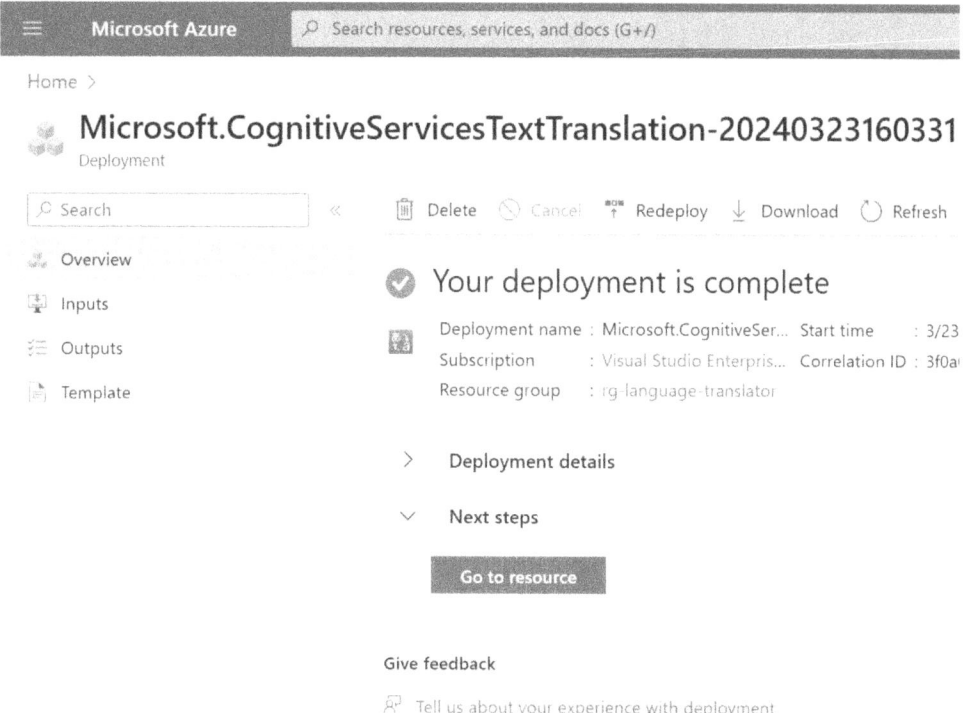

Figure 3-5. *Click Go to resource*

Now that we have provisioned our AI Translator service in the Azure Portal, we will need to fetch the access key and endpoint to interact with it from our solution. Access keys are just one way of authenticating our calls to the Translator service. We can use other methods like Managed Identity–based authentication which is recommended for production workloads. For the purpose of our PoC, we are going to use key-based authentication.

To fetch the key and endpoint for our translator resource, click Keys and Endpoint as shown in Figure 3-6.

CHAPTER 3   BUILD A MULTI-LANGUAGE TEXT TRANSLATOR APP WITH AZURE FUNCTIONS

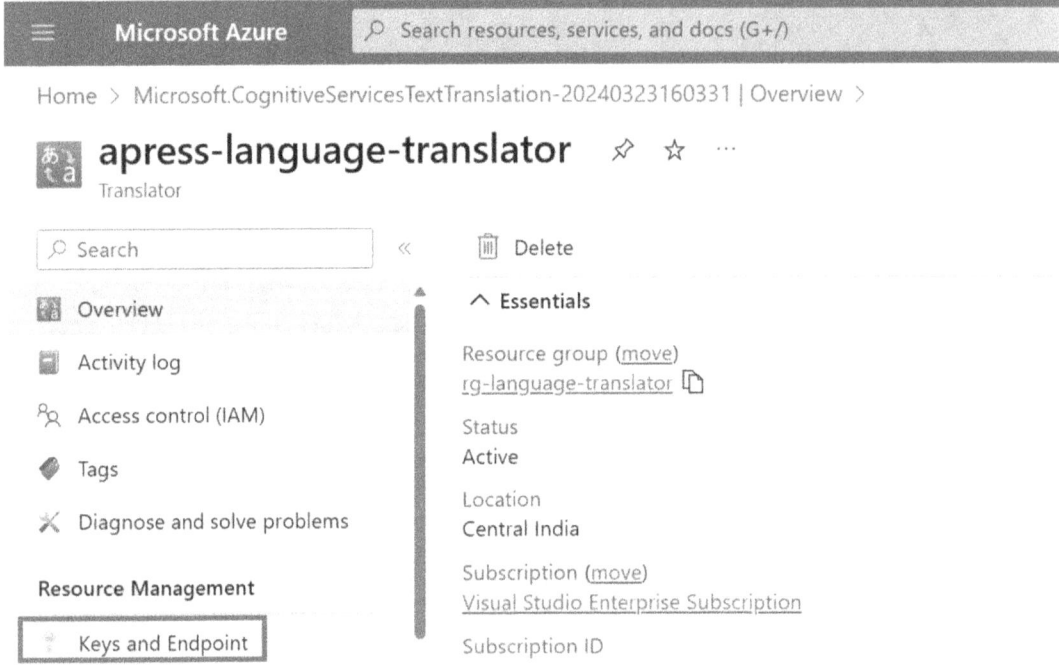

Figure 3-6. Click Keys and Endpoint

We will have to fetch either one of the primary or secondary key and the resource region from the screen shown in Figure 3-7. We will use these values later in our application for authentication purposes.

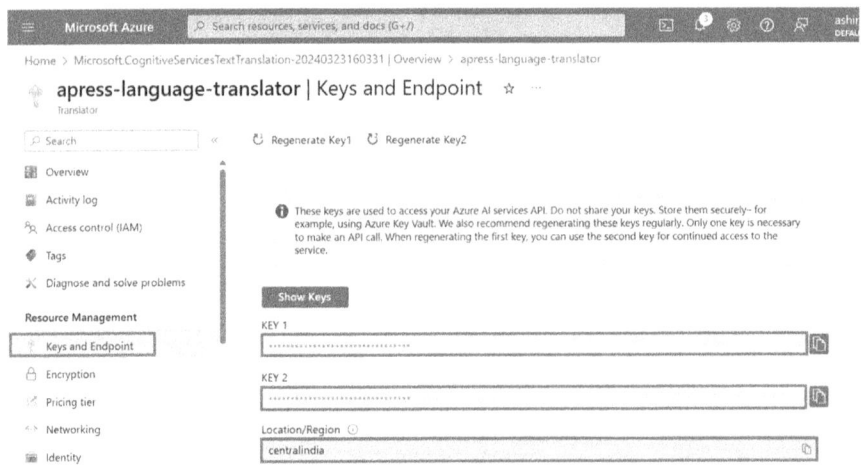

Figure 3-7. Get the key and region

CHAPTER 3   BUILD A MULTI-LANGUAGE TEXT TRANSLATOR APP WITH AZURE FUNCTIONS

Now that we have provisioned the translator resource and have the required information to authenticate requests from our application to the Translator service, we have completed the prerequisites. In the next section, we will build the multi-language text translator app for our proof of concept.

Create a Multi-language Text Translator App

In this section, we are going to complete the proof of concept for our fictional company to build a feature for our product as briefly discussed in the "Proposed Solution" section.

As we have already discussed the business requirement and provisioned the required resources, let's start building our multi-language text translator app using the Azure Function template. Open Visual Studio 2022 and click **Create a new project** as shown in Figure 3-8.

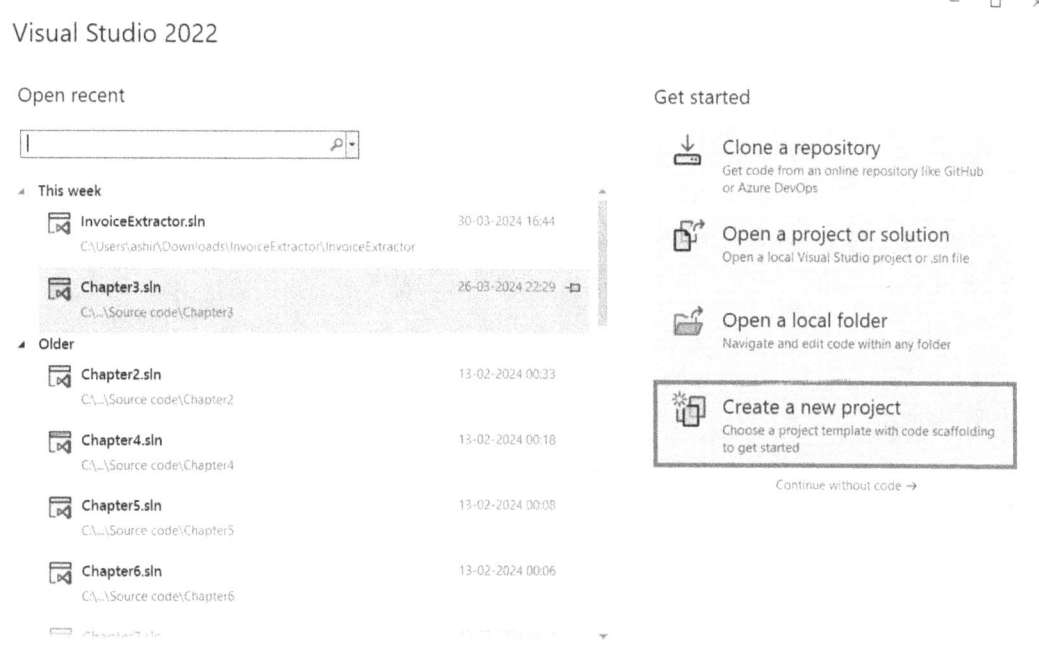

Figure 3-8.   *Create a new project*

Select the **Azure Functions** project template as shown in Figure 3-9 and click **Next**.

CHAPTER 3   BUILD A MULTI-LANGUAGE TEXT TRANSLATOR APP WITH AZURE FUNCTIONS

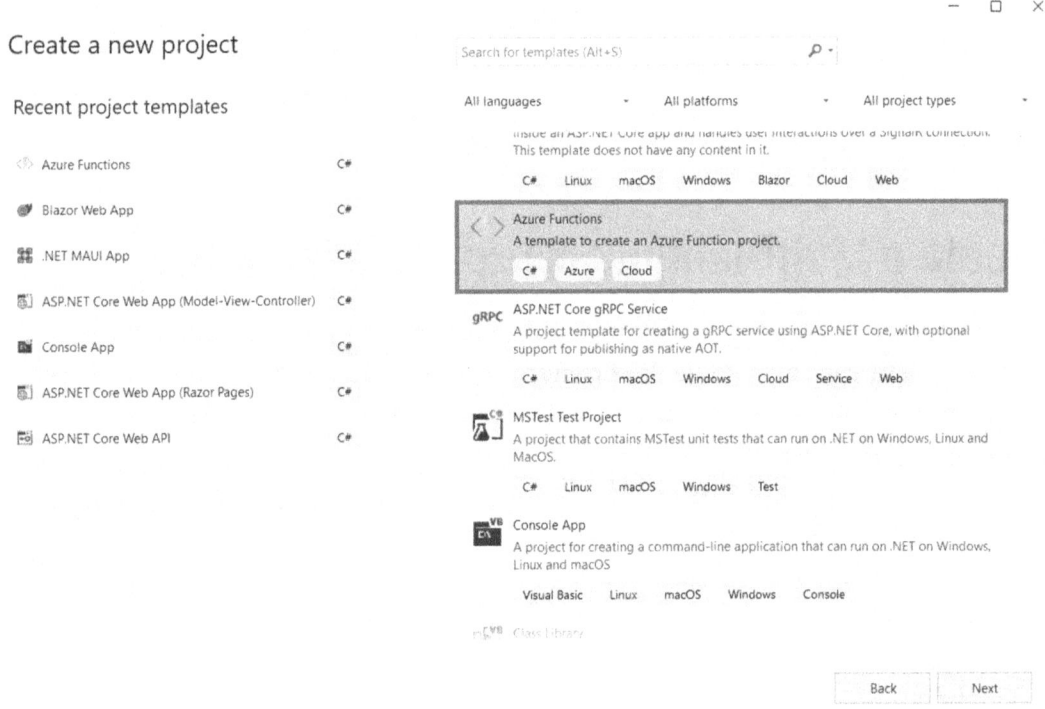

Figure 3-9. Click Next

Enter the **project name**, **location**, and **solution name** as shown in Figure 3-10 and click **Next**.

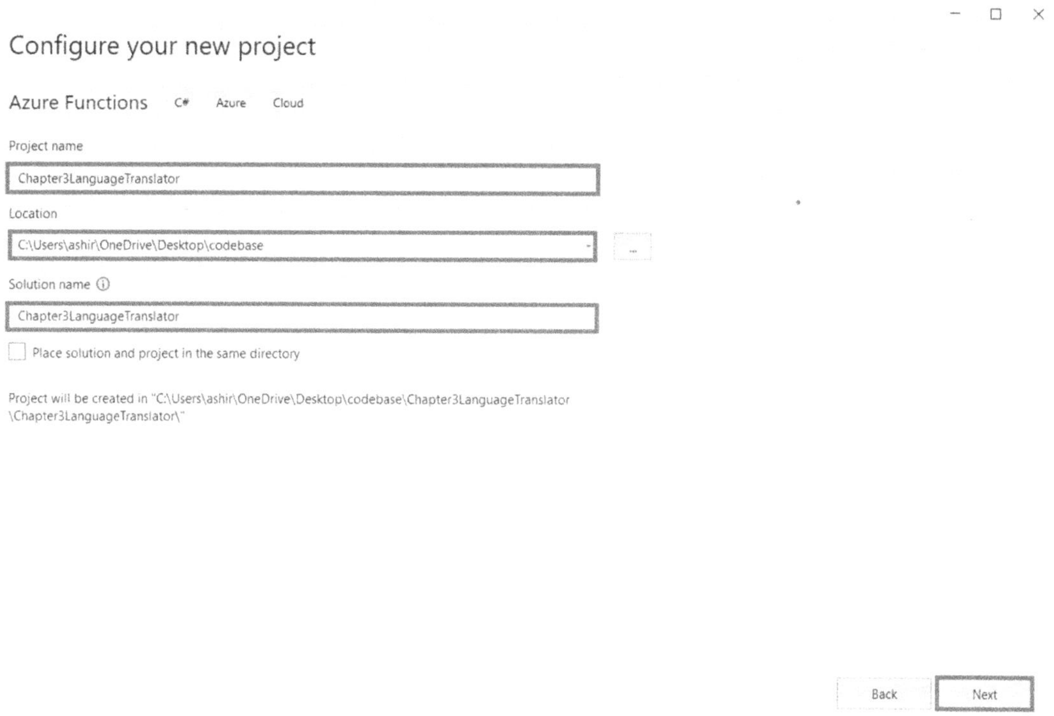

CHAPTER 3   BUILD A MULTI-LANGUAGE TEXT TRANSLATOR APP WITH AZURE FUNCTIONS

Figure 3-10. Enter the project name, location, and solution name

Now select the **.NET 8.0 Isolated** as the Functions worker and **Http trigger** as the Function trigger type, check the **Use Azurite for runtime storage account**, and define the authorization level as **Function**. Once you are done, click **Create** as shown in Figure 3-11.

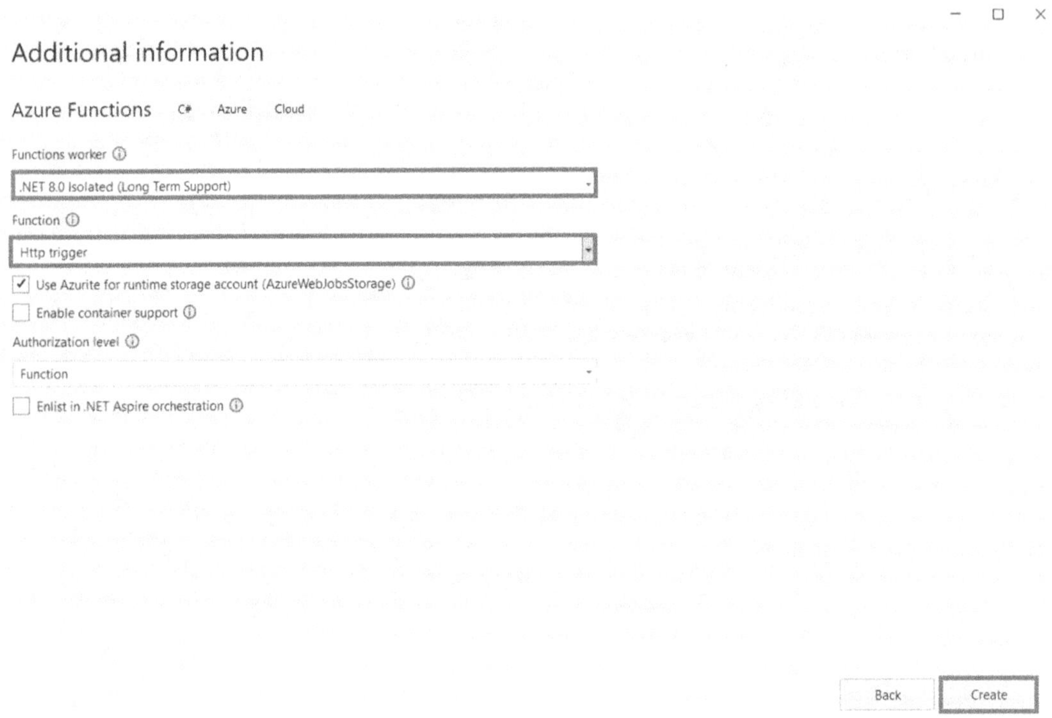

Figure 3-11. Click Create

Now Visual Studio will generate an HTTP-triggered Azure Function named **Function1** out of the box. Let's rename the function as **Translator** and update the function attribute with the same. As a next step, let's add all the packages that we would need to build our solutions. To do so, open the NuGet package manager and install the following packages:

1. Azure.AI.Translation.Text

2. Newtonsoft.Json

3. Microsoft.Extensions.Azure

Azure.AI.Translation.Text is the official SDK for the Azure AI Translator service. We will leverage its capabilities to perform text translations in our application.

Newtonsoft.Json is a popular JSON framework in the .NET ecosystem. We will leverage it to serialize and deserialize objects.

Microsoft.Extensions.Azure is a set of extension libraries of Azure services which enables an easier life cycle management for resources. We will leverage it to inject Azure clients into our DI container.

CHAPTER 3   BUILD A MULTI-LANGUAGE TEXT TRANSLATOR APP WITH AZURE FUNCTIONS

After installing all the abovementioned NuGet packages, let's open the local. settings.json and then add the **TranslatorKey** and **TranslatorRegion** keys. These values are required to authenticate our requests to the Translator service. We had fetched these values in the previous section. Let's add these two keys and their values as demonstrated in Listing 3-1.

Listing 3-1. Add TranslatorKey and TranslatorRegion

```
{
  "IsEncrypted": false,
  "Values": {
    "AzureWebJobsStorage": "AzureWebJobsStorageConnectionStringValue",
    "FUNCTIONS_WORKER_RUNTIME": "dotnet-isolated",
    "TranslatorKey": "enter your resource key",
    "TranslatorRegion": "enter your resource region"
  }
}
```

Please do note that storing function secrets or sensitive information in the local. settings.json file or hard-coding such information in a variable is not advisable. We recommend using a key vault to store function secrets.

Now that we have added our key and endpoint in the local.settings.json file, let's open the Program.cs file and update it with the lines shown in Listing 3-2.

Listing 3-2. Code for Program.cs

```
using Microsoft.Extensions.Azure;
using Microsoft.Extensions.DependencyInjection;
using Microsoft.Extensions.Hosting;

var host = new HostBuilder()
    .ConfigureFunctionsWorkerDefaults()
    .ConfigureServices(
    services =>
    {
        services.AddAzureClients(builder =>
        {
            builder.AddTextTranslationClient(
```

```
            new AzureKeyCredential(Environment.GetEnvironmentVariable
            ("TranslatorKey")),
            Environment.GetEnvironmentVariable("TranslatorRegion"));
        });
    })
    .Build();
host.Run();
```

In Listing 3-2, we are injecting an instance of the TextTranslation client in the DI container by fetching the credentials from the local.settings.json. We are using the AddAzureClients method available as part of Microsoft.Extensions.Azure SDK to configure the Azure Translator client.

Now that we have injected the instance of the TextTranslation client, let's move our focus to explore ways to consume them. To do so, create a folder called **Business** in your solution. As a next step, add an interface called **ITranslatorBusiness** and a class **TranslatorBusiness**. TranslatorBusiness is going to implement the ITranslatorBusiness. Add the code mentioned in Listing 3-3 in the ITranslatorBusiness interface.

Listing 3-3. Code for ITranslatorBusiness.cs

```
public interface ITranslatorBusiness
{
    Task<string> TranslateMessageAsync(string message, string
    targetLanguage);
}
```

The **ITranslatorBusiness** contains the definition of one method called **TranslateMessageAsync**. This method will take two parameters – message and targetLanguage. **message** represents the message that the user wants to translate, and **targetLanguage** refers to the language in which the user wants to translate the message. Using the message and targetLanguage, the TranslateMessageAsync method will return you the translated text.

As we have understood the purpose of the TranslateMessageAsync method, let's look at its implementation in the TranslatorBusiness class which is present in Listing 3-4.

Listing 3-4. Code for TranslatorBusiness.cs

```
using Azure.AI.Translation.Text;
using System;
using System.Collections.Generic;
using System.Linq;
using System.Text;
using System.Threading.Tasks;

namespace Chapter3_LanguageTranslator.Business
{
    public class TranslatorBusiness : ITranslatorBusiness
    {
        private readonly TextTranslationClient _textTranslationClient;
        public TranslatorBusiness(TextTranslationClient
        textTranslationClient)
        {
            _textTranslationClient = textTranslationClient;
        }
        public async Task<string> TranslateMessageAsync(string message,
        string targetLanguage)
        {
            string languageCode = String.Empty;

            switch (targetLanguage.ToLower())
            {
                case "french":
                    languageCode = "fr";
                    break;
                case "spanish":
                    languageCode = "es";
                    break;
                case "hindi":
                    languageCode = "hi";
                    break;
                case "german":
                    languageCode = "de";
```

CHAPTER 3   BUILD A MULTI-LANGUAGE TEXT TRANSLATOR APP WITH AZURE FUNCTIONS

```
                break;
            default:
                throw new Exception(message: "Invalid target
                language");
        }

        var result = await _textTranslationClient.
        TranslateAsync(languageCode, message);

        IReadOnlyList<TranslatedTextItem> translations = result.Value;
        TranslatedTextItem translation = translations.FirstOrDefault();

        return translation.Translations.FirstOrDefault().Text;
        }
    }
}
```

In Listing 3-4, we have initialized a client of **TextTranslationClient** using Construction injection and later leverage its **TranslateAsync** method to translate messages to the target language defined by the user. As per the business requirement, we are only supporting language translation into four languages, that is, French, German, Hindi, and Spanish. If the user provides any language that is supported as per the business requirements, then the method throws an exception.

Now that we have written the code for ITranslatorBusiness and TranslatorBusiness, let's go back to Program.cs and update the code to register the TranslatorBusiness class as a singleton service for the ITranslatorBusiness interface in the DI container. The updated code for Program.cs is present in Listing 3-5.

Listing 3-5. Updated code for Program.cs

```
using Azure;
using Azure.AI.Translation.Text.Custom;
using Chapter3_LanguageTranslator.Business;
using Microsoft.Extensions.Azure;
using Microsoft.Extensions.DependencyInjection;
using Microsoft.Extensions.Hosting;

var host = new HostBuilder()
    .ConfigureFunctionsWorkerDefaults()
```

```
    .ConfigureServices(
    services =>
    {
        services.AddAzureClients(builder =>
        {
            builder.AddTextTranslationClient(
                new AzureKeyCredential(Environment.GetEnvironmentVariable
                ("TranslatorKey")),
                Environment.GetEnvironmentVariable("TranslatorRegion"));
        });
        services.AddSingleton<ITranslatorBusiness, TranslatorBusiness>();
    })
    .Build();
host.Run();
```

As part of the next step, let's create a folder called **Model** in our solution and add a class called **payload.cs** in it. Add the code shown in Listing 3-6 in the payload.cs class. This class will represent the data model of the request payload by deserializing it. We are going to leverage it in the Translator.cs function.

Listing 3-6. Code for Payload.cs

```
using System;
using System.Collections.Generic;
using System.Linq;
using System.Text;
using System.Threading.Tasks;

namespace Chapter3_LanguageTranslator.Model
{
    public class Payload
    {
        public string Message { get; set; }
        public string TargetLanguage { get; set; }
    }
}
```

CHAPTER 3   BUILD A MULTI-LANGUAGE TEXT TRANSLATOR APP WITH AZURE FUNCTIONS

Having completed the business implementation, injected the required services into the DI container, configured the key and endpoint in our local.settings.json file, and defined the payload class, we can now finalize the Translator.cs function by integrating the business logic into it. Let's open the Translator.cs class and update it with the code mentioned in Listing 3-7.

Listing 3-7. Code for Translator.cs

```
using System.Net;
using Chapter3_LanguageTranslator.Business;
using Chapter3_LanguageTranslator.Model;
using Microsoft.Azure.Functions.Worker;
using Microsoft.Azure.Functions.Worker.Http;
using Microsoft.Extensions.Logging;
using Newtonsoft.Json;

namespace Chapter3_LanguageTranslator
{
    public class Translator
    {
        private readonly ILogger<Translator> _logger;
        private readonly ITranslatorBusiness _translatorBusiness;

        public Translator(ILogger<Translator> logger, ITranslatorBusiness translatorBusiness)
        {
            _logger = logger;
            _translatorBusiness = translatorBusiness;
        }

        [Function("Translator")]
        public async Task<HttpResponseData> RunAsync([HttpTrigger(AuthorizationLevel.Function, "get", "post")] HttpRequestData req)
        {
            try
            {
                string requestBody = await new StreamReader(req.Body).ReadToEndAsync();
```

```csharp
            var payload = JsonConvert.DeserializeObject<Payload>
            (requestBody);

            _logger.LogInformation("C# HTTP trigger function processed 
            a request.");

            var result = await _translatorBusiness.
            TranslateMessageAsync(payload.Message, payload.
            TargetLanguage);

            _logger.LogInformation($"Translation: {result}");

            var response = req.CreateResponse(HttpStatusCode.OK);

            response.WriteString(result);

            return response;
        }
        catch (Exception ex)
        {
            _logger.LogError(ex, $"An error occurred - {ex.Message}");
            var response = req.CreateResponse(HttpStatusCode.
            BadRequest);
            response.WriteString(ex.Message);
            return response;
        }
    }
  }
}
```

In Listing 3-7, we are injecting an instance of the **ITranslatorBusiness** and **ILogger** using constructor injection. Then in the **RunAsync** method, we are deserializing the content present in the request body into an object of **Payload** type. Next, we call the TranslateMessageAsync method from the injected instance of the ITranslateBusiness to translate the message present in the payload to the target language specified in the request. Once the processing is done, the function returns the translated text back to the end user.

Now that we have written the code for our solution, in the next section we will test it out using postman.

Test the Multi-language Text Translator Function with Postman

To test the Translator function, we will have to run the function project and start the Azure Functions Core tool. Once you are able to see the Azure Functions Core tool running, copy the endpoint of the Translator function from there as highlighted in Figure 3-12.

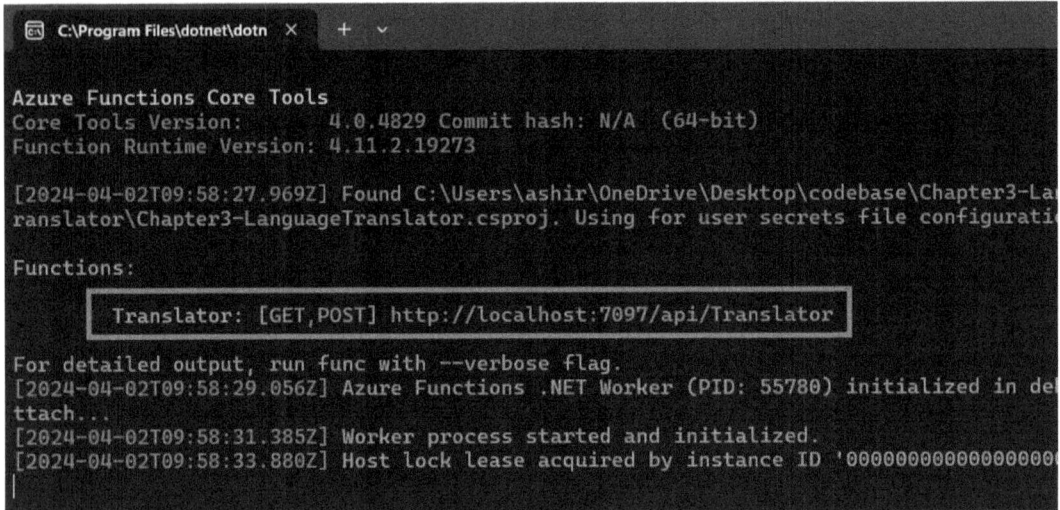

Figure 3-12. *Get the endpoint of the Translator function*

With the endpoint in our hands, let's open postman and create a new collection. Then, add a post request to test our **Translator** function. In the URL of the request, add the endpoint, and in the request body, pass the json shown in Listing 3-8 and click Send.

Listing 3-8. Request payload for the Translator function

```
{
    "message":"Hello",
    "targetLanguage":"hindi"
}
```

The response from our Translator function can be seen in Figure 3-13.

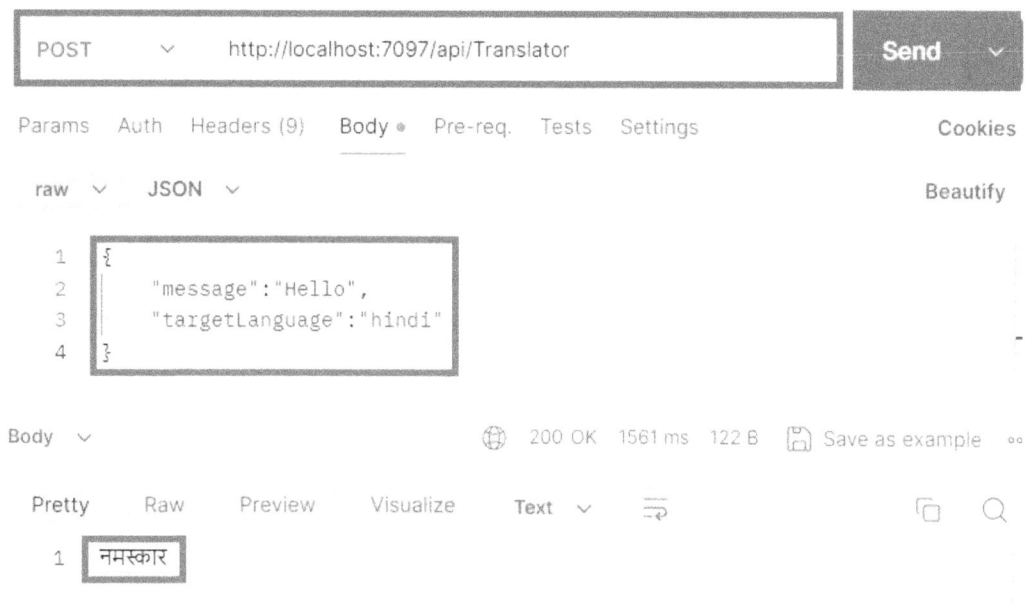

Figure 3-13. *Response from the Translator function*

As can be seen from Figure 3-13, our Translator function was able to accurately translate the message in Hindi. I hope you enjoyed the chapter.

Summary

In this chapter, you've gained insights into creating intelligent solutions using Azure Functions and the Azure AI Translator service through the development of a multi-language translator app. Our exploration delved into the Azure AI Translator service, uncovering its features and applications. Additionally, we navigated through the steps of provisioning an Azure AI Translator service within the Azure Portal. Throughout this process, we've acquired knowledge on constructing an intelligent solution by harnessing the capabilities of the Azure AI Translator service. The primary focus of this chapter centered around the language translation feature offered by the Azure AI Translator service. In the forthcoming chapter, our attention will shift toward investigating the speech-to-text feature provided by the Azure AI Speech service.

CHAPTER 4

Build a Desktop App with .NET MAUI to Generate Texts from Audio Files

Understanding human speech and interpreting it has been an interesting problem in the world of AI. It holds immense value in various domains and industries. Whether it is improving the user experience for consumers of voice assistants like Siri or Alexa or addressing accessibility issues for people with disabilities, speech processing has a significant role to play. A lot of progress into this area has been made over the years, but to build applications with speech capabilities from scratch often is resource intensive and time-consuming. This may not be feasible for organizations that may not have the domain expertise or capital resources at their disposal. In such scenarios, we can leverage speech solutions provided by various vendors. One such offering is the Azure AI Speech service from Microsoft Azure. This service enables us to process and analyze speech and gather insights from audio data. In this chapter, we are going to briefly discuss about the Azure AI Speech service and its use cases and build a desktop app to transcribe audio content by leveraging its client SDKs.

Structure

In this chapter, we will explore the following aspects of Azure:

- Introduction to the Azure AI Speech service
- Create your first Azure AI Speech service in the Azure Portal
- Create a desktop app to transcribe audio content with the Azure AI Speech service

Objectives

After studying this chapter, you should be able to

- Grasp the essentials of the Azure AI Speech service
- Add the capabilities of the Azure AI Speech service to your applications

Introduction to Azure AI Speech Service

The Azure AI Speech service is a fully managed cloud-based speech synthesis and recognition service of Microsoft Azure. It enables developers and organizations to build speech-enabled applications. It comes up with various capabilities such as text to speech, speech to text, speech translation, and voice recognition. The Speech service is a production-grade service which is leveraged for various scenarios in Microsoft products. Some of the examples are live captions in Teams, dictations in Office/Windows, subtitles/translations in PowerPoint, and Read Aloud on Edge. You can deploy an instance of the Azure AI Speech service in different environments like the cloud or the edge with the help of containers. You can also create custom voices or build your own model with the Speech service. It comes up with a flexible pricing model where you can either opt for a pay-as-you-go model or avail any of the commitment tiers. You are priced as on the volume of characters/second that you have performed text to speech/speech to text.

Some of the key features of the Azure AI Speech service are as follows:

1. **Speech to Text** – With this capability, we can transcribe audio data into textual format with high accuracy. It is widely used for scenarios involving note taking, captioning, etc.

2. **Text to Speech** – With this feature, we can generate audio content from the textual data. It enables applications to be voice enabled and helps in building inclusive apps. A classic example where text to speech is widely used is screen readers.

3. **Speech Translations** – With this functionality, you can perform near real-time audio translation for over 30+ languages. It is extremely useful for applications that need to provide real-time translations to different users. One of the popular cases can be facilitating communications during diplomatic missions.

4. **Speaker Recognition** – With this functionality, we enable our applications with the ability to detect speakers by recognizing their voices present in the audio stream or file. It is really useful for scenarios involving voice-based biometrics.

5. **Custom Model and Voices** – With this functionality, teams and organizations can create unique, customized voices for their own applications. Some examples where custom models and voices can be useful are in building virtual customer support agents or for creating voices for fictional characters.

6. **Supports Client SDKs** – The service provides client SDKs in various languages and frameworks like Python, Node.js, C#, and Java. It enables developers to easily integrate the Translator service in their applications. For the language for which the SDKs are not available, they can use the REST APIs to integrate the capabilities of the Azure AI Translator service in their application.

Now that we have explored some of the key features of the Azure AI Speech service, let's explore some of the potential use cases where it can come in handy:

1. **Call Center Automation** – We can leverage the power of the Azure AI Speech service to automate call center operations like transcribing customer calls in real time.

2. **Accessibility Solutions** – We can leverage the text-to-speech and speech-to-text capabilities of the Azure AI Speech service to build accessible solutions for people with disabilities. It can be integrated with screen readers or communication devices to enable users to access digital content and communicate effectively.

As we have explored what Azure AI Speech service is and what its key features and use cases are, let's explore ways to integrate it in our solutions by building a desktop app to transcribe audio files.

CHAPTER 4   BUILD A DESKTOP APP WITH .NET MAUI TO GENERATE TEXTS FROM AUDIO FILES

Problem Statement

You are working for a fictional company, AS Media Times. The company is a media firm which deals with newspapers and magazines. Oftentimes, your company conducts interviews, press conferences, and events. A large volume of audio content is generated during such occasions. Currently, your company manually transcribes content. But this is a cumbersome process which takes a lot of time. Your management has decided to build a system to automate the process of transcribing text from such audio files to reduce the manual efforts. The architect of your team has identified the Azure AI Speech service to be a perfect solution to solve this problem. As part of the development team, you are tasked with the proof of concept to explore ways to extract textual data from audio files by leveraging the power of the Azure AI Speech service. Your team is going to leverage your proof of concept as the base for the further development of the functionality.

Proposed Solution

After going through the requirement, you have broken down the problem into two tasks:

1. Transcribe audio files
2. Provide an interface to interact with the solution

To solve both of the abovementioned problems, you have decided to use .NET MAUI and the Azure AI Speech service to develop the solution. With the help of .NET MAUI, we are going to provide a desktop app to the end users where they can upload their audio and view the transcribed text. The desktop app is going to take the audio file provided by the user, then leverage the power of the Azure AI Speech service to transcribe the audio content and then display back the result on the screen.

Before we start building the desktop app, we need a couple of things in place. The following are the prerequisites to start the development activities:

1. Create an Azure AI Speech service
2. Fetch the endpoint and key of the Azure AI Speech service

Once we have these two things in place, we can start building our solution using Visual Studio 2022. Let's get started.

CHAPTER 4   BUILD A DESKTOP APP WITH .NET MAUI TO GENERATE TEXTS FROM AUDIO FILES

Create an Azure AI Speech Service

To create an Azure AI Speech service, go to the Azure Portal and type Speech in the search box. Click the **Speech services** in the search results as shown in Figure 4-1.

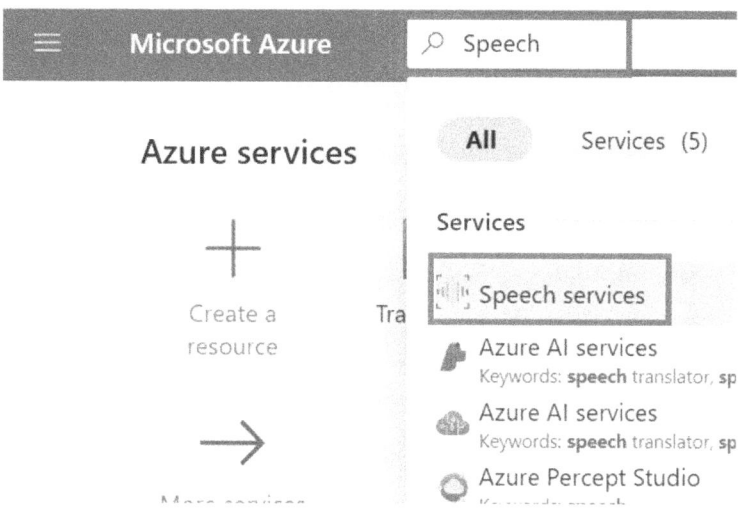

Figure 4-1. *Search for Speech*

On the screen shown in Figure 4-2, you can view the list of Speech services that you have provisioned. Click **Create** to provision our Speech service in Azure.

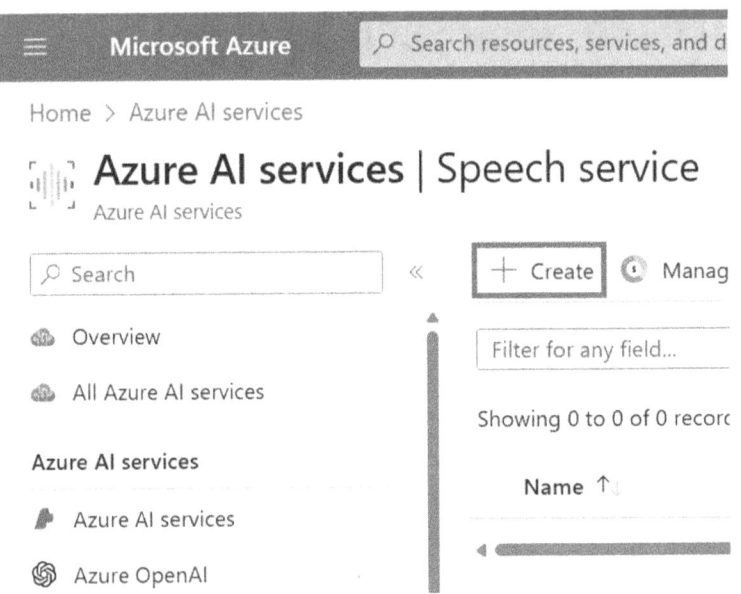

Figure 4-2. *Click Create*

Next, select your subscription and resource group from the drop-downs available on the screen as can be seen in Figure 4-3. If you don't have a resource group, you can create a new one on this screen. After that, select the region, provide the resource name, and select the pricing tier. The resource name needs to be a unique one. For the purpose of building this solution, we are going to use the **Free F0** tier. This tier provides us with the capability to perform speech to text for five audio hours per month, which should be enough to build and test our proof of concept (PoC). For workloads running in a production environment, it is advised to use higher tiers. Once you have entered the preceding details, click **Review + create**.

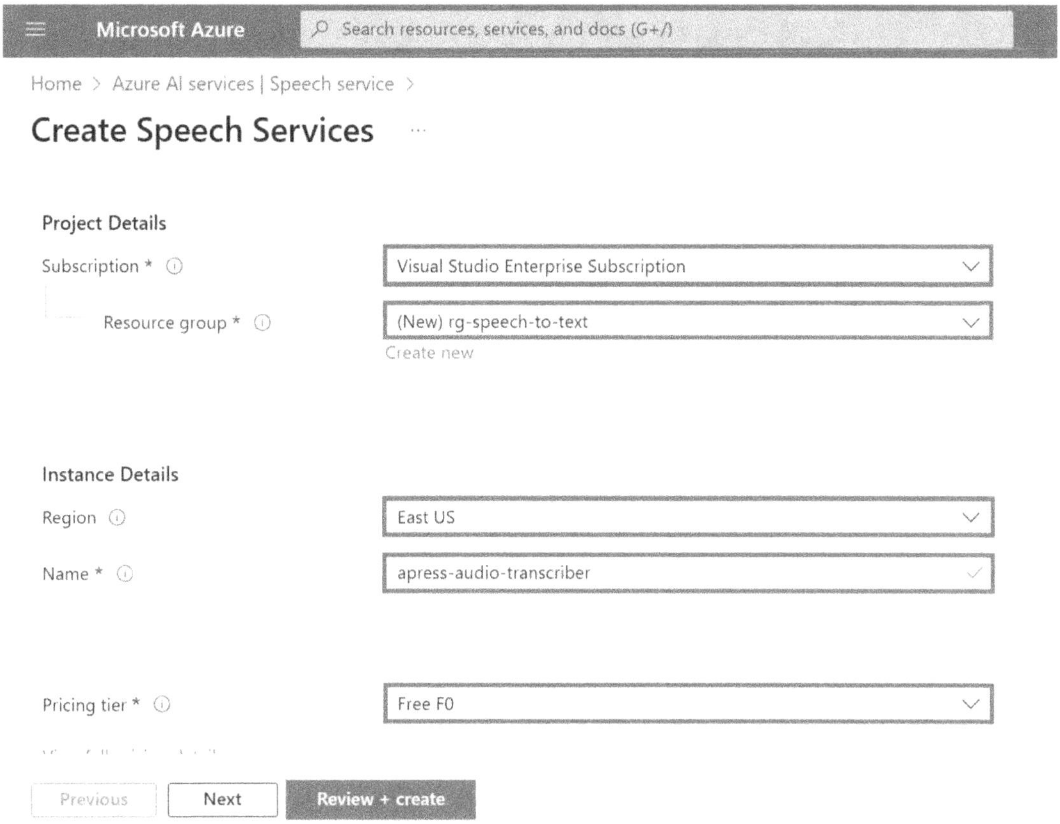

CHAPTER 4 BUILD A DESKTOP APP WITH .NET MAUI TO GENERATE TEXTS FROM AUDIO FILES

Figure 4-3. Click Review + create

Now you will see a summary of the configuration for the speech resource that you had entered on the previous screen. A validation check will be done on the configurations. Once the validation of the configuration is done, click **Create** to provision the resource as shown in Figure 4-4. If you wanted to make any changes, you could click **Previous** and make the necessary changes for the resource.

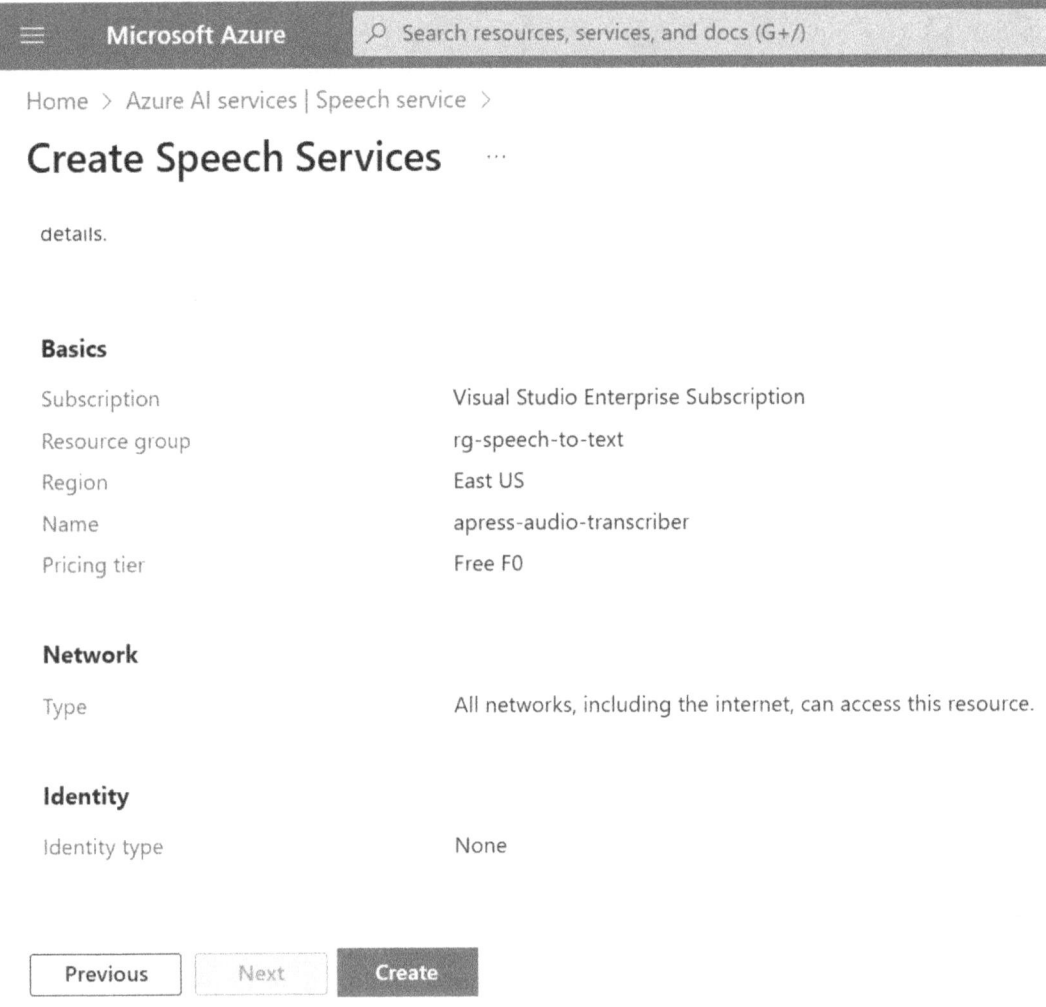

Figure 4-4. Click Create

Once the resource has been created successfully, you will see the message "Your deployment is complete," as shown in Figure 4-5. Once you see that message, click **Go to resource** to view the newly provisioned speech resource.

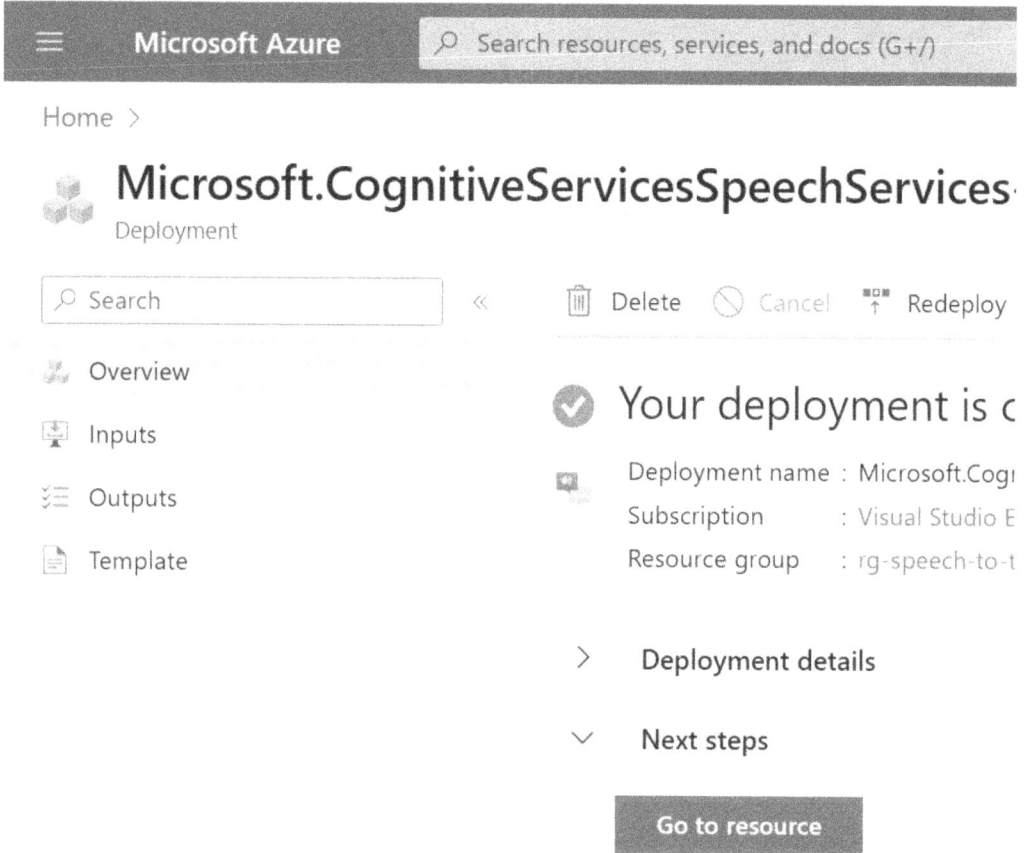

Figure 4-5. *Click Go to resource*

Now that we have provisioned our AI Speech service in the Azure Portal, we will need to fetch the access key and endpoint to interact with it from our solution. Access keys are just one way of authenticating our calls to the Speech service. We can use other methods like Managed Identity–based authentication which is recommended for production workloads. For the purpose of our PoC, we are going to use key-based authentication.

To fetch the key and endpoint for our language, click Keys and Endpoint as shown in Figure 4-6.

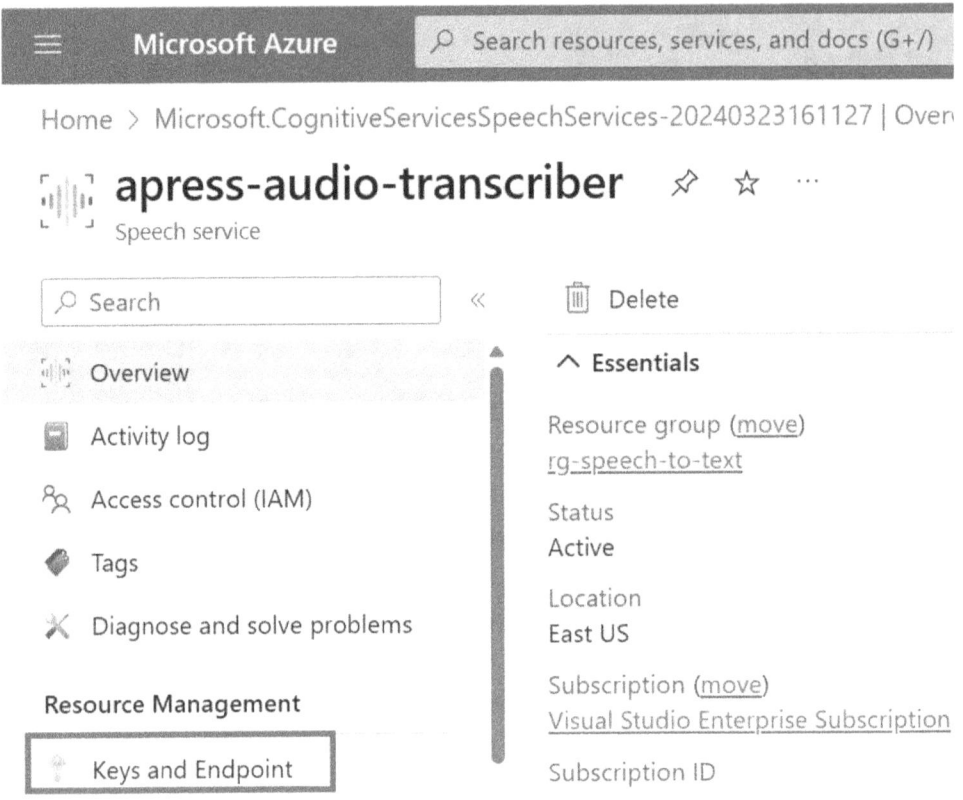

Figure 4-6. *Click Keys and Endpoint*

We will have to fetch either one of the primary or secondary key, the resource endpoint, and the region from the screen shown in Figure 4-7. We will use these values later in our application for authentication purposes.

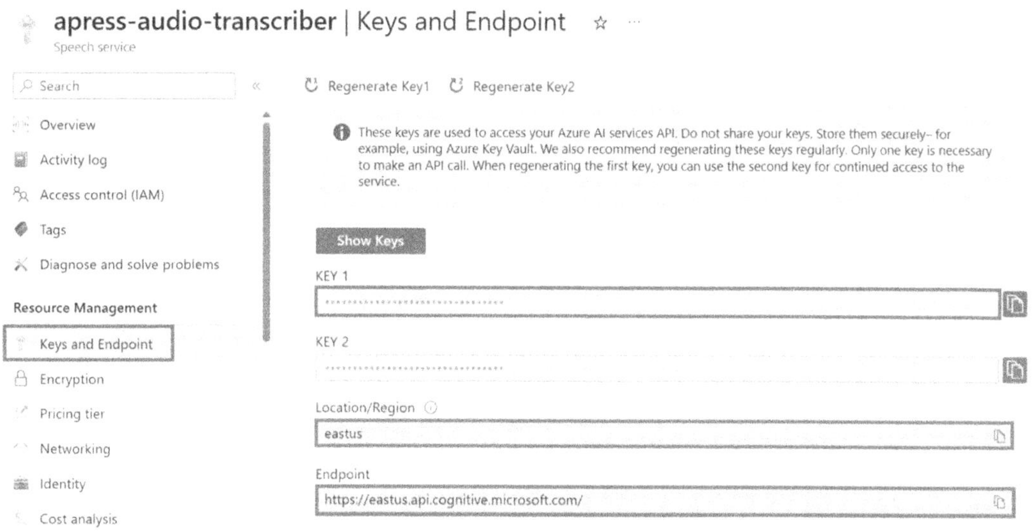

Figure 4-7. Get the key, endpoint, and region

Now that we have provisioned the speech resource and have the required information to authenticate requests from our application to the language service, we have completed the prerequisites. In the next section, we will build the desktop app to generate text from audio files.

Create a Desktop App with .NET MAUI to Generate Texts from Audio Files

In this section, we are going to complete the proof of concept for our fictional company to build a feature for our product as briefly discussed in the "Proposed Solution" section.

As we have already discussed the business requirement and provisioned the required resources, let's start building our desktop app to generate texts from audio files using the **.NET MAUI app** template.

Chances are that you may not be able to view the .NET MAUI template unless you added the **.NET Multi-platform App UI development** workload. If you have not added it previously, open the Visual Studio installer, click Modify, check the **.NET Multi-platform App UI development** workload, and click **Install** as highlighted in Figure 4-8.

CHAPTER 4   BUILD A DESKTOP APP WITH .NET MAUI TO GENERATE TEXTS FROM AUDIO FILES

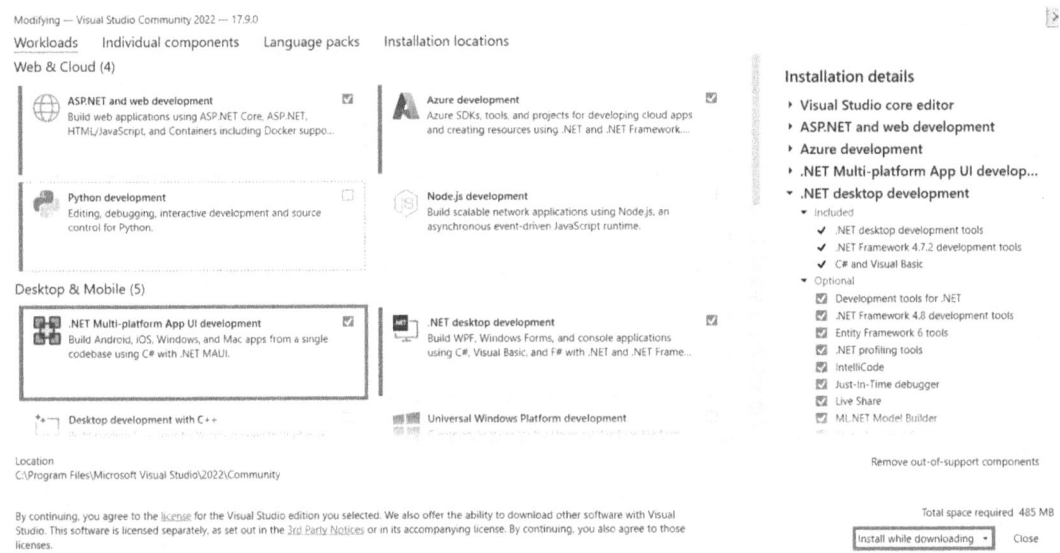

Figure 4-8. *Install the .NET Multi-platform App UI development workload*

Once the workload has been installed, open Visual Studio 2022 and click **Create a new project** as shown in Figure 4-9.

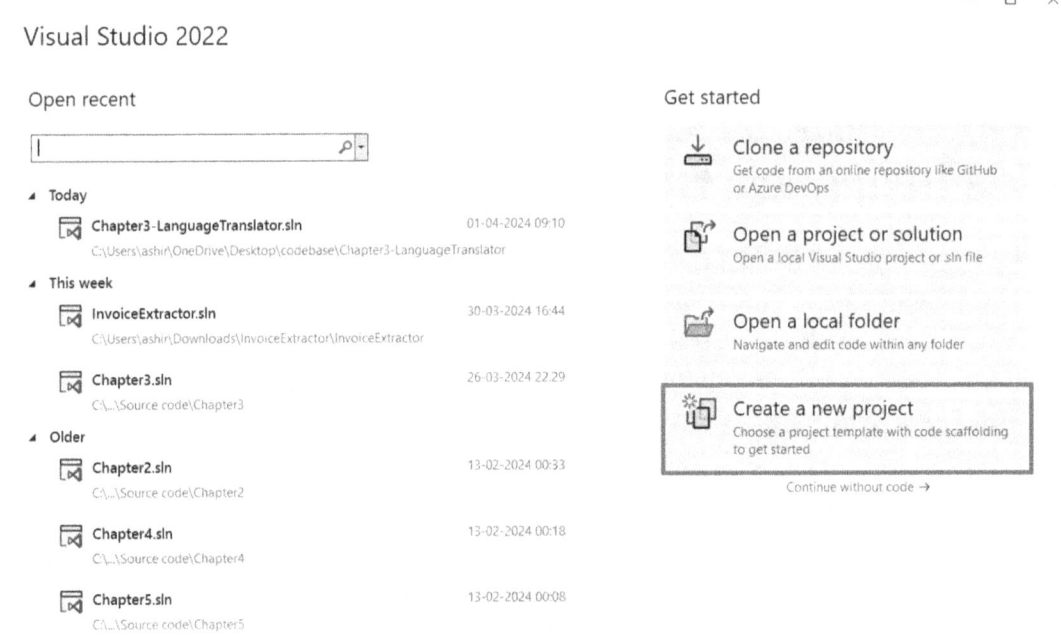

Figure 4-9. *Create a new project*

Select the **.NET MAUI App** project template as shown in Figure 4-10 and click **Next**.

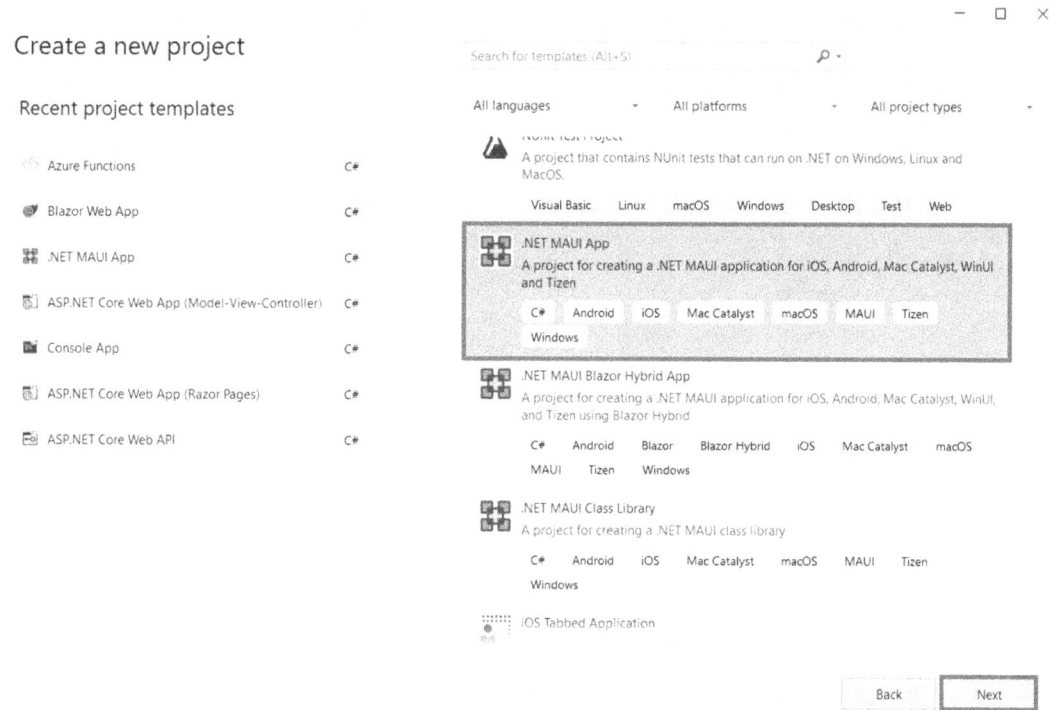

Figure 4-10. *Click Next*

Enter the **project name**, **location**, and **solution name** as shown in Figure 4-11 and click **Next**.

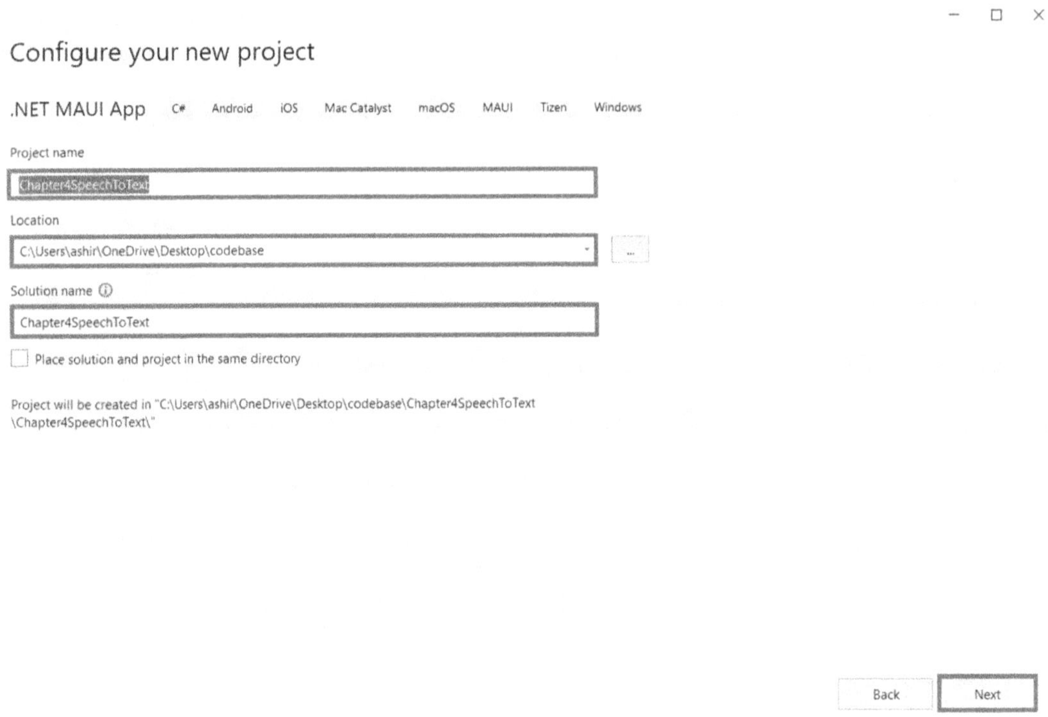

CHAPTER 4   BUILD A DESKTOP APP WITH .NET MAUI TO GENERATE TEXTS FROM AUDIO FILES

Figure 4-11. Enter the project name, location, and solution name

Now select the **.NET 8.0** as the runtime and click **Create** as shown Figure 4-12.

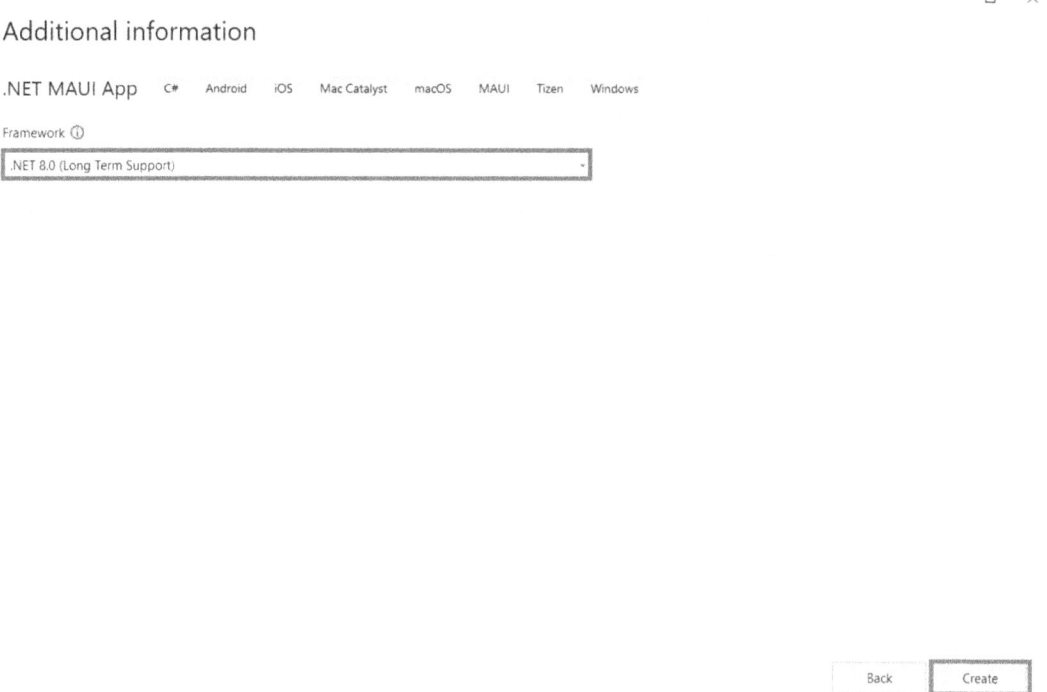

Figure 4-12. *Click Create*

Now Visual Studio will generate a sample .NET MAUI app out of the box. As a next step, let's add all the packages that we would need to build our solutions. To do so, open the NuGet package manager and install the following package:

1. Microsoft.CognitiveServices.Speech

Microsoft.CognitiveServices.Speech is the official SDK for interacting with the Azure AI Speech service. We will leverage this SDK to add the capability of transcribing audio files in our application.

After installing the abovementioned NuGet package, let's open the MainPage.xaml and update it with the code mentioned in Listing 4-1.

Listing 4-1. Code for MainPage.xaml

```
<?xml version="1.0" encoding="utf-8" ?>
<ContentPage xmlns="http://schemas.microsoft.com/dotnet/2021/maui"
             xmlns:x="http://schemas.microsoft.com/winfx/2009/xaml"
             x:Class="Chapter4SpeechToText.MainPage">
```

CHAPTER 4   BUILD A DESKTOP APP WITH .NET MAUI TO GENERATE TEXTS FROM AUDIO FILES

```xml
<ScrollView>
    <VerticalStackLayout
        Padding="30,0"
        Spacing="25">
        <Image
            Source="dotnet_bot.png"
            HeightRequest="155"
            Aspect="AspectFit"
            SemanticProperties.Description="dot net bot in a race car
            number eight" />

        <Label
            Text="Welcome to AS Media Times!"
            Style="{StaticResource Headline}" />
        <Entry
            x:Name="entAbsolutePath"
            Text=""
            Placeholder="Please provide the absolute path of your .wav
            file"></Entry>
        <Entry
            x:Name="entSubscriptionKey"
            Text=""
            Placeholder="Please provide the subscription key of your
            speech resource"></Entry>
        <Entry
             x:Name="entRegion"
            Text=""
            Placeholder="Please provide the region of your speech
            resource"></Entry>

        <Button
            x:Name="btnTranscribe"
            Text="Transcribe"
            Clicked ="btnTranscribe_Clicked"
            HorizontalOptions="Fill" />

        <Label
```

```
                x:Name="lblTranscribeResult"
                Text=""
                Style="{StaticResource SubHeadline}" />
        </VerticalStackLayout>
    </ScrollView>

</ContentPage>
```

In Listing 4-1, we are defining the UI layout and component of our app. We have an image, two labels, three entry fields, and one button. The image used here is the dotnet image that comes out of the box when we create a .NET MAUI app. We have one label which mentions **Welcome to AS Media Times!**. Next, we have three entry fields in our app. Entry fields are like text boxes. We are going to leverage them to fetch the absolute path of the audio file, region, and key of the Speech service. Then, we have a button called **Transcribe**. This button has an event handler configured, that is, **btnTranscribe_Clicked**. Every time someone clicks this button, the btnTranscribe_Clicked method will be invoked. Lastly, we have one more label. This label is going to display the result after the execution of the **btnTranscribe_Clicked** method.

As we have explored the XAML code which defined the UI of our application, let's implement the business logic in the code-behind file to make the app functional. Replace the code of MainPage.xaml.cs with the code shown in Listing 4-2.

Listing 4-2. Code for MainPage.xaml.cs

```
using Microsoft.CognitiveServices.Speech.Audio;
using Microsoft.CognitiveServices.Speech;

namespace Chapter4SpeechToText
{
    public partial class MainPage : ContentPage
    {
        public MainPage()
        {
            InitializeComponent();
        }

        private async void btnTranscribe_Clicked(object sender,
        EventArgs e)
```

```csharp
        {
            var absolutePathToWavFile = entAbsolutePath.Text;
            var speechKey = entSubscriptionKey.Text;
            var speechRegion = entRegion.Text;

            var speechConfig = SpeechConfig.FromSubscription(speechKey,
            speechRegion);
            speechConfig.SpeechRecognitionLanguage = "en-US";

            using var audioConfig = AudioConfig.FromWavFileInput(absolute
            PathToWavFile);

            using var speechRecognizer = new SpeechRecognizer(speechConfig,
            audioConfig);

            var speechRecognitionResult = await speechRecognizer.
            RecognizeOnceAsync();

            var result = OutputSpeechRecognitionResult(speechRecognition
            Result);

            lblTranscribeResult.Text = $"Transcribed text - {result}";
        }
        static string OutputSpeechRecognitionResult(SpeechRecognitionResult
        speechRecognitionResult)
        {
            string result = string.Empty;
            switch (speechRecognitionResult.Reason)
            {
                case ResultReason.RecognizedSpeech:
                    result = speechRecognitionResult.Text;
                    break;
                case ResultReason.NoMatch:
                    result = "NOMATCH: Speech could not be recognized.";
                    break;
                case ResultReason.Canceled:
```

```
            result = $"CANCELED: Operation cancelled";
            break;
    }
    return result;
  }
 }
}
```

Listing 4-2 contains the implementation of the **btnTranscribe_Clicked** method. This method is called every time the user clicks the **Transcribe** button. Inside this method, we fetch the absolute path of the audio file, key, and region of the Speech service by using the text property of the respective entry fields. Once we have these values, we create an instance of the **SpeechRecognizer** to interact with our Azure AI Speech service. Once we have created the instance, we leverage the power of the **RecognizeOnceAsync** method to transcribe the audio file into text. We later check the outcome of the result, and if the **ResultReason** was **RecognizedSpeech**, then we bind the value to the text property of the **lblTranscribeResult** label to show the result in the app.

Now that we have implemented the business of our app and defined the UI, let's test the app in the next section.

Test the .NET MAUI App

To test the web app, let's run it on the Windows machine. Before you run the solution as a desktop app on Windows, you will have to turn on the Developer Mode in your system. To do so, you can go to the **For developers** section present inside the **System** section of your settings on Windows 11. Once there, toggle the **Developer** mode as **On**. This is only required for the first time. Once done, run your app with the **Windows machine**. This will start your app. The app would look similar to the one shown in Figure 4-13.

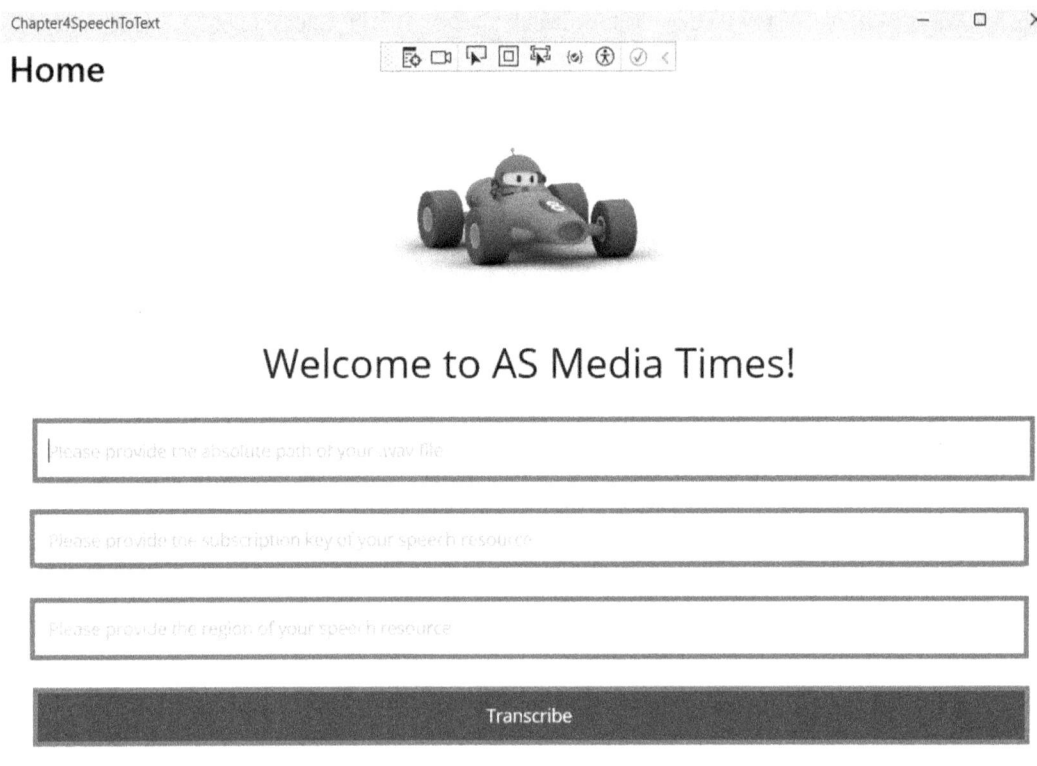

Figure 4-13. *Our .NET MAUI app*

As the app is up and running, let's provide the details and click Transcribe. Currently, this solution only supports audio files of .wav format. I have used the audio sample available at `https://github.com/Azure-Samples/cognitive-services-speech-sdk/blob/master/sampledata/audiofiles/TalkForAFewSeconds16.wav`; please feel free to use any .wav file that you might have. To test the app, let's provide the absolute path of the audio file, the region, and the key of the speech resource and click the **Transcribe** button. After processing the request, the app should display the transcribed text in a label as shown in Figure 4-14.

CHAPTER 4 BUILD A DESKTOP APP WITH .NET MAUI TO GENERATE TEXTS FROM AUDIO FILES

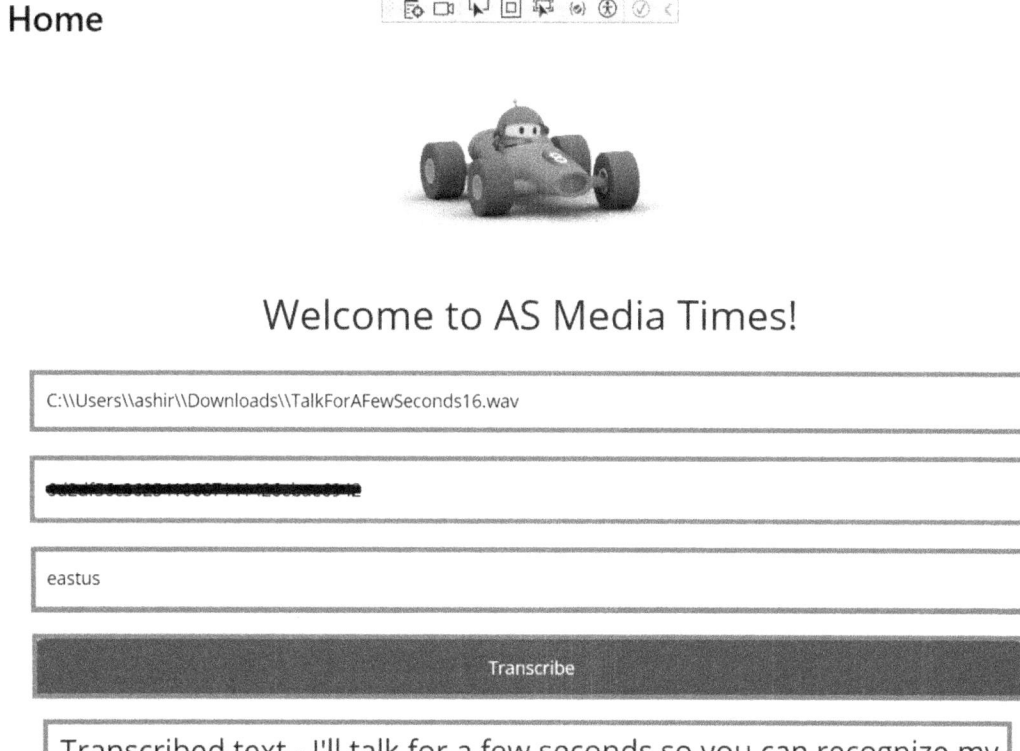

Figure 4-14. Demo of our .NET MAUI app

As can be seen from Figure 4-14, our desktop app was able to accurately transcribe the audio file.

Summary

In this chapter, you've gained insights into creating intelligent solutions using .NET MAUI and the Azure AI Speech service through the development of a desktop app to transcribe audio files. Our exploration delved into the Azure AI Speech service, uncovering its features and applications. Additionally, we navigated through the steps of provisioning an Azure AI Speech service within the Azure Portal. Throughout this process, we've acquired knowledge on constructing an intelligent solution by harnessing the capabilities of the Azure AI Speech service. The primary focus of this chapter centered around the speech-to-text feature offered by the Azure AI Speech service. In the forthcoming chapter, our attention will shift toward investigating the OCR feature provided by the Azure AI Vision service.

CHAPTER 5

Build a Desktop App with .NET MAUI to Extract Text from Images

As per estimates, over 3.2 billion photos are uploaded to the Internet from different sources. With the advent of smartphone, click photos are just a click away. All these photos can have informational insights or memories of loved ones. A lot of information can be derived from such pictures which can aid in taking better business decisions or in enhancing customer experiences. But building image processing systems from scratch needs a lot of resources and domain expertise. To mitigate these hurdles, we can leverage third-party AI solutions and add cognitive capability of interpreting images in our applications. One such service is Azure AI Vision of Microsoft Azure which can analyze images and perform various operations around images. In this chapter, we are going to briefly discuss about the Azure AI Vision service and its use cases and build a desktop app to extract textual content from images by leveraging its client SDKs.

Structure

In this chapter, we will explore the following aspects of Azure:

- Introduction to the Azure AI Vision service
- Create your first Azure AI Vision service in the Azure Portal
- Create a desktop app to extract textual content from images with the Azure AI Vision service

Objectives

After studying this chapter, you should be able to

- Grasp the essentials of the Azure AI Vision service
- Add the capabilities of the Azure AI Vision service to your applications

Introduction to Azure AI Vision Service

The Azure AI Vision service is a fully managed cloud-based image analysis service of Microsoft Azure. It enables developers and organizations to build applications which can process and gather insights from visual data without requiring deep expertise in computer vision. The Azure AI Vision service provides a unified platform to perform various computer vision tasks, such as analyzing images, reading text, detecting faces, as well as facial recognition. The applications of the Azure AI Vision service are widespread. For specific scenarios where you want to customize existing models for specific scenarios, exploring Azure Custom Vision would be a good idea. The Azure AI Vision service comes up with a guaranteed SLA of 99.9% like other Azure AI Services. You can deploy an instance of the Azure AI Vision service in different environments like the cloud or the edge with the help of containers. It comes up with a flexible pricing model where you can either opt for a pay-as-you-go model or avail any of the commitment tiers.

Some of the key features of the Azure AI Vision service are as follows:

1. **Analyze Images** – With this feature, we can build applications that can analyze a visual content and gather insights such as object detection, classification, caption generation, etc.

2. **Read Text** – With this feature, we can extract textual content present in images or documents. It supports both printed and handwritten text from images. It supports text extraction for multiple languages at the moment. We are going to explore this functionality in the later section of this chapter.

3. **Detect Faces** – With this functionality, we can detect, recognize, and analyze human faces in images. It is useful for scenarios involving touchless access control, facial identification, or facial blurring capability to safeguard the user's privacy.

4. **Spatial Analysis** – With this feature, we can detect the presence of a person in video streams. There are various use cases of this feature, a prominent use case being analyzing if people are abiding to social distancing rules and wearing masks in a video stream.

5. **Supports Client SDKs** – The service provides client SDKs in various languages like Python, JavaScript, C#, and Java. It enables developers to easily integrate the Vision service in their applications. For the languages for which the SDKs are not available, they can use the REST APIs to integrate the capabilities of the Azure AI Vision service in their application.

Now that we have explored some of the key features of the Azure AI Vision service, let's explore some of the potential use cases where it can come in handy:

1. **Document Digitization and Processing** – A lot of industries like finance, insurance, and legal services have a lot of information stored in physical documents. We can leverage the OCR capabilities of the Azure AI Vision service to extract data from scanned documents and store them in meaningful manner to derive insights. It will help in reducing manual efforts in data entry-related activities and significantly improve productivity.

2. **Smart Traffic Solution** – Managing traffic in cities and towns is often a challenging task. Traffic congestions and safety are major concerns for any city/town authorities. With the help of Azure AI Vision services, we can analyze video streams and derive insights, such as identifying traffic violations like illegal parking or running on red light or incident detection. This will help in ensuring road safety and identifying offenders easily.

As we have explored what Azure AI Vision service is and what its key features and use cases are, let's explore ways to integrate it in our solutions by building a desktop app to extract textual content from images.

Problem Statement

You are working for a fictional company, AT Corp. The company has multiple museums under its umbrella. The museums are dedicated to preserve and showcase cultural artifacts and historical documents. Most of the documents are a few centuries old and hold significant historical importance. Currently, the company is facing a challenge in digitizing its extensive collection of archive material. To address this issue, the company created a team which can extract content from the images of the historical documents and show it in digital text format. As part of the development team, you are tasked to build a proof of concept to extract textual content from images by leveraging the power of the Azure AI Vision service. The proof of concept will later be leveraged to build a full-fledged system to extract data from all the documents in digitized format and to share it with a wider audience.

Proposed Solution

After going through the requirement, you have broken down the problem into two tasks:

1. Extract texts from images
2. Provide an interface to interact with the solution

To solve both of the abovementioned problems, you have decided to use .NET MAUI and the Azure AI Vision service to develop the solution. With the help of the .NET MAUI, we are going to provide a desktop app to the end users where they can upload their images and view the text extracted from them. The desktop app is going to take the image file provided by the user, then leverage the power of the Azure AI Vision service to perform text extraction and then display back the result on the screen.

Before we start building the desktop app, we need a couple of things in place. The following are the prerequisites to start the development activities:

1. Create an Azure AI Vision service
2. Fetch the endpoint and key of the Azure AI Vision service

CHAPTER 5   BUILD A DESKTOP APP WITH .NET MAUI TO EXTRACT TEXT FROM IMAGES

Once we have these two things in place, we can start building our solution using Visual Studio 2022. Let's get started.

Create an Azure AI Computer Vision Service

To create an Azure AI Vision service, go to the Azure Portal and type Computer Vision in the search box. Click the **Computer vision** in the search results as shown in Figure 5-1.

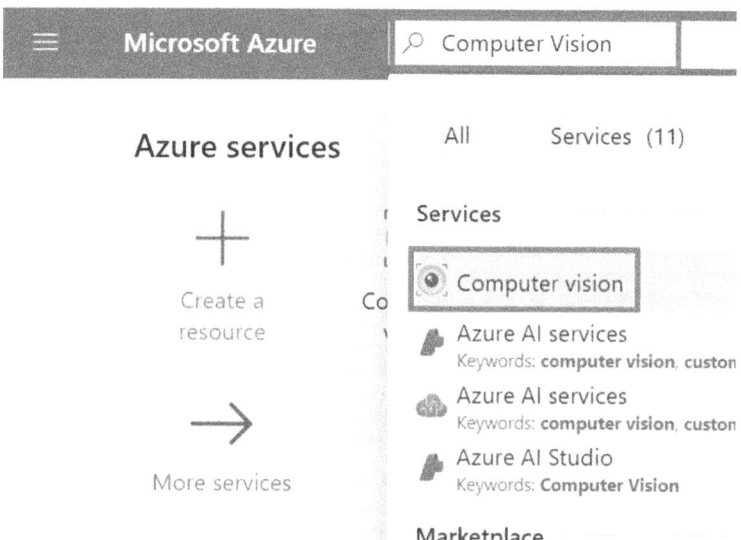

Figure 5-1. *Search for computer vision*

On the screen shown in Figure 5-2, you can view the list of Computer Vision services that you have provisioned. Click **Create** to provision our Computer Vision service in Azure.

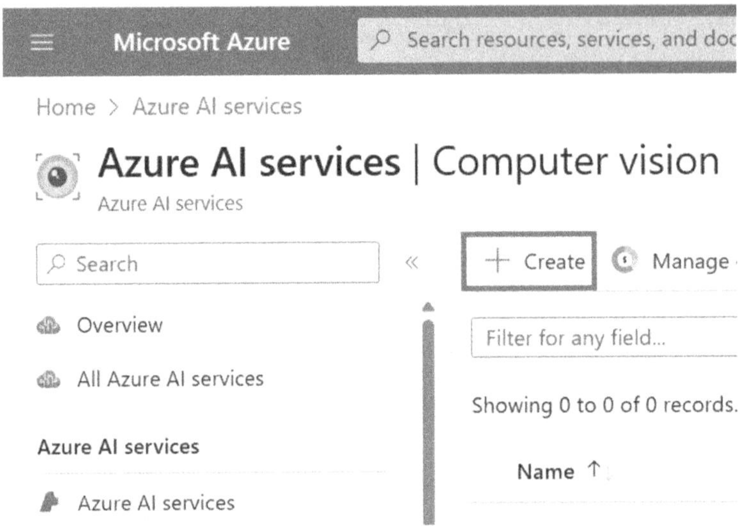

CHAPTER 5   BUILD A DESKTOP APP WITH .NET MAUI TO EXTRACT TEXT FROM IMAGES

Figure 5-2.   Click Create

Next, select your subscription and resource group from the drop-downs available on the screen as can be seen in Figure 5-3. If you don't have a resource group, you can create a new one on this screen. After that, select the region, provide the resource name, and select the pricing tier. The resource name needs to be a unique one. For the purpose of building this solution, we are going to the **Free F0** tier. This tier provides us with the capability to perform 20 calls per minute and overall 5K calls per month, which should be enough to build and test our proof of concept (PoC). For workloads running in a production environment, it is advised to use higher tiers. Once you have entered the preceding details, you will have to check the tick box stating that you have reviewed and acknowledge the terms in the Responsible AI Notice. Once done, click **Review + create**.

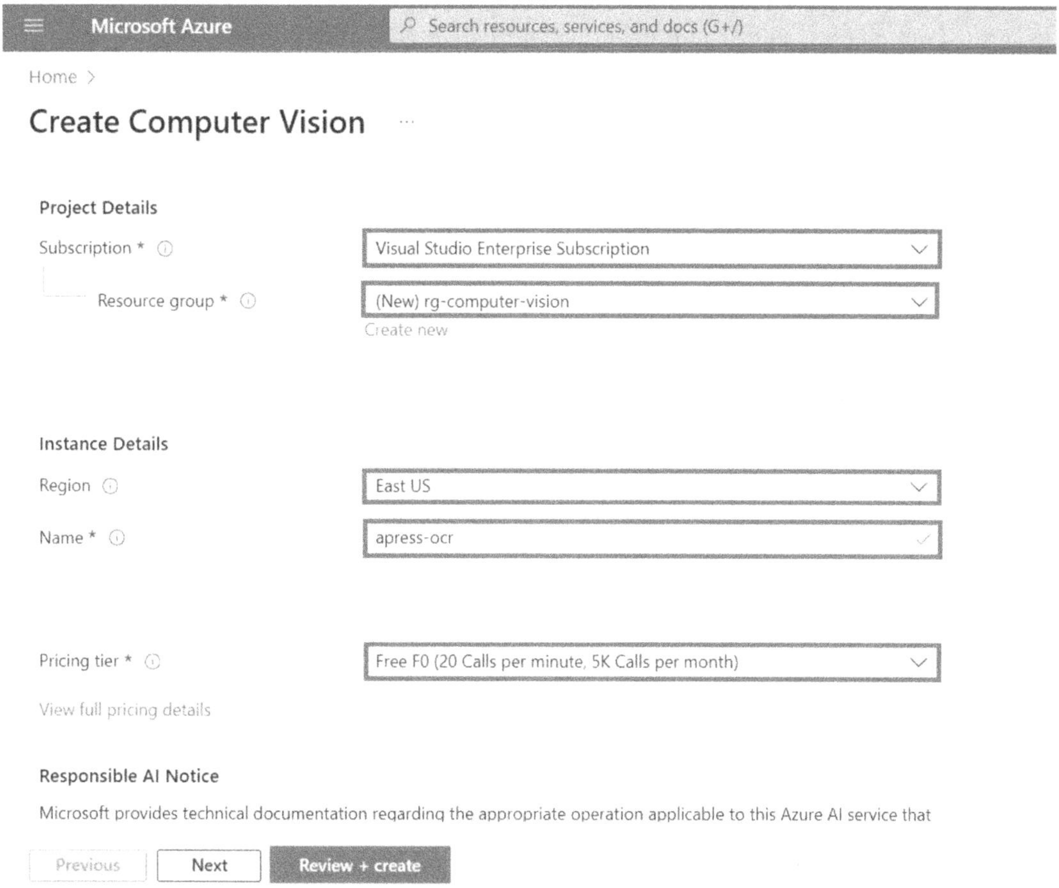

CHAPTER 5 BUILD A DESKTOP APP WITH .NET MAUI TO EXTRACT TEXT FROM IMAGES

Figure 5-3. Click Review + create

Now you will see a summary of the configuration for the computer vision resource that you had entered on the previous screen. A validation check will be done on the configurations. Once the validation of the configuration is done, click **Create** to provision the resource as shown in Figure 5-4. If you wanted to make any changes, you could click **Previous** and make the necessary changes for the resource.

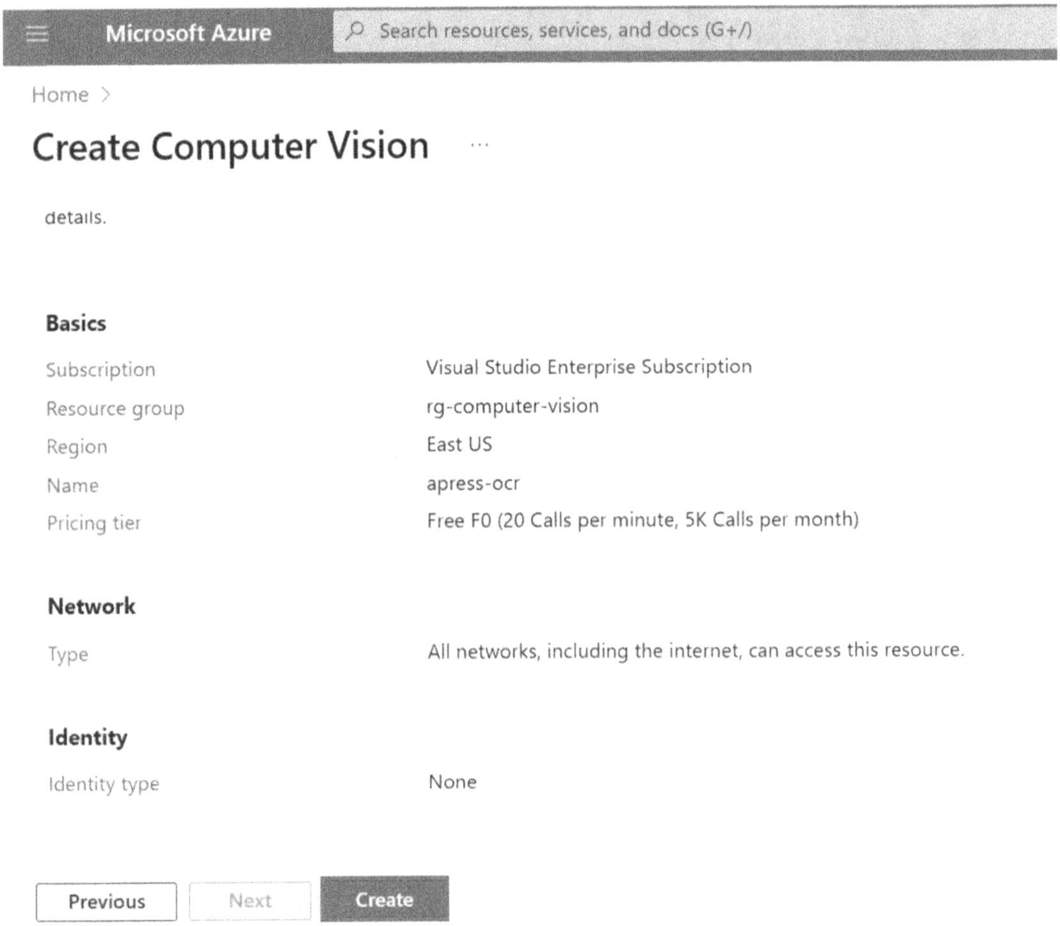
Microsoft Azure
Search resources, services, and docs (G+/)
Home >
Create Computer Vision
details.
Basics
Subscription
Visual Studio Enterprise Subscription
Resource group
rg-computer-vision
Region
East US
Name
apress-ocr
Pricing tier
Free F0 (20 Calls per minute, 5K Calls per month)
Network
Type
All networks, including the internet, can access this resource.
Identity
Identity type
None
Previous
Next
Create

Figure 5-4. *Click Create*

Once the resource has been created successfully, you will see the message "Your deployment is complete," as shown in Figure 5-5. Once you see that message, click **Go to resource** to view the newly provisioned computer vision resource.

CHAPTER 5 BUILD A DESKTOP APP WITH .NET MAUI TO EXTRACT TEXT FROM IMAGES

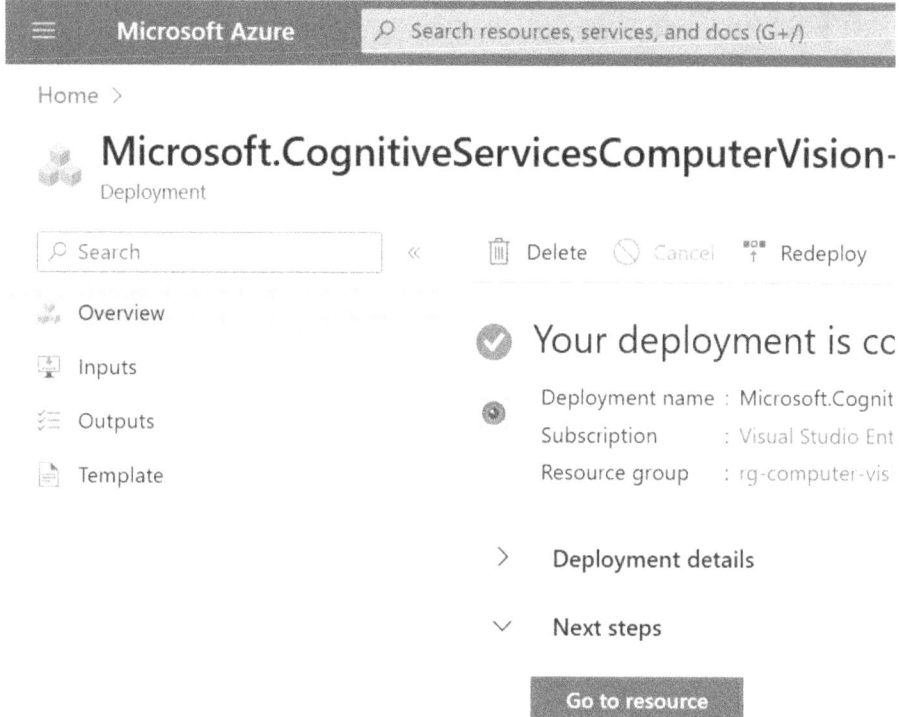

Figure 5-5. *Click Go to resource*

Now that we have provisioned our AI Computer Vision service in the Azure Portal, we will need to fetch the access key and endpoint to interact with it from our solution. Access keys are just one way of authenticating our calls to the Computer Vision service. We can use other methods like Managed Identity-based authentication which is recommended for production workloads. For the purpose of our PoC, we are going to use key-based authentication.

To fetch the key and endpoint for our computer vision, click Keys and Endpoint as shown in Figure 5-6.

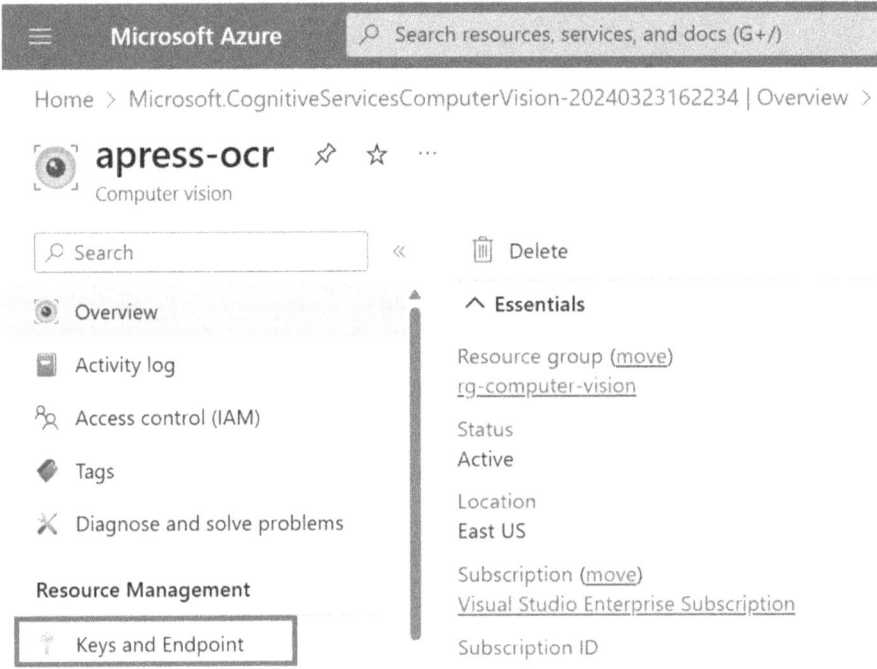

Figure 5-6. Click Keys and Endpoint

We will have to fetch either one of the primary or secondary key, the resource endpoint, and the region from the screen shown in Figure 5-7. We will use these values later in our application for authentication purposes.

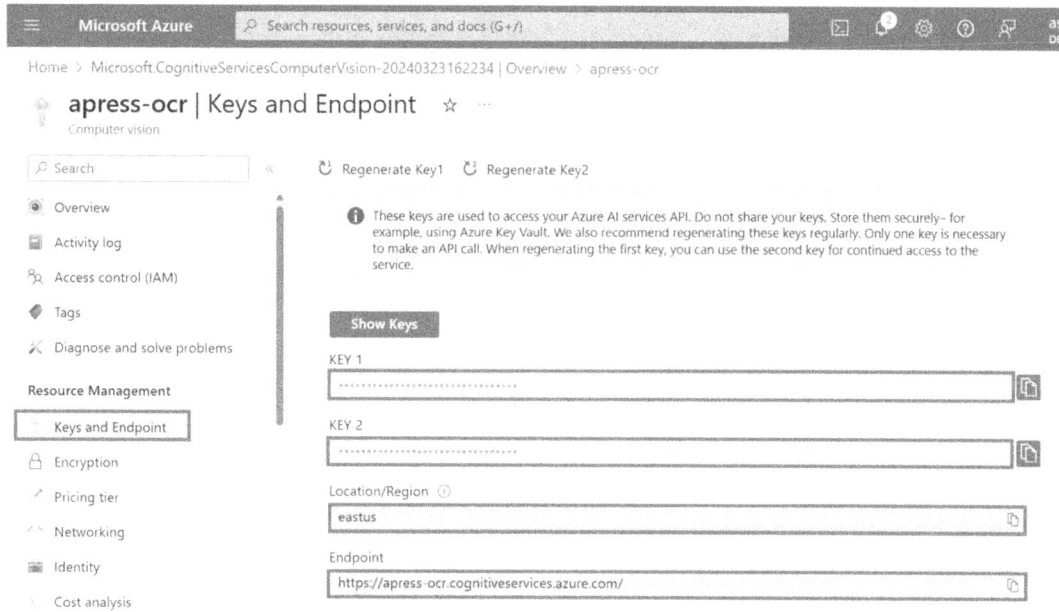

Figure 5-7. *Get the key, endpoint, and region*

Now that we have provisioned the computer vision resource and have the required information to authenticate requests from our application to the Computer Vision service, we have completed one of the prerequisites. In the next section, we will create a desktop app with .NET MAUI to extract text from images.

Create a Desktop App with .NET MAUI to Extract Text from Images

In this section, we are going to complete the proof of concept for our fictional company to build a feature for our product as briefly discussed in the "Proposed Solution" section.

As we have already discussed the business requirement and provisioned the required resources, let's start building our desktop app to extract texts from image files by using the **.NET MAUI app** template.

Chances are that you may not be able to view the .NET MAUI template unless you added the **.NET Multi-platform App UI development** workload. If you have not added it previously, open the Visual Studio installer, click Modify, check the **.NET Multi-platform App UI development** workload, and click **Install** as highlighted in Figure 5-8.

CHAPTER 5   BUILD A DESKTOP APP WITH .NET MAUI TO EXTRACT TEXT FROM IMAGES

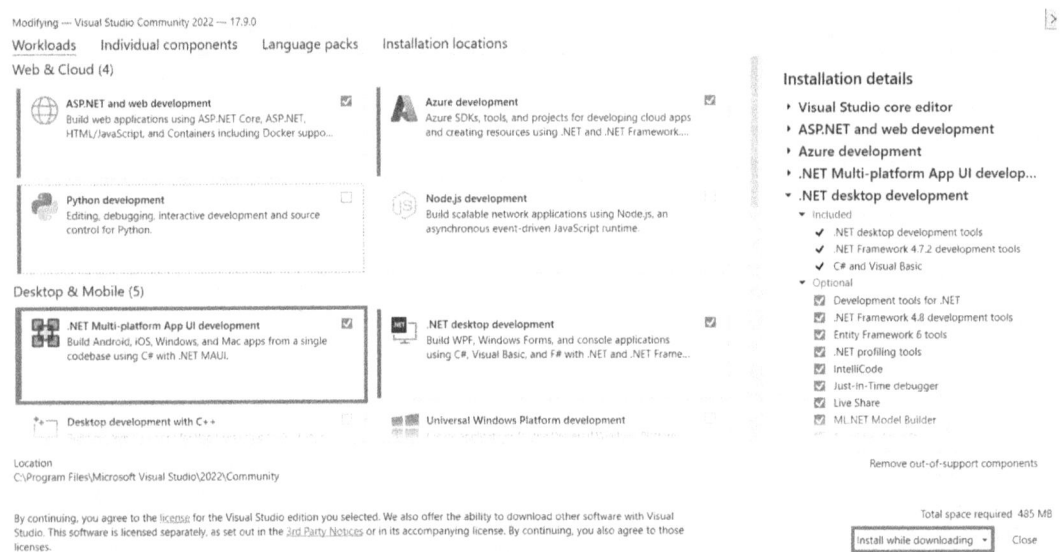

Figure 5-8. Install the .NET Multi-platform App UI development workload

Once the workload has been installed, open Visual Studio 2022 and click **Create a new project** as shown in Figure 5-9.

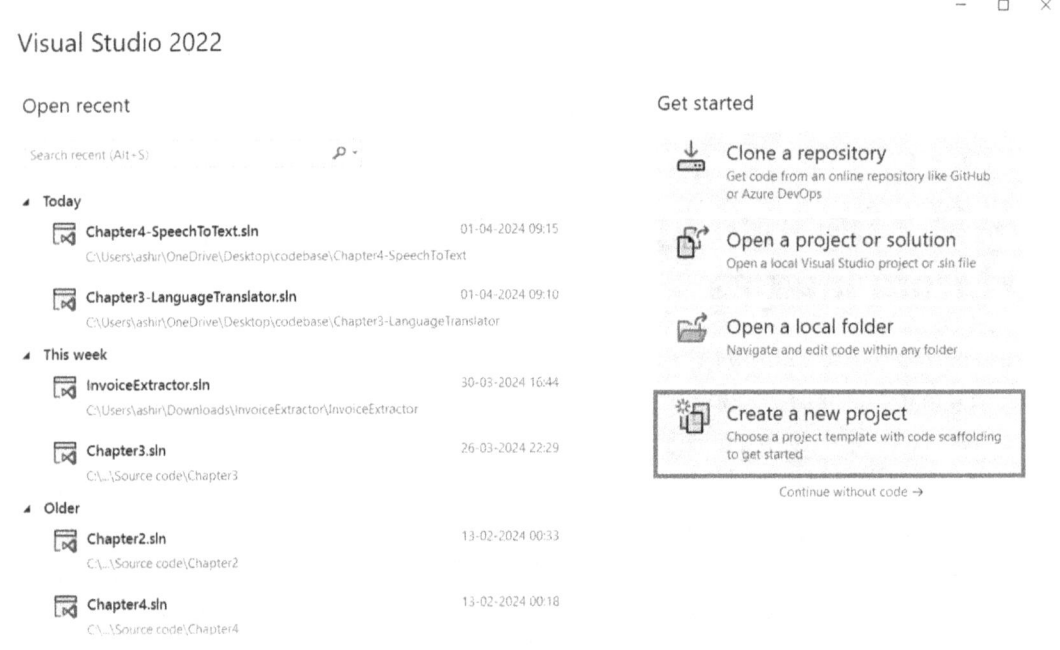

Figure 5-9. Create a new project

CHAPTER 5 BUILD A DESKTOP APP WITH .NET MAUI TO EXTRACT TEXT FROM IMAGES

Select the **.NET MAUI App** project template as shown in Figure 5-10 and click **Next**.

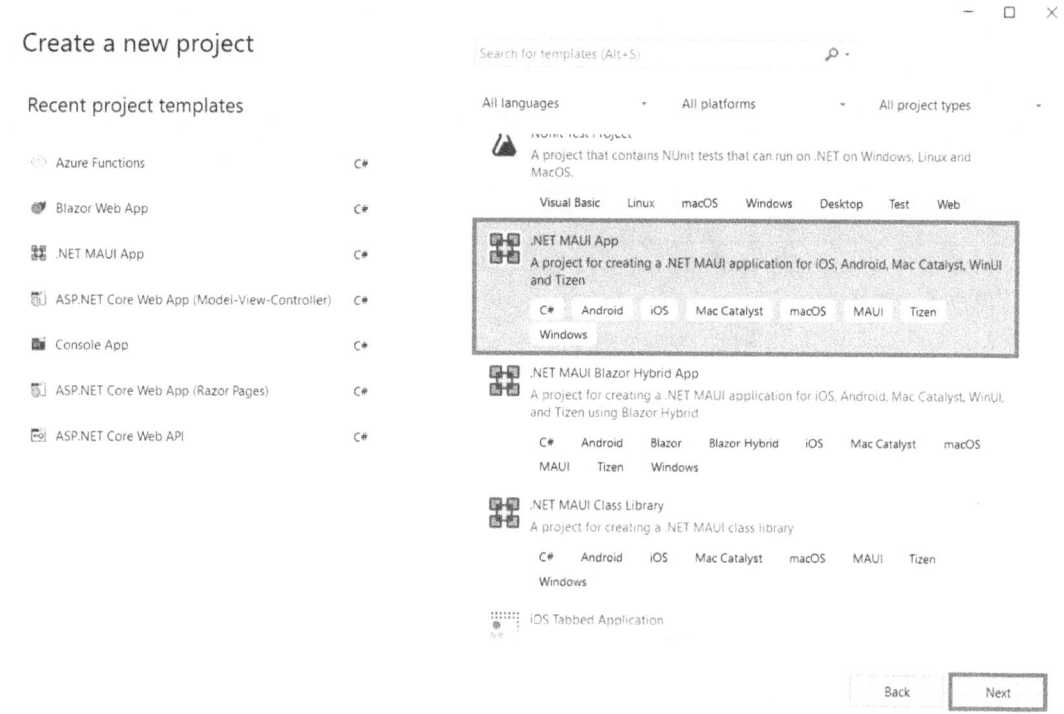

Figure 5-10. *Click Next*

Enter the **project name**, **location**, and **solution name** as shown in Figure 5-11 and click **Next**.

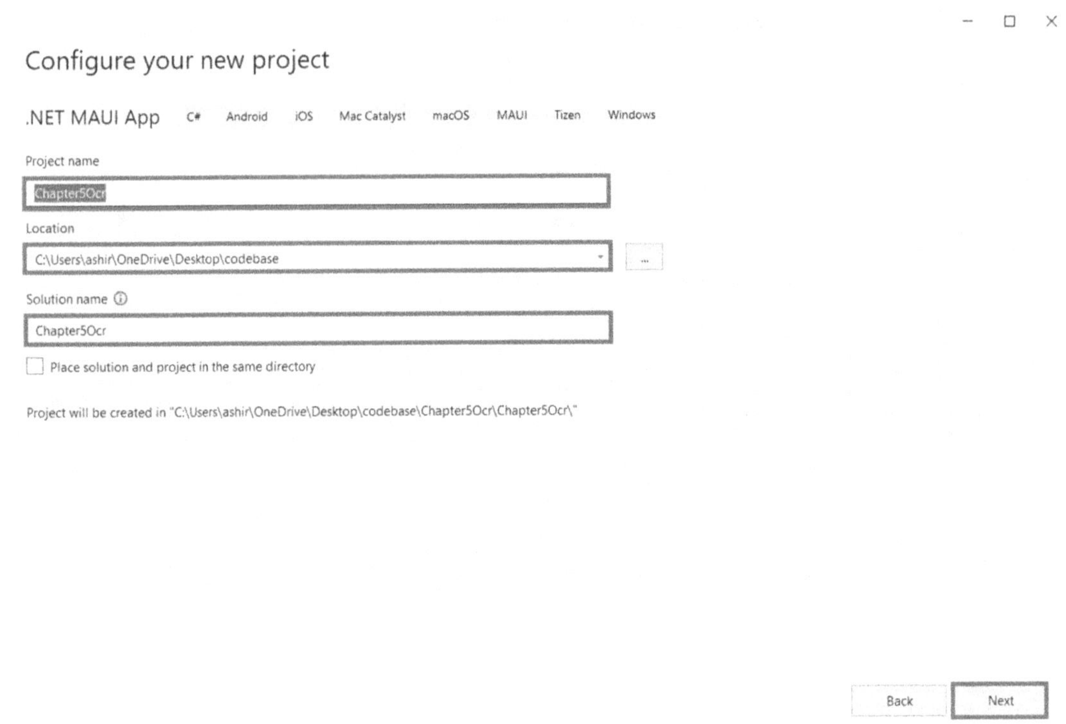

CHAPTER 5 BUILD A DESKTOP APP WITH .NET MAUI TO EXTRACT TEXT FROM IMAGES

Figure 5-11. *Enter the project name, location, and solution name*

Now select the **.NET 8.0** as the runtime and click **Create** as shown in Figure 5-12.

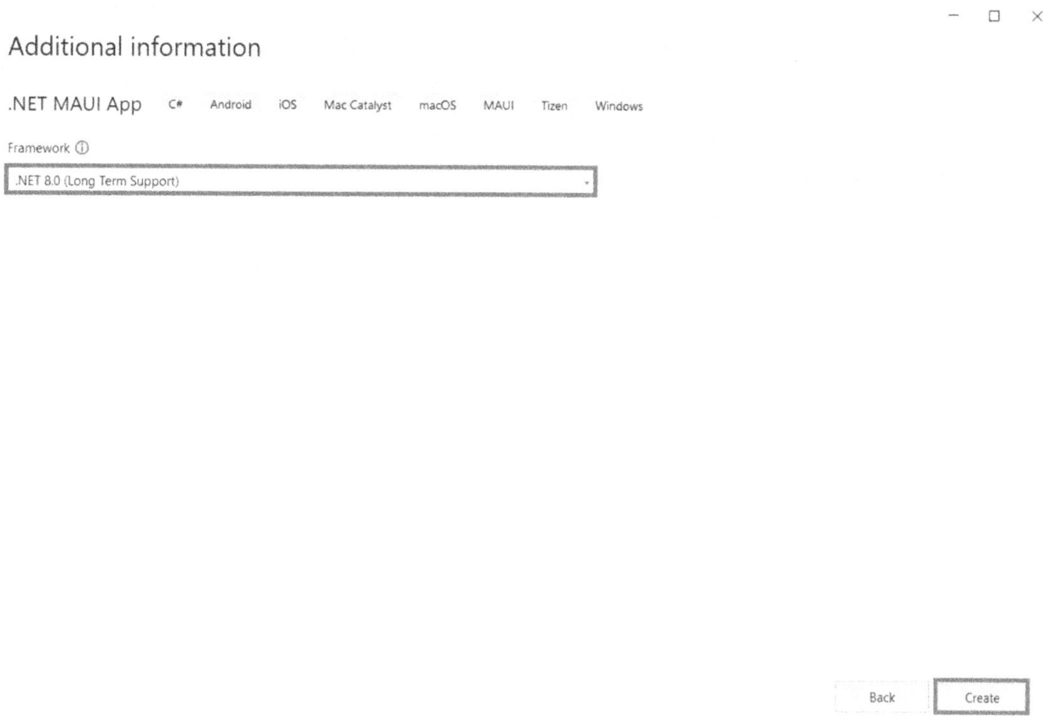

Figure 5-12. Click Create

Now Visual Studio will generate a sample .NET MAUI app out of the box. As a next step, let's add all the packages that we would need to build our solutions. To do so, open the NuGet package manager and install the following package:

1. Azure.AI.Vision.ImageAnalysis

Azure.AI.Vision.ImageAnalysis is the official SDK for interacting with the Azure AI Vision service to perform any kind of image analysis. We will leverage this SDK to add the capability of extracting textual content from images in our application.

After installing the abovementioned NuGet package, let's open the MainPage.xaml and update it with the code mentioned in Listing 5-1.

Listing 5-1. Code for MainPage.xaml

```
<?xml version="1.0" encoding="utf-8" ?>
<ContentPage xmlns="http://schemas.microsoft.com/dotnet/2021/maui"
             xmlns:x="http://schemas.microsoft.com/winfx/2009/xaml"
             x:Class="Chapter5Ocr.MainPage">
```

```xml
<ScrollView>
    <VerticalStackLayout
        Padding="30,0"
        Spacing="25">
        <Image
            Source="dotnet_bot.png"
            HeightRequest="155"
            Aspect="AspectFit"
            SemanticProperties.Description="dot net bot in a race car number eight" />

        <Label
        Text="Welcome to AT Corp!"
        Style="{StaticResource Headline}" />

        <Entry
        x:Name="entAbsolutePath"
        Text=""
        Placeholder="Please provide the absolute path of your image file"></Entry>
        <Entry
        x:Name="entSubscriptionKey"
        Text=""
        Placeholder="Please provide the subscription key of your AI vision resource"></Entry>
        <Entry
        x:Name="entEndpoint"
        Text=""
        Placeholder="Please provide the endpoint of your vision AI resource"></Entry>

        <Button
        x:Name="btnExtractText"
        Text="Extract text"
        Clicked ="btnExtractText_Clicked"
        HorizontalOptions="Fill" />
```

```
        <Label
        x:Name="lblExtractedTextResult"
        Text=""
        Style="{StaticResource SubHeadline}" />
    </VerticalStackLayout>
  </ScrollView>
</ContentPage>
```

In Listing 5-1, we are defining the UI layout and component of our app. We have an image, two labels, three entry fields, and one button. The image used here is the dotnet image that comes out of the box when we create a .NET MAUI app. We have one label which mentions **Welcome to AT Corp!**. Next, we have three entry fields in our app. Entry fields are like text boxes. We are going to leverage them to fetch the absolute path of the image file, endpoint, and key of the AI Vision service. Then, we have a button called **Extract Text**. This button has an event handler configured, that is, **btnExtractText_Clicked**. Every time someone clicks this button, the btnExtractText_Clicked method will be invoked. Lastly, we have one more label. This label is going to display the result after the execution of the btnExtractText_Clicked method.

As we have explored the XAML code which defined the UI of our application, let's implement the business logic in the code-behind file to make the app functional. Replace the code of MainPage.xaml.cs with the code shown in Listing 5-2.

Listing 5-2. Code for MainPage.xaml

```
using Azure.AI.Vision.ImageAnalysis;
using Azure;
using System.Net;

namespace Chapter5Ocr
{
    public partial class MainPage : ContentPage
    {
        public MainPage()
        {
            InitializeComponent();
        }
```

```csharp
private void btnExtractText_Clicked(object sender, EventArgs e)
{
    var absolutePathToImageFile = entAbsolutePath.Text;
    var visionKey = entSubscriptionKey.Text;
    var visionEndpoint = entEndpoint.Text;

    ImageAnalysisClient client = new ImageAnalysisClient(
        new Uri(visionEndpoint),
        new AzureKeyCredential(visionKey));

    using FileStream stream = new FileStream(absolutePathToImageFile, FileMode.Open);
    BinaryData imageData = BinaryData.FromStream(stream);

    ImageAnalysisResult result = client.Analyze(imageData,
    VisualFeatures.Read);

    string extractedText = String.Empty;
    foreach (DetectedTextBlock block in result.Read.Blocks)
        foreach (DetectedTextLine line in block.Lines)
        {
            extractedText = extractedText + "\n" + line.Text;
        }

    lblExtractedTextResult.Text = extractedText;
    }
  }
}
```

Listing 5-2 contains the implementation of the **btnExtractText_Clicked** method. This method is called every time the user clicks the **Extract Text** button. Inside this method, we fetch the absolute path of the image file, key, and endpoint of the Vision service by using the text property of the respective entry fields. We then convert the content of the image into **BinaryData** type. Once we have these values, we create an instance of the **ImageAnalysisResult** class to interact with our Azure AI Vision service. Once we have created the instance, we leverage the power of the **Analyze** method to extract texts from image files. Please do note that we have **VisualFeatures.Read** as the value of the parameter for the Analyze method. This is required for performing text extraction operation. We later iterate through all the lines that were detected as a result of the Analyze operation and then concatenate it in a string. And finally, we bind the result with the text property of the lblExtractedTextResult label to show the result in the app.

Now that we have implemented the business of our app and defined the UI, let's test the app in the next section.

Test the .NET MAUI App

To test the web app, let's run it on a Windows machine. Before you run the solution as a desktop app on Windows, you will have to turn on the Developer Mode in your system. To do so, you can go to the **For developers** section present inside the **System** section of your settings on Windows 11. Once there, toggle the **Developer** mode as **On**. This is only required for the first time. Once done, run your app with the **Windows machine**. This will start your app. The app would look similar to the one shown in Figure 5-13.

CHAPTER 5 BUILD A DESKTOP APP WITH .NET MAUI TO EXTRACT TEXT FROM IMAGES

Figure 5-13. Our .NET MAUI app

As the app is up and running, let's provide the details and click the **Extract text** button. I have used the image shown in Figure 5-14; please feel free to use any image file that you might have.

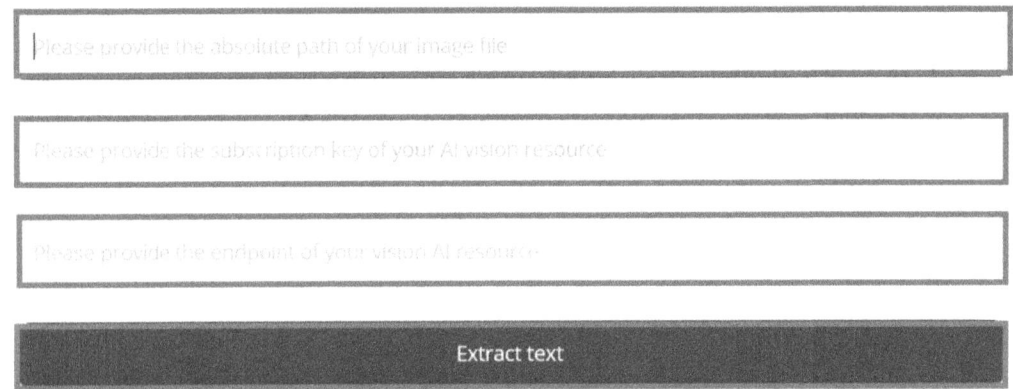

Figure 5-14. Sample image used for the test

To test the app, let's provide the absolute path of the image file, the endpoint, and the key of the vision resource and click the **Extract text** button. After processing the request, the app should display the extracted text in a label as shown in Figure 5-15.

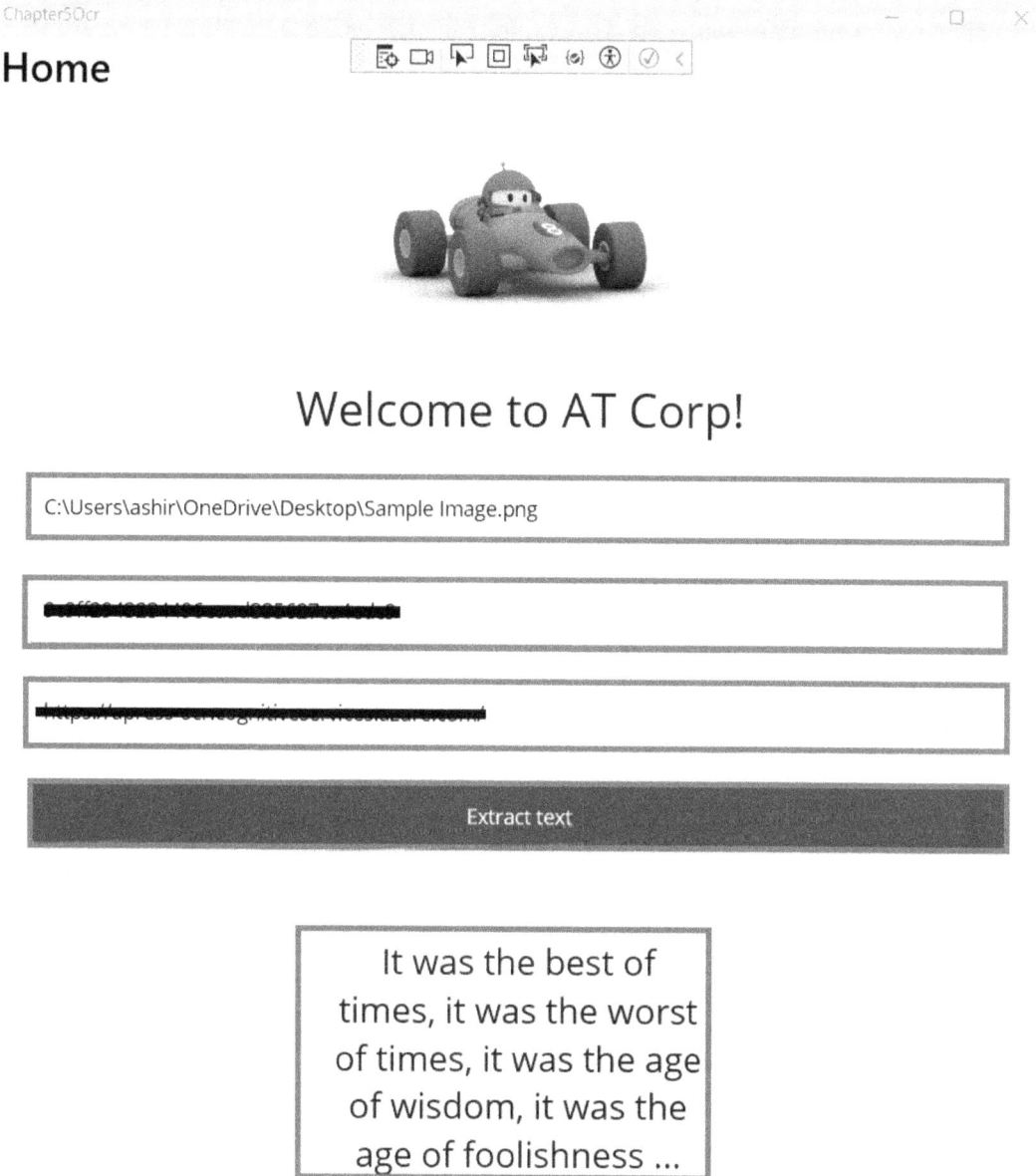

Figure 5-15. *Demo of our .NET MAUI app*

As can be seen from Figure 5-15, our desktop app was able to accurately extract text from the image file.

Summary

In this chapter, you've gained insights into creating intelligent solutions using .NET MAUI and the Azure AI Vision service through the development of a desktop app to extract textual content from images. Our exploration delved into the Azure AI Vision service, uncovering its features and applications. Additionally, we navigated through the steps of provisioning an Azure AI Vision service, a.k.a. Computer Vision service, within the Azure Portal. Throughout this process, we've acquired knowledge on constructing an intelligent solution by harnessing the capabilities of the Azure AI Vision service. The primary focus of this chapter centered around the OCR feature offered by the Azure AI Vision service. In the forthcoming chapter, our attention will shift toward investigating the features provided by the Azure AI Document Intelligence service to extract data from receipts.

CHAPTER 6

Build a Web App to Extract Data from Invoices Using Azure AI Document Intelligence

In the current digital world, a lot of data is generated and is present in unstructured format. Some common examples of data in such format can be data lying in documents such as invoices, receipts, and contracts. This makes it difficult to derive insights from such data easily. Extracting data from such sources can be time-consuming, resource intensive, and error prone. With Azure AI Document Intelligence, we can extract data from these documents in an automated manner by leveraging prebuilt or custom models. As part of this chapter, we are going to briefly discuss about the Azure AI Document Intelligence service and its use cases and build an invoice data extractor by leveraging its client SDKs.

Structure

In this chapter, we will explore the following aspects of Azure:

- Introduction to the Azure AI Document Intelligence service
- Create your first Azure AI Document Intelligence service in the Azure Portal
- Create a web app to fetch data from invoices using Azure AI Document Intelligence

CHAPTER 6 BUILD A WEB APP TO EXTRACT DATA FROM INVOICES USING AZURE AI DOCUMENT INTELLIGENCE

Objectives

After studying this chapter, you should be able to

- Grasp the essentials of the Azure AI Document Intelligence service
- Add the capabilities of the Azure AI Document Intelligence service to your applications

Introduction to Azure AI Document Intelligence Service

The Azure AI Document Intelligence service is a fully managed cloud-based service of Microsoft Azure which enables businesses to extract key insights from a range of documents which can be forms, receipts, or invoices. It was previously known as Azure Form Recognizer. Document Intelligence uses advanced machine learning algorithms to extract data, key-value pairs, and tables from structured, semi-structured, or unstructured documents. This makes it an invaluable tool for document processing. It comes up with a set of prebuilt models to analyze different kinds of documents. Along with that, you can create your custom models tailored to cater to your specific documents. It comes up with a guaranteed SLA of 99.9% like other Azure AI Services. You can deploy an instance of Azure AI Document Intelligence at your environment of choice, which can be either the cloud or the edge.

Some of the key features of the Azure AI Document Intelligence service are as follows:

1. **Document Analysis** – With this feature, we can build applications which can seamlessly extract data from forms and documents in structured format for your organizations to consume and derive insights using the prebuilt models. We don't need to manually label data to extract insights. Prebuilt models cover most of the common scenarios like IDs, receipts, and invoices.

2. **Custom Models** – We can build custom models which are trained on our data to increase the efficiency of the data extraction process for documents with specific format and layout.

3. **Security and Compliance** – Azure AI Document Intelligence adheres to various industry standards like GDPR and HIPAA for data security and compliances.

4. **Supports Client SDKs** – The service provides client SDKs in various languages like Python, JavaScript, C#, and Java. It enables developers to easily integrate the Document Intelligence service in their applications. For the languages for which the SDKs are not available, they can use the REST APIs to integrate the capabilities of the Azure AI Document Intelligence service in their application.

Now that we have explored some of the key features of the Azure AI Document Intelligence service, let's explore some of the potential use cases where it can come in handy:

1. **Financial Document Processing** – Take an example of a financial institution. It receives large numbers of documents such as bank statements, loan applications, and financial reports from customers which are mostly in physical format. To process and extract such a large number of documents manually is a resource- and time-intensive operation. We can leverage the power of Azure AI Document Intelligence to process these records and store in a meaningful format to derive insights. It results in reduced manual efforts and faster processing of documents.

2. **Healthcare Record Analysis** – Similar to a financial institution, a healthcare provider manages a number of patient records which can be documents like medical charts, prescriptions, lab reports, or insurance forms. Most of the documents like prescriptions are usually handwritten, while other reports come in physical/digital format. To process all these data manually, it would take a considerable amount of time. We can leverage Azure AI Document Intelligence over here to automate the process of medical data extraction. This in turn will help in faster billing and claim processing.

As we have explored what Azure AI Document Intelligence service is and what its key features and use cases are, let's explore ways to integrate it in our solutions by building a web app to extract data from invoices.

Problem Statement

You are working for a fictional company, AccountExt Corp. Your company is currently having a document processing system which helps the admin and operations team to add invoice- and billing-related information. In the current system, end users, that is, admin and operations team, need to manually sort, categorize, and extract data from documents. Manual extraction of key information from documents is both resource-intensive and time-consuming process. To address this concern, your team is tasked to build a proof of concept which can extract key information from company invoices. As part of the development team, you are tasked to develop a solution to extract key information like invoice number, invoice date, total cost, etc., from invoices. The success of this proof of concept will streamline the work of the admin and operations team in processing documents by enhancing their productivity and compliance.

Proposed Solution

After going through the requirement, you have broken down the problem into two tasks:

1. Extract key information from invoices
2. Provide an interface to interact with the solution

To solve both of the abovementioned problems, you have decided to use the ASP. NET Core web app and the Azure AI Document Intelligence service to develop the solution. With the help of the web app, we are going to provide an interface to the end users to upload the invoice and view the extracted information. The web app is going to take invoices from the user's request, then leverage the power of Azure AI Document Intelligence to extract key insights from the invoice and display the values on the screen.

Before we start building the web app, we need a couple of things in place. The following are the prerequisites to start the development activities:

1. Create an Azure AI Document Intelligence service
2. Fetch the endpoint and key of the Azure AI Document Intelligence service

Once we have these two things in place, we can start building our solution using Visual Studio 2022. Let's get started.

CHAPTER 6   BUILD A WEB APP TO EXTRACT DATA FROM INVOICES USING AZURE AI DOCUMENT INTELLIGENCE

Create an Azure AI Document Intelligence Service

To create an Azure AI Document Intelligence service, go to the Azure Portal and type Document Intelligence in the search box. Click the **Document intelligences** in the search results as shown in Figure 6-1.

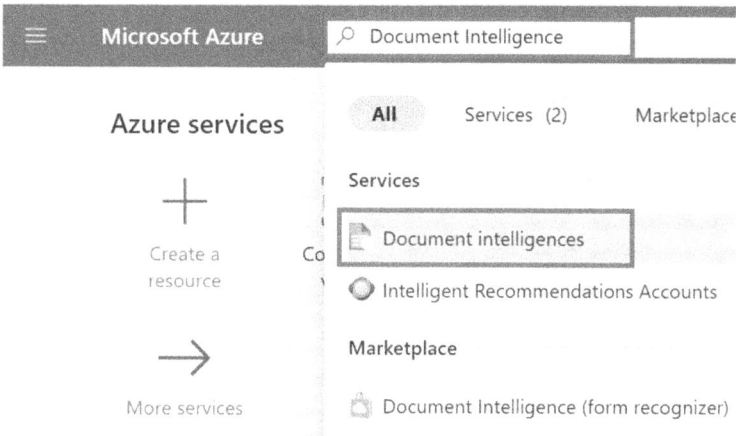

Figure 6-1. *Search for Document Intelligence*

On the screen shown in Figure 6-2, you can view the list of Document Intelligence services that you have provisioned. Click **Create** to provision our Document Intelligence service in Azure.

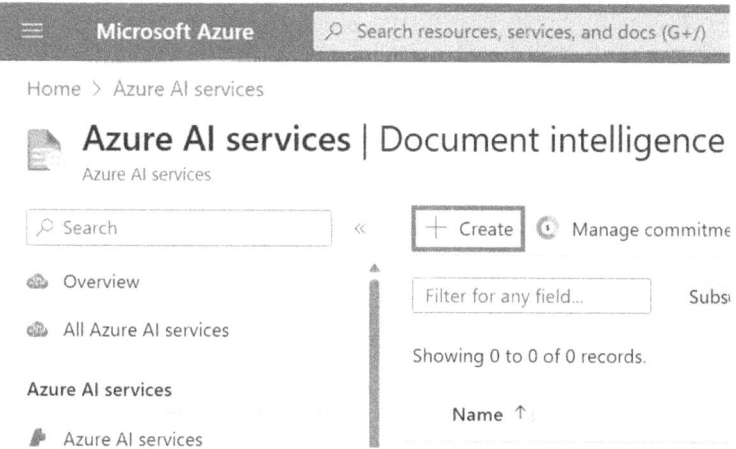

Figure 6-2. *Click Create*

115

CHAPTER 6 BUILD A WEB APP TO EXTRACT DATA FROM INVOICES USING AZURE AI DOCUMENT INTELLIGENCE

Next, select your subscription and resource group from the drop-downs available on the screen as can be seen in Figure 6-3. If you don't have a resource group, you can create a new one on this screen. After that, select the region, provide the resource name, and select the pricing tier. The resource name needs to be a unique one. For the purpose of building this solution, we are going to the **Free F0** tier. This tier provides us with the capability to perform 20 calls per minute and 500 pages per month which should be enough to build and test our proof of concept (PoC). For workloads running in a production environment, it is advised to use higher tiers. Once you have entered the preceding details, click **Review + create**.

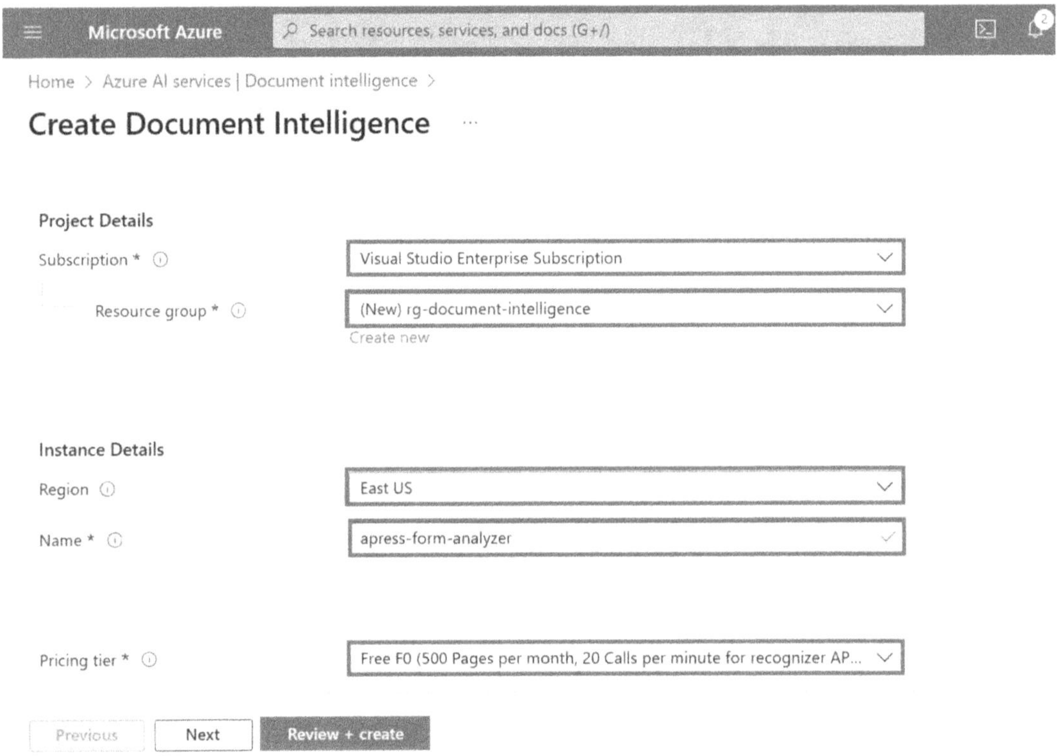

Figure 6-3. Click Review + create

Now you will see a summary of the configuration for the Document Intelligence resource that you had entered on the previous screen. A validation check will be done on the configurations. Once the validation of the configuration is done, click **Create** to provision the resource as shown in Figure 6-4. If you wanted to make any changes, you could click **Previous** and make the necessary changes for the resource.

116

CHAPTER 6   BUILD A WEB APP TO EXTRACT DATA FROM INVOICES USING AZURE AI DOCUMENT INTELLIGENCE

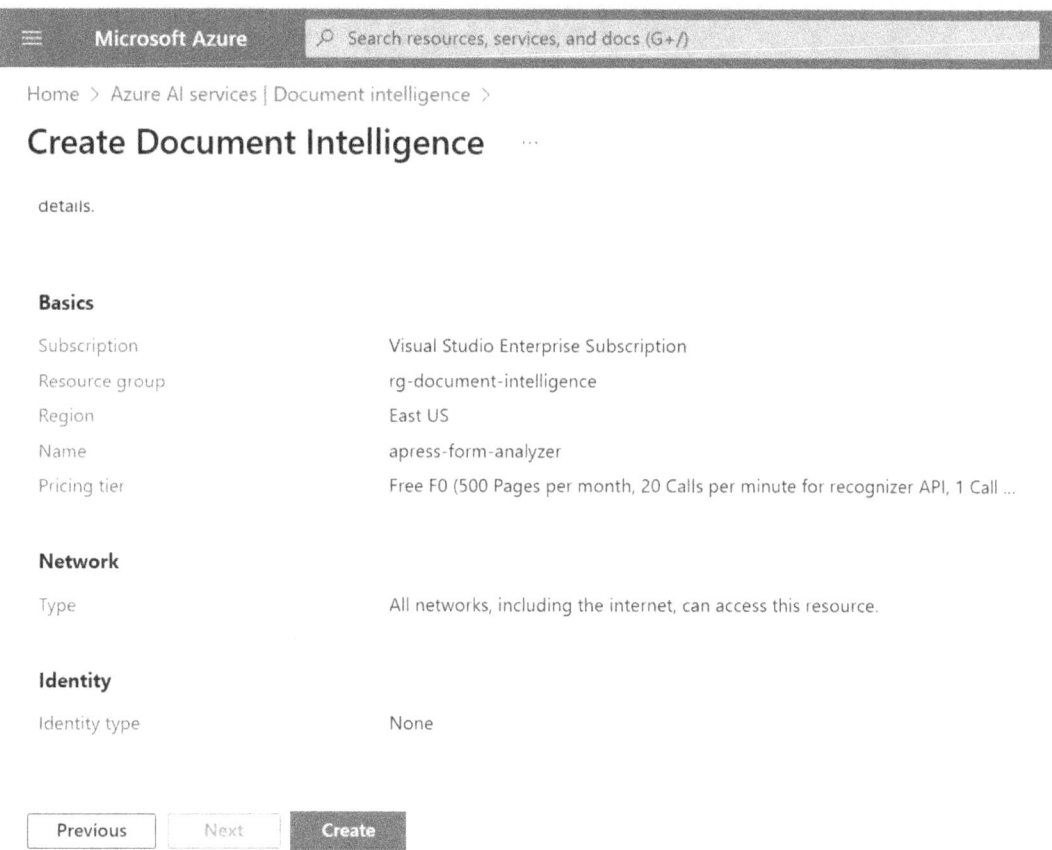

Figure 6-4.   Click Create

Once the resource has been created successfully, you will see the message "Your deployment is complete," as shown in Figure 6-5. Once you see that message, click **Go to resource** to view the newly provisioned Document Intelligence resource.

CHAPTER 6   BUILD A WEB APP TO EXTRACT DATA FROM INVOICES USING AZURE AI DOCUMENT INTELLIGENCE

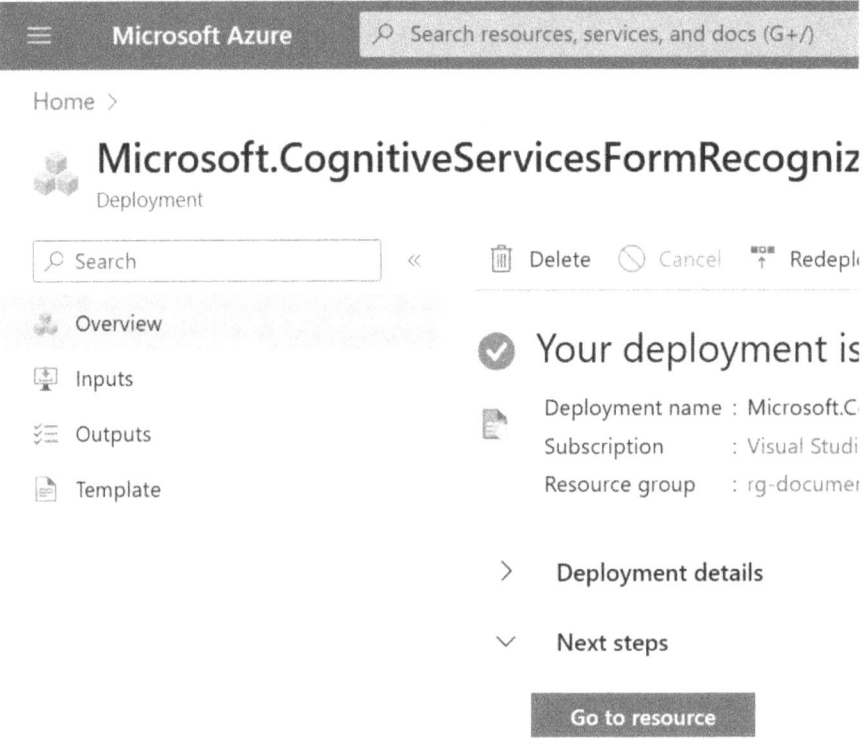

Figure 6-5. *Click Go to resource*

Now that we have provisioned our AI Document Intelligence service in the Azure Portal, we will need to fetch the access key and endpoint to interact with it from our solution. Access keys are just one way of authenticating our calls to the Document Intelligence service. We can use other methods like Managed Identity–based authentication which is recommended for production workloads. For the purposes of our PoC, we are going to use key-based authentication.

To fetch the key and endpoint for our Document Intelligence service, click Keys and Endpoint as shown in Figure 6-6.

CHAPTER 6   BUILD A WEB APP TO EXTRACT DATA FROM INVOICES USING AZURE AI DOCUMENT INTELLIGENCE

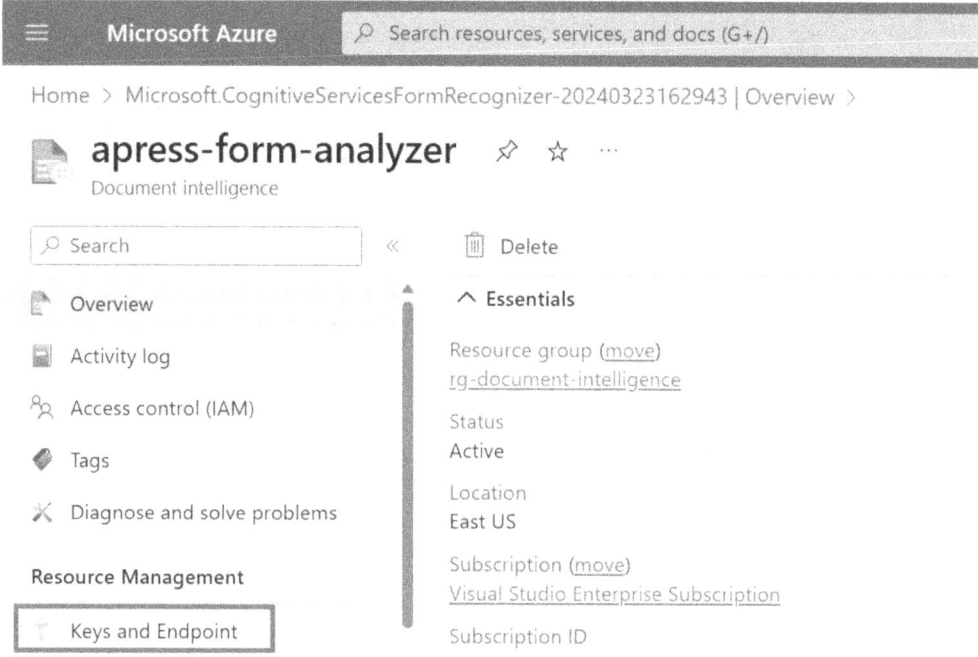

Figure 6-6. *Click Keys and Endpoint*

We will have to fetch either one of the primary or secondary key, the resource endpoint, and the region from the screen shown in Figure 6-7. We will use these values later in our application for authentication purposes.

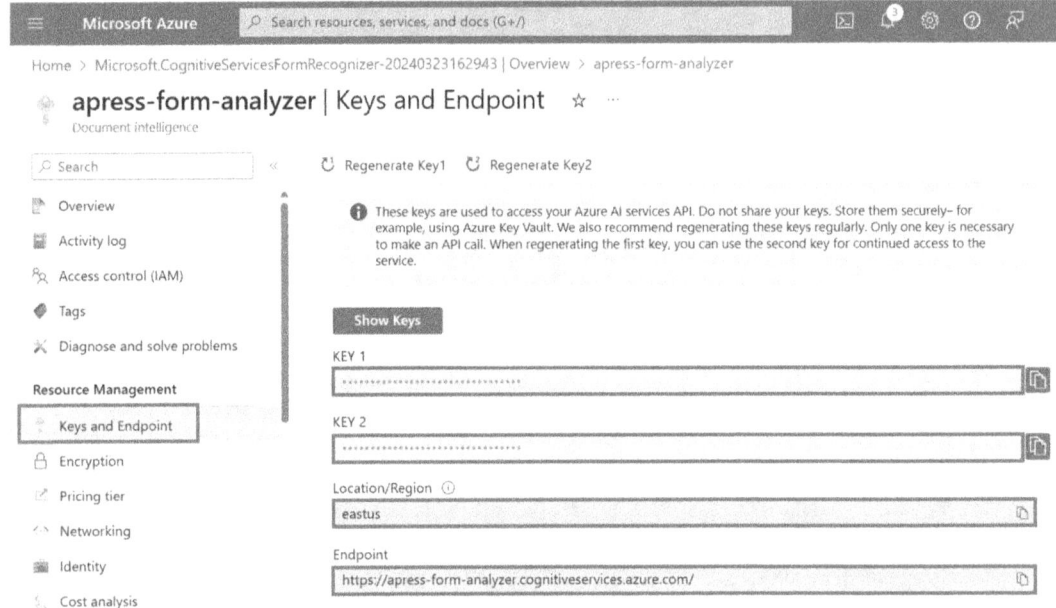

Figure 6-7. *Get the key, endpoint, and region*

Now that we have provisioned the Document Intelligence resource and have the required information to authenticate request from our application to the Document Intelligence service. Thus, we have completed the prerequisites required to move to build our app. In the next section, we will build a web app to extract data from receipts using Azure AI Document Intelligence.

Build a Web App to Extract Data from Receipts Using Azure AI Document Intelligence

In this section, we are going to complete the proof of concept for our fictional company to build a feature for our product as briefly discussed in the "Proposed Solution" section.

As we have already discussed the business requirement and provisioned the required resources, let's start building our web app to extract data from receipts by leveraging the power of Azure AI Document Intelligence. Open Visual Studio 2022 and click **Create a new project** as shown in Figure 6-8.

CHAPTER 6   BUILD A WEB APP TO EXTRACT DATA FROM INVOICES USING AZURE AI DOCUMENT INTELLIGENCE

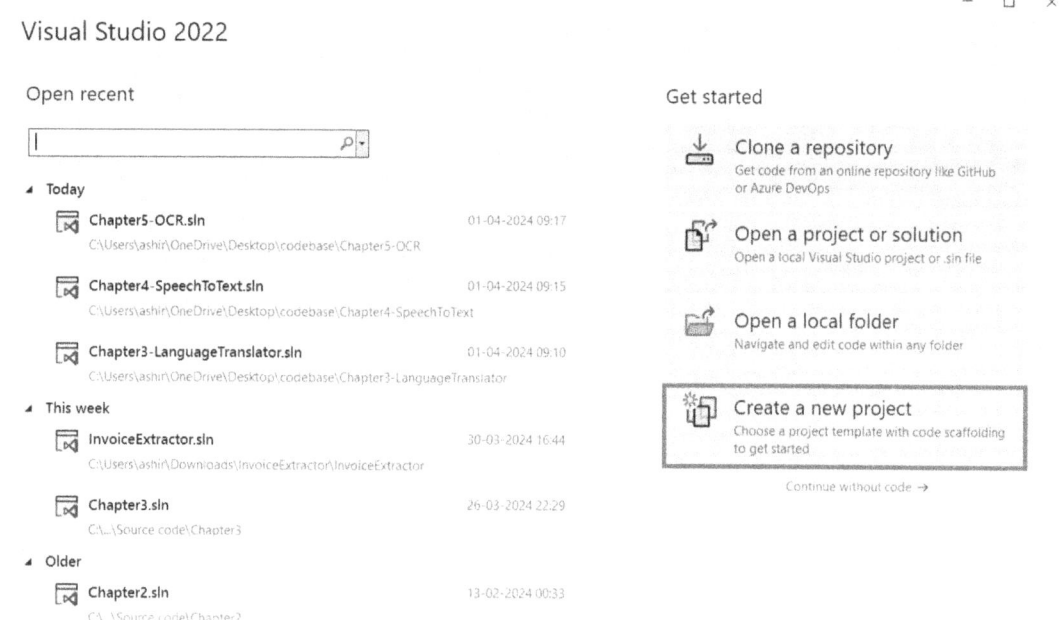

Figure 6-8. *Create a new project*

Select the **ASP.NET Core Web App (Razor Pages)** project template as shown in Figure 6-9 and click **Next**.

CHAPTER 6 BUILD A WEB APP TO EXTRACT DATA FROM INVOICES USING AZURE AI DOCUMENT INTELLIGENCE

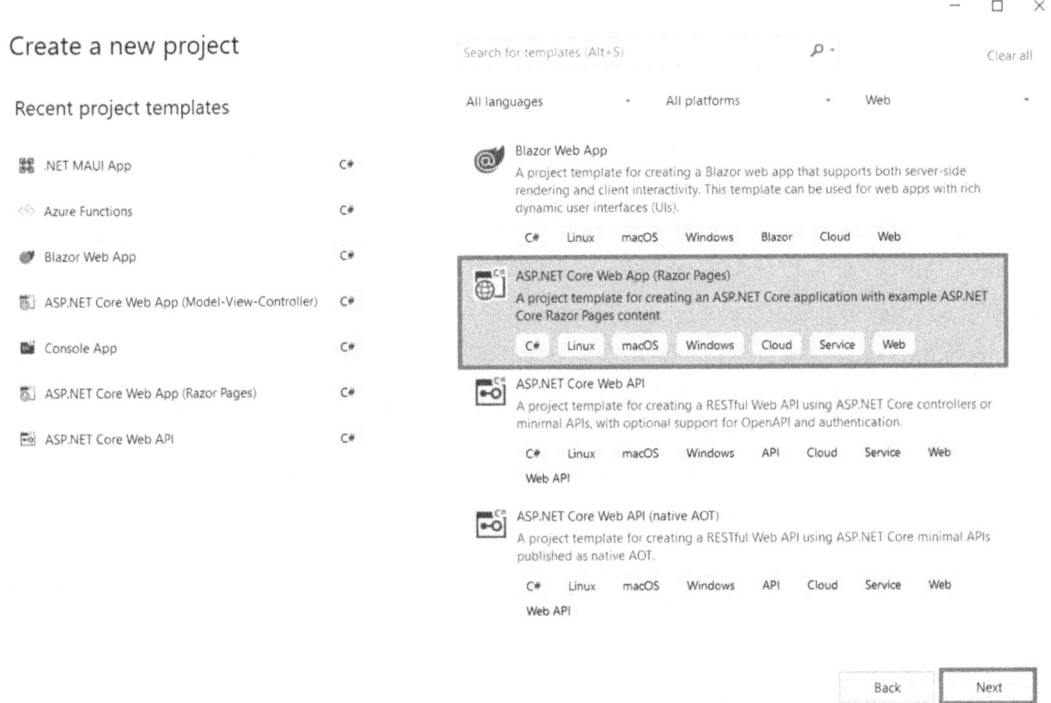

Figure 6-9. *Click Next*

Enter the **project name**, **location**, and **solution name** as shown in Figure 6-10 and click **Next**.

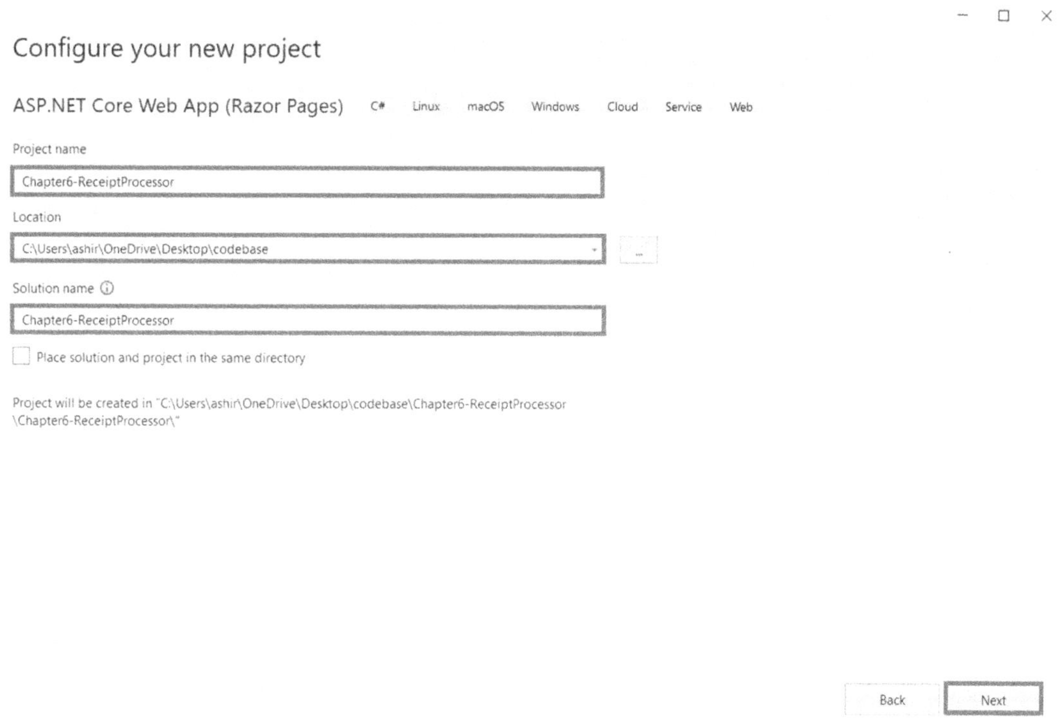

CHAPTER 6   BUILD A WEB APP TO EXTRACT DATA FROM INVOICES USING AZURE AI DOCUMENT INTELLIGENCE

Figure 6-10. *Enter the project name, location, and solution name*

Now select the **.NET 8** as the framework and **None** as the authentication type, then check the **Configure for HTTPS** and **Do not use top-level statements**. Once you are done, click **Create** as shown in Figure 6-11.

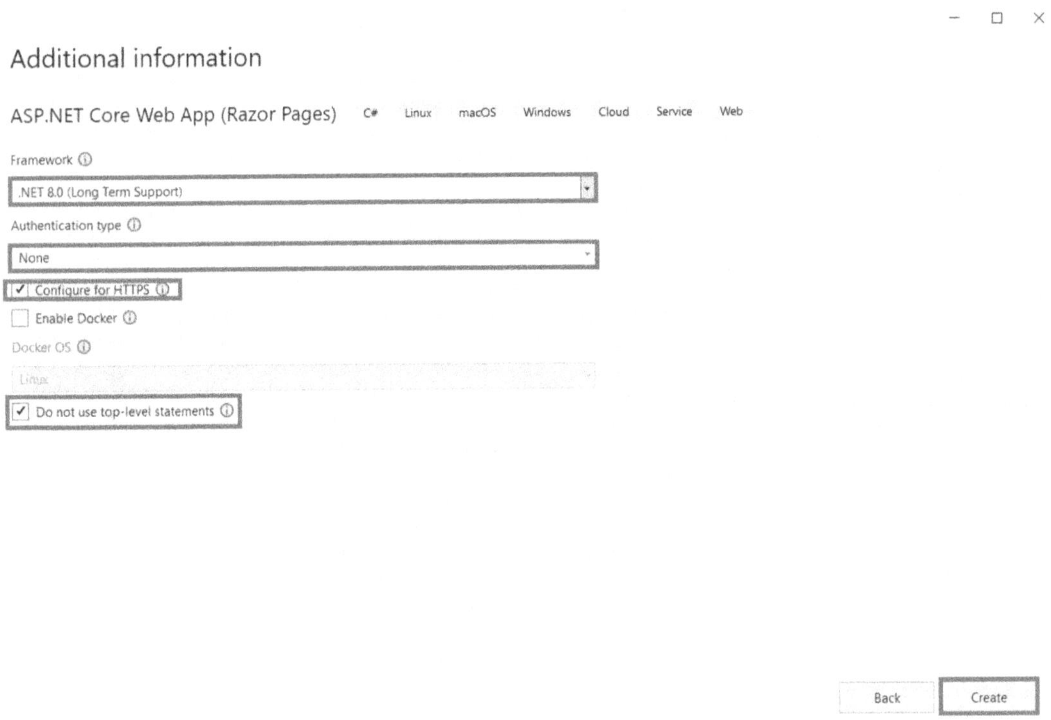

CHAPTER 6   BUILD A WEB APP TO EXTRACT DATA FROM INVOICES USING AZURE AI DOCUMENT INTELLIGENCE

Figure 6-11. Click Create

Now Visual Studio will generate an ASP.NET Core web app with razor pages out of the box. As a next step, let's add all the packages that we would need to build our solutions. To do so, open the NuGet package manager and install the following package:

1. Azure.AI.FormRecognizer

Azure.AI.FormRecognizer is the official SDK for Azure AI Document Intelligence service and the erstwhile Form Recognizer service at the time of writing this book. We will leverage its powers to add the capability of data extraction from invoices in our app. In the future, we can use the Azure.AI.DocumentIntelligence package once it's no longer in preview.

After installing the abovementioned NuGet package, let's open the **appsettings.json** file and then add the following key-value pairs: **UploadDirectory**, **DocumentIntelligenceKey**, and **DocumentIntelligenceEndpoint**. These values are required to authenticate our requests to the Azure Document Intelligence service. We had fetched these values in the previous section. **UploadDirectory** is required to configure the **IFileProvider** that we will do later in the chapter. Let's add these three keys and their values as demonstrated in Listing 6-1.

CHAPTER 6   BUILD A WEB APP TO EXTRACT DATA FROM INVOICES USING AZURE AI DOCUMENT INTELLIGENCE

Listing 6-1. Add the required key-value pairs in appsettings.json

```
{
  "Logging": {
    "LogLevel": {
      "Default": "Information",
      "Microsoft.AspNetCore": "Warning"
    }
  },
  "AllowedHosts": "*",
  "UploadDirectory": "wwwroot/uploads",
  "DocumentIntelligenceKey": "enter your resource key",
  "DocumentIntelligenceEndpoint": "enter your endpoint"
}
```

Please do note that storing function secrets or sensitive information in the appsettings.json file or hard-coding such information in a variable is not advisable. I recommend using a key vault to store application secrets.

Now that we have added our UploadDirectory, key, and endpoint of the Document Intelligence service in the appsettings.json file, let's open the Program.cs file and update it with the lines shown in Listing 6-2.

Listing 6-2. Code for Program.cs

```
using Microsoft.Extensions.FileProviders;

namespace Chapter6_ReceiptProcessor
{
    public class Program
    {
        public static void Main(string[] args)
        {
            var builder = WebApplication.CreateBuilder(args);

            // Add services to the container.
            builder.Services.AddRazorPages();

            var uploadDirectory = builder.Configuration.
            GetSection("UploadDirectory").Value;
```

```
            var fileProvider = new PhysicalFileProvider(Path.
            Combine(Directory.GetCurrentDirectory(), uploadDirectory));

            builder.Services.AddSingleton<IFileProvider>(fileProvider);

            var app = builder.Build();

            // Configure the HTTP request pipeline.
            if (!app.Environment.IsDevelopment())
            {
                app.UseExceptionHandler("/Error");

                app.UseHsts();
            }

            app.UseHttpsRedirection();
            app.UseStaticFiles();

            app.UseRouting();

            app.UseAuthorization();

            app.MapRazorPages();

            app.Run();
        }
    }
}
```

In Listing 6-2, we retrieve a directory path for file uploads from the application's configuration settings, then create a **PhysicalFileProvider** object to access the physical file system for that directory. Finally, it registers this file provider as a singleton service, allowing other parts of the application to easily access and manipulate files within the specified directory.

Before we move forward, we need to create a folder inside the **wwwroot** folder called **uploads**. This is the folder where all our invoices will be stored.

As a next step, let's create a folder called **Model** in our solution. Add a class called **Invoice**. We will be leveraging this class to represent the properties of the invoices that the user uploads in our system. The definition of the invoice model can be found in Listing 6-3.

Listing 6-3. Code for Invoice.cs

```
namespace Chapter6_ReceiptProcessor.Model
{
    public class Invoice
    {
        public string FileName { get; set; }
        public string InvoiceNumber { get; set; }
        public string InvoiceDate { get; set; }
        public string Gstin { get; set; }
        public string InvoiceAmount { get; set; }
        public string GstAmount { get; set; }
        public string TotalAmount { get; set; }
    }
}
```

Now that we have the invoice model in place, let's focus on implementing the business logic. To do so, let's create a folder called **Business** in our solution. As a next step, add an interface called **IInvoiceProcessor** and a class **InvoiceProcessor**. InvoiceProcessor is going to implement the IInvoiceProcessor interface. Add the code mentioned in Listing 6-4 in the IInvoiceProcessor interface.

Listing 6-4. Code for IInvoiceProcessor.cs

```
using Chapter6_ReceiptProcessor.Model;

namespace Chapter6_ReceiptProcessor.Services
{
    public interface IInvoiceProcessor
    {
        public Invoice GetInvoice(Stream fileContent);
    }
}
```

The IInvoiceProcessor contains the definition of one method called GetInvoice. This method will take one parameter – fileContent of stream type. fileContent represents the invoice that the user wants to process and extract insights from. Using the fileContent, the GetInvoice method will return data like GST No, Invoice No, and Total Amount from the invoice.

CHAPTER 6   BUILD A WEB APP TO EXTRACT DATA FROM INVOICES USING AZURE AI DOCUMENT INTELLIGENCE

As we have understood the purpose of the GetInvoice method, let's look at its implementation in the InvoiceProcessor class which is present in Listing 6-5.

Listing 6-5. Code for InvoiceProcessor.cs

```
using Azure;
using Azure.AI.FormRecognizer.DocumentAnalysis;
using Chapter6_ReceiptProcessor.Model;
using Microsoft.Extensions.Configuration;

namespace Chapter6_ReceiptProcessor.Services
{
    public class InvoiceProcessor : IInvoiceProcessor
    {
        private readonly IConfiguration _configuration;
        private DocumentAnalysisClient client;
        public InvoiceProcessor(IConfiguration configuration)
        {
            _configuration = configuration;
            string endpoint = _configuration["DocumentIntelligence
            Endpoint"];
            string apiKey = _configuration["DocumentIntelligenceKey"];
            var credential = new AzureKeyCredential(apiKey);
            client = new DocumentAnalysisClient(new Uri(endpoint),
            credential);
        }
        public Invoice GetInvoice(Stream fileContent)
        {
            AnalyzeDocumentOperation operation = client.
            AnalyzeDocument(waitUntil: WaitUntil.Completed, "prebuilt-
            document", fileContent);
            AnalyzeResult result = operation.Value;

            Invoice invoice = new Invoice();

            foreach (DocumentKeyValuePair kvp in result.KeyValuePairs)
            {
                if (kvp.Value == null)
```

```csharp
        {
            Console.WriteLine($"   Found key with no value: '{kvp.
            Key.Content}'");
        }
        else
        {
            if (kvp.Key.Content.Contains("Invoice Number"))
            {
                invoice.InvoiceNumber = kvp.Value.Content;
                continue;
            }
            if (kvp.Key.Content.Contains("Invoice Date"))
            {
                invoice.InvoiceDate = kvp.Value.Content;
                continue;
            }
            if (kvp.Key.Content.Contains("GSTIN"))
            {
                invoice.Gstin = kvp.Value.Content;
                continue;
            }
            if (kvp.Key.Content.Contains("Invoice Amount"))
            {
                invoice.InvoiceAmount = kvp.Value.Content;
                continue;
            }
            if (kvp.Key.Content.Contains("GST"))
            {
                invoice.GstAmount = kvp.Value.Content;
                continue;
            }
            if (kvp.Key.Content.Contains("Total"))
            {
                invoice.TotalAmount = kvp.Value.Content;
                continue;
```

```
                    }
                }
            }
            return invoice;
        }
    }
}
```

In Listing 6-5, the **InvoiceProcessor** class implements an interface **IInvoiceProcessor**. It uses the Azure Form Recognizer SDK to interact with the Azure AI Document Intelligence service to extract key information from the invoice provided as a stream of content. The constructor initializes the Form Recognizer client with the endpoint and API key obtained from configuration settings. The **GetInvoice** method processes the document content, extracts relevant key-value pairs, and populates the data in the instance of an **invoice** object with fields such as invoice number, date, GSTIN, invoice amount, GST amount, and total amount. Finally, it returns the populated "Invoice" object.

Now that we have defined both the IInvoiceProcessor and InvoiceProcessor class, let's go back to our Program.cs class. Update the Program.cs class as shown in Listing 6-6 to register the **InvoiceProcessor** class as a singleton service that implements the **IInvoiceProcessor** interface in the DI container.

Listing 6-6. Updated code for Program.cs

```
using Chapter6_ReceiptProcessor.Services;
using Microsoft.Extensions.FileProviders;

namespace Chapter6_ReceiptProcessor
{
    public class Program
    {
        public static void Main(string[] args)
        {
            var builder = WebApplication.CreateBuilder(args);

            // Add services to the container.
            builder.Services.AddRazorPages();
```

```
            var uploadDirectory = builder.Configuration.
            GetSection("UploadDirectory").Value;

            var fileProvider = new PhysicalFileProvider(Path.
            Combine(Directory.GetCurrentDirectory(), uploadDirectory));

            builder.Services.AddSingleton<IFileProvider>(fileProvider);

            builder.Services.AddSingleton<IInvoiceProcessor,
            InvoiceProcessor>();

            var app = builder.Build();

            // Configure the HTTP request pipeline.
            if (!app.Environment.IsDevelopment())
            {
                app.UseExceptionHandler("/Error");

                app.UseHsts();
            }

            app.UseHttpsRedirection();
            app.UseStaticFiles();

            app.UseRouting();

            app.UseAuthorization();

            app.MapRazorPages();

            app.Run();
        }
    }
}
```

As we implemented business logic, let's create the razor pages to take files as input and then display the extracted data. For this purpose, we need to add two empty razor pages – DisplayFile.cshtml and FileUpload.cshtml.

DisplayFile.cshtml is responsible for displaying all the values extracted by business logic for the invoice submitted by the end user and for providing the ability to download the invoice. FileUpload.cshtml is responsible for providing the interface for the end user to upload the document, invoke the business logic, extract the values, and pass them to the DisplayFile.cshtml page.

Let's start with the DisplayFile.cshtml razor page. Add an empty razor page with the name DisplayFile inside the Pages folder. Add the code shown in Listing 6-7 in the DisplayFile.cshtml.

Listing 6-7. Code for DisplayFile.cshtml

```
@page "{fileName}"
@model Chapter6_ReceiptProcessor.Pages.DisplayFileModel
@{
    ViewData["Title"] = "Display File";
}
<div class="container">
    <div class="row">
        <div class="col-md-6">
            @if (Model.FilePath != null)
            {
                <div class="form-group">
                    <label for="InvoiceNo">Invoice No.</label>
                    <input type="text" id="InvoiceNo" name="InvoiceNo"
                    class="form-control" value="@Model.Invoice.
                    InvoiceNumber" />
                </div>
                <div class="form-group">
                    <label for="InvoiceDate">Invoice Date:</label>
                    <input type="text" id="InvoiceDate" name="InvoiceDate"
                    class="form-control" value="@Model.Invoice.
                    InvoiceDate" />
                </div>
                <div class="form-group">
                    <label for="gstin">GSTIN</label>
```

```html
                <input type="text" id="gstin" name="gstin" class="form-
                control" value="@Model.Invoice.Gstin" />
            </div>
            <div class="form-group">
                <label for="gstAmount">GST Amount</label>
                <input type="text" id="gstAmount" name="gstAmount"
                class="form-control" value="@Model.Invoice.
                GstAmount" />
            </div>
            <div class="form-group" >
                <label for="totalAmount">Total Amount</label>
                <input type="text" id="totalAmount" name="totalAmount"
                class="form-control" value="@Model.Invoice.
                TotalAmount" />
            </div>

            <div class="form-group" style="padding-top:10px">
                <a class="btn btn-success" href="/uploads/@Model.
                FileName" download>Download File</a>
            </div>

            <div class="form-group" style="padding-top:10px">
                <a class="btn btn-warning" href="/FileUpload">Go
                Back</a>
            </div>
    }
    else
    {
        <p>File not found.</p>
    }
</div>
<div class="col-md-6">
    @if (Model.FilePath != null)
    {
```

```
                <div>
                    <embed src="/uploads/@Model.Invoice.FileName"
                        width="100%" height="500px" />
                </div>
            }
        </div>
    </div>
</div>
```

In the razor code, we are displaying the details of the invoice that was uploaded by the user. It checks if the file exists, and if so, it displays various input fields populated with information extracted from the uploaded file like GSTIN, Invoice No, Invoice Date, and Total Amount alongside buttons to download the file and navigate back to the file upload page. Additionally, it displays a preview of the uploaded file, such as an embedded PDF document, in the page layout. We have used a bootstrap class to design the UI.

Now that we have understood what the UI for the DisplayFile razor page has, let's explore the code-behind file for the DisplayFile razor page. The code for the code-behind file can be found in Listing 6-8.

Listing 6-8. Code for DisplayFile.cshtml.cs

```
using Chapter6_ReceiptProcessor.Model;
using Microsoft.AspNetCore.Mvc;
using Microsoft.AspNetCore.Mvc.RazorPages;
using Microsoft.Extensions.FileProviders;

namespace Chapter6_ReceiptProcessor.Pages
{
    public class DisplayFileModel : PageModel
    {
        private readonly IWebHostEnvironment _environment;
        public string FilePath { get; private set; }
        public string FileName { get; private set; }
        public long FileSize { get; private set; }
        public Invoice Invoice = new Invoice();
        public DisplayFileModel(IWebHostEnvironment environment)
        {
```

```csharp
        _environment = environment;
    }
    public IActionResult OnGet(string FileName, string InvoiceNumber,
    string InvoiceDate, string Gstin, string GstAmount, string
    TotalAmount)
    {
        if (!string.IsNullOrEmpty(FileName))
        {
            var uploadsFolder = Path.Combine(_environment.WebRootPath,
            "uploads");
            var filePath = Path.Combine(uploadsFolder, FileName);

            var fileProvider = new PhysicalFileProvider(uploadsFolder);
            var fileInfo = fileProvider.GetFileInfo(FileName);

            if (fileInfo.Exists)
            {
                FilePath = filePath;
                FileSize = fileInfo.Length;
                Invoice.FileName = FileName;
                Invoice.InvoiceNumber = InvoiceNumber;
                Invoice.InvoiceDate = InvoiceDate;
                Invoice.TotalAmount = TotalAmount;
                Invoice.GstAmount = GstAmount;
                Invoice.Gstin = Gstin;
                return Page();
            }
        }
        return RedirectToPage("/Index");
    }
  }
}
```

The DisplayFile.cshtml.cs has four properties, namely, FilePath, FileName, FileSize, and instance of type invoice. In the constructor, it injects IWebHostEnvironment to access information about the web hosting environment. Every time the page gets a GET request, it retrieves information about the uploaded file and populates the properties accordingly. If the file exists, it sets the properties and returns the page view. Otherwise, it redirects to the index page.

As we have explored the DisplayFile razor page, let's move our focus to the FileUpload razor page. Create an empty razor page with the name FileUpload inside the Pages folder. Next, add the code shown in Listing 6-9 in the FileUpload.cshtml.

Listing 6-9. Code for FileUpload.cshtml

```
@page
@model Chapter6_ReceiptProcessor.Pages.FileUploadModel
@{
    ViewData["Title"] = "Upload Invoice";
}
<h2>@ViewData["Title"]</h2>
<form method="post" enctype="multipart/form-data">
    <div class="form-group">
        <label for="file">Select a file:</label>
        <input type="file" name="file" class="form-control-file" />
    </div>
    <button type="submit" class="btn btn-primary">Upload</button>
</form>

@if (Model.Message != null)
{
    <div class="alert alert-success mt-3">
        @Model.Message
    </div>
}
```

With the code in Listing 6-9, the razor page provides a user interface for uploading invoices to the user. It includes a form with a file input field and a submit button, allowing users to select a file and upload it. Additionally, it displays a success message if the upload operation is successful to inform users of the outcome. We are using bootstrap classes here to design the UI.

CHAPTER 6   BUILD A WEB APP TO EXTRACT DATA FROM INVOICES USING AZURE AI DOCUMENT INTELLIGENCE

Now that we have understood what the UI for the FileUpload razor page has, let's explore the code-behind file for the FileUpload razor page. The code for the code-behind file can be found in Listing 6-10.

Listing 6-10. Code for FileUpload.cshtml.cs

```csharp
using Chapter6_ReceiptProcessor.Model;
using Chapter6_ReceiptProcessor.Services;
using Microsoft.AspNetCore.Mvc;
using Microsoft.AspNetCore.Mvc.RazorPages;

namespace Chapter6_ReceiptProcessor.Pages
{
    public class FileUploadModel : PageModel
    {
        private readonly IWebHostEnvironment _environment;
        private readonly IInvoiceProcessor _invoiceProcessor;
        public FileUploadModel(IWebHostEnvironment environment,
        IInvoiceProcessor invoiceProcessor)
        {
            _environment = environment;
            _invoiceProcessor = invoiceProcessor;
        }
        [TempData]
        public string Message { get; set; }
        public async Task<IActionResult> OnPostAsync(IFormFile file)
        {
            if (file != null && file.Length > 0)
            {
                var uploadsFolder = Path.Combine(_environment.WebRootPath,
                "uploads");
                Directory.CreateDirectory(uploadsFolder);
                var fileName = Guid.NewGuid().ToString() + Path.
                GetExtension(file.FileName);
                var filePath = Path.Combine(uploadsFolder, fileName);

                Invoice invoice = new Invoice();
```

```csharp
        using (var stream = new FileStream(filePath, FileMode.
        Create))
        {
            await file.CopyToAsync(stream);
        }

        Stream data = ConvertFormFileToStream(file);

        invoice = _invoiceProcessor.GetInvoice(data);
        invoice.FileName = fileName;

        return RedirectToPage("/DisplayFile", new { invoice.
        FileName, invoice.InvoiceNumber, invoice.InvoiceDate,
        invoice.Gstin, invoice.GstAmount, invoice.TotalAmount });
    }
    else
    {
        Message = "Please select a file to upload.";
    }

    return Page();
}
public Stream ConvertFormFileToStream(IFormFile file)
{
    // Check if the file is null
    if (file == null)
    {
        return null;
    }

    // Open a stream to read the contents of the IFormFile
    var stream = new MemoryStream();
    file.CopyTo(stream);
    stream.Seek(0, SeekOrigin.Begin); // Rewind the stream to the
                                        beginning
```

```
            return stream;
        }
    }
}
```

In Listing 6-10, we inject the instances of IWebHostEnvironment and IInvoiceProcessor using constructor injection. When a file is uploaded via a POST request (OnPostAsync method), it saves the file to the server, converts it to a stream, extracts invoice information using the injected IInvoiceProcessor, and then redirects to a display page (DisplayFile razor page) with the extracted information. The class contains a method called ConvertFormFileToStream to convert an uploaded file into a stream for processing. We leverage this method to convert the uploaded invoice to a stream to pass the file content to the GetInvoice method of the IInvoiceProcessor instance.

Now that we have the business class, configured the Program.cs class, added the required key-value pairs in our appsettings.json, and added the required razor pages, we are close to completing the solution. As a last step, we need to add a navigation link to the FileUpload razor page. To do so, replace the _Layout.cshtml class with the code shown in Listing 6-11.

Listing 6-11. Updated code for _Layout.cshtml

```html
<!DOCTYPE html>
<html lang="en">
<head>
    <meta charset="utf-8" />
    <meta name="viewport" content="width=device-width, initial-scale=1.0" />
    <title>@ViewData["Title"] - Chapter6_ReceiptProcessor</title>
    <link rel="stylesheet" href="~/lib/bootstrap/dist/css/bootstrap.min.css" />
    <link rel="stylesheet" href="~/css/site.css" asp-append-version="true" />
    <link rel="stylesheet" href="~/Chapter6_ReceiptProcessor.styles.css" asp-append-version="true" />
</head>
<body>
    <header>
```

```html
<nav class="navbar navbar-expand-sm navbar-toggleable-sm navbar-
light bg-white border-bottom box-shadow mb-3">
    <div class="container">
        <a class="navbar-brand" asp-area="" asp-page="/
        Index">Chapter6_ReceiptProcessor</a>
        <button class="navbar-toggler" type="button"
        data-bs-toggle="collapse" data-bs-target=".navbar-collapse"
        aria-controls="navbarSupportedContent"
                aria-expanded="false" aria-label="Toggle
                navigation">
            <span class="navbar-toggler-icon"></span>
        </button>
        <div class="navbar-collapse collapse d-sm-inline-flex
        justify-content-between">
            <ul class="navbar-nav flex-grow-1">
                <li class="nav-item">
                    <a class="nav-link text-dark" asp-area=""
                    asp-page="/Index">Home</a>
                </li>
                <li class="nav-item">
                    <a class="nav-link text-dark" asp-area=""
                    asp-page="/FileUpload">Invoices</a>
                </li>
                <li class="nav-item">
                    <a class="nav-link text-dark" asp-area=""
                    asp-page="/Privacy">Privacy</a>
                </li>
            </ul>
        </div>
    </div>
</nav>
</header>
<div class="container">
    <main role="main" class="pb-3">
        @RenderBody()
```

CHAPTER 6   BUILD A WEB APP TO EXTRACT DATA FROM INVOICES USING AZURE AI DOCUMENT INTELLIGENCE

```
        </main>
    </div>

    <footer class="border-top footer text-muted">
        <div class="container">
            &copy; 2024 - Chapter6_ReceiptProcessor - <a asp-area=""
            asp-page="/Privacy">Privacy</a>
        </div>
    </footer>
    <script src="~/lib/jquery/dist/jquery.min.js"></script>
    <script src="~/lib/bootstrap/dist/js/bootstrap.bundle.min.js"></script>
    <script src="~/js/site.js" asp-append-version="true"></script>

    @await RenderSectionAsync("Scripts", required: false)
</body>
</html>
```

In Listing 6-11, we have added the nav link called **Invoices**, routing to the FileUpload razor page. With this, our solution is ready. Let's test it out in the next section.

Test the Web App

To test the web app, we will have to run our project. Once you are able to view the index page, click Invoices. This will route us to our FileUpload razor page as shown in Figure 6-12.

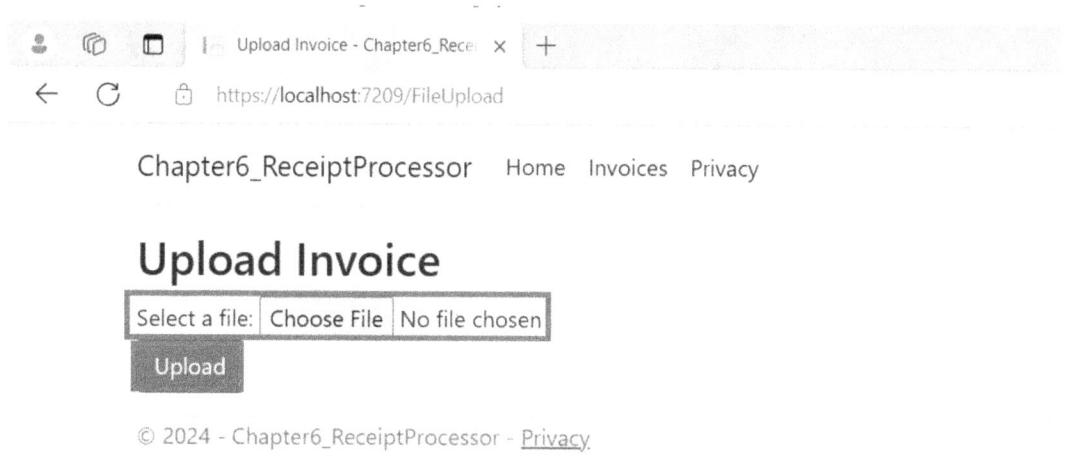

Figure 6-12. *Go to the Invoices page*

141

CHAPTER 6   BUILD A WEB APP TO EXTRACT DATA FROM INVOICES USING AZURE AI DOCUMENT INTELLIGENCE

I will be using the invoice shown in Figure 6-13 for testing purposes. Please feel free to use the invoices that you have at hand. We can click the Choose file button to select the invoice from our file system. Once selected, click Upload. When you click this button, the application saves the invoice in the server and then processes it. Once the processing is completed, it redirects you to the DisplayFile razor page.

INVOICE

Millets Private Limited
Elephant Road, Kormangla
Bengaluru 560 077,
Karnataka, Code: 29, India
accounts@millets.com
GSTIN: 234AACDG0237H1ZE

Bill To:
Abhishek Corp
40-11, FatehPuri Community, Kailash Colony
Extn, New Delhi-110048
State Name: Delhi, Code: 07

Invoice Number: 01
Invoice Date: 11/04/2024
Invoice Amount: Rs. 8543.3/-

No	Item	HSN/SAC	GST Rate	Quantity	Amount in Rs.
1	Millet Chocolate Pancake mix			1 kg	325
2	Millet Banana Choco Chip Pancake mix			1 kg	345.8
3	Millet Banana Blueberry Pancake mix			1 kg	357.5
4	Millet Vanilla Cake Mix			450 gm	325
5	Millet Chocolate Cake Mix			450 gm	325
6	Millet Chocolate Muesli			1 kg	410.8
7	Millet Mawa Muesli			1 kg	520
8	Millet Peanut Butter Muesli			1 kg	390
9	Millet Banana Granola			1 kg	405.6
10	Millet Balls - Cheese oregano			1 kg	487.5
11	Millet Balls - Peri Peri			450 gm	487.5
12	Millet Balls - Cheddar Cheese			450 gm	487.5
13	Millet Pops - Tomato			450 gm	487.5
14	Millet Pops - Pudina			450 gm	487.5
				Total	5842.2
				GST 12%	701.1
				Transportation	2000
				Total	8543.3

Amount chargeable in words: Rupees: Eight thousand five hundred forty-three rupees thirty paise only

Declaration: We declare that this invoice shows the actual price of the goods described and that all particulars are true and correct.

Company's Bank Details

Bank Name: HDFC Bank
A/c No.: 94783871298651
IFSC Code: HQRC0008886

Ashirwad
Millets Private Limited
Authorised Signatory

Figure 6-13. *Sample invoice*

After the processing of the invoice is completed, you should be able to view the results as shown in Figure 6-14.

CHAPTER 6 BUILD A WEB APP TO EXTRACT DATA FROM INVOICES USING AZURE AI DOCUMENT INTELLIGENCE

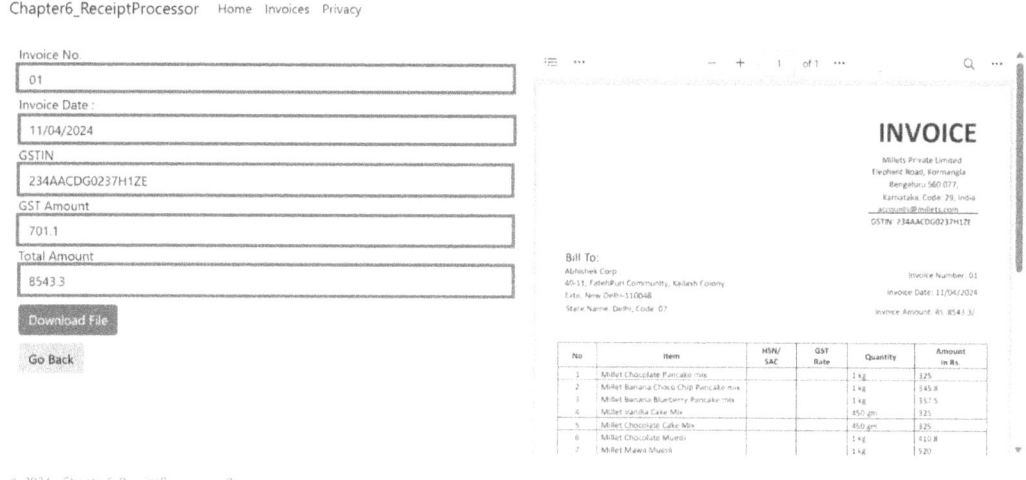

Figure 6-14. *Values extracted from the invoice*

As can be seen from Figure 6-14, our web app was able to accurately extract various values like Invoice No, Invoice Date, GSTIN, GST Amount, and Total Amount.

Summary

In this chapter, you've gained insights into creating intelligent solutions using ASP.NET Core web app and the Azure AI Document Intelligence service through the development of a web app to extract values from receipts. Our exploration delved into the Azure AI Document Intelligence service, uncovering its features and applications. Additionally, we navigated through the steps of provisioning an Azure AI Document Intelligence service within the Azure Portal. Throughout this process, we've acquired knowledge on constructing an intelligent solution by harnessing the capabilities of the Azure AI Document Intelligence service. The primary focus of this chapter centered around extracting textual data as key-value pair functionality offered by the Azure AI Document Intelligence service. In the forthcoming chapter, our attention will shift toward investigating the features provided by the Azure AI Content Safety service to flag texts containing harmful content.

CHAPTER 7

Build a Content-Flagging App with Azure AI Content Safety

As per reports, we stay in a world where almost 500 million tweets and 95 million photos are posted on Twitter and Instagram per day, respectively. The number is only going to increase as time passes by as seen in the rise of their user base. With this growth, creating a safer online space for people to communicate and socialize becomes important. To enable this, content moderation is essential for all social media companies. The Azure AI Content Safety service is one such offering by Microsoft Azure which enables applications to flag content containing harmful content. In this chapter, we are going to briefly discuss about the Azure AI Content Safety service and its use cases and build a content flagger to identify inappropriate content in textual data by leveraging its client SDKs.

Structure

In this chapter, we will explore the following aspects of Azure:

- Introduction to the Azure AI Content Safety service
- Create your first Azure AI Content Safety service in the Azure Portal
- Create a content flagger with the Azure AI Content Safety service

CHAPTER 7 BUILD A CONTENT-FLAGGING APP WITH AZURE AI CONTENT SAFETY

Objectives

After studying this chapter, you should be able to

- Grasp the essentials of the Azure AI Content Safety service
- Add the capabilities of the Azure AI Content Safety service to your applications

Introduction to Azure AI Content Safety Service

The Azure AI Content Safety service is a fully managed cloud-based service of Microsoft Azure which enables businesses to detect harmful user- or AI-generated content in applications and services. It is slated to succeed the Azure Content Moderator service which was deprecated on February 2024. With the Azure AI Content Safety service, we can moderate textual as well as visual content by using its Text and Image APIs. These APIs allow us to detect material which can be harmful or disturbing in nature. It also boasts certain features like Prompt shields and Protected material text detection which are still in public preview. With the protected material text, we can find and stop well-known text, like song lyrics or recipes, from appearing in the language model's output. There are primarily four harm categories in which content is classified by the Azure AI Content Safety service: hate and fairness, sexual, violence, and self-harm. The severity level for each of these categories ranges from 0 to 7. The higher the level, the more profanity a content might contain. This functionality is currently limited to only for content in English. It comes up with a guaranteed SLA of 99.9% like other Azure AI Services.

Some of the key features of the Azure AI Content Safety service are as follows:

1. **Analyze Text** – With this feature, the service is able to analyze text and scan for things like sexual content, violence, hate speech, and self-harm, each with different levels of seriousness. For example, it might detect a mild swear word or a graphic description of violence.

2. **Analyze Image** – With this feature, the service is able to analyze images for sexual content, violence, hate speech, and self-harm with varying levels of severity detection. For example, the system might flag a graphic depiction of violence that could be labeled as high severity.

3. **Supports Client SDKS** – The service provides client SDKs in various languages like Python, JavaScript, C#, and Java. It enables developers to easily integrate the Content Safety service in their applications. For the languages for which the SDKs are not available, they can use the REST APIs to integrate the capabilities of the Azure AI Content Safety service in their application.

Now that we have explored some of the key features of the Azure AI Content Safety service, let's explore some of the potential use cases where it can come in handy:

1. **Social Media Platforms** – This service can be leveraged in social media platforms to automatically filter out or flag content from user-uploaded images and comments to create a safer online environment for its users.

2. **Ecommerce Websites** – With a large number of users posting product reviews and feedback, an ecommerce website can leverage this service to ensure that product reviews and product images are free from offensive content and ensure a safe shopping experience for its customers.

As we have explored what Azure AI Content Safety service is and what its key features and use cases are, let's explore ways to integrate it in our solutions by building a content-flagging app.

Problem Statement

You are working for a fictional social media company, FashBash Inc. Over the past few quarters, the user base of the company has grown substantially. With the growth, a concerning trend has also emerged. The amount of inappropriate content circulating over the platform has increased by 40%, and a lot of users have complaints regarding the same. To make the platform a safe place for the end users, the company has decided to explore ways to moderate the content. As part of this, your team is assigned with the task to develop a proof of concept to moderate content containing inappropriate text. Your dev lead has asked you to build a solution by leveraging Azure AI Content Safety to identify textual data with inappropriate content. The proof of concept is crucial and a business-critical requirement. Your team is going to leverage your proof of concept as the base for the further development of the functionality.

Proposed Solution

After going through the requirement, you have broken down the problem into two tasks:

1. Flag text containing inappropriate content
2. Provide an interface to interact with the solution

To solve both of the abovementioned problems, you have decided to use the ASP. NET Core Web API and the Azure AI Content Safety service to develop the solution. With the help of the Web API, we are going to provide a REST endpoint to the end users to make requests and receive the desired responses. The API is going to take the textual content from the user's request, then leverage the power of the Azure AI Content Safety service to identify if the content has any inappropriate content and return back the result as a response.

Before we start building the Web API, we need a couple of things in place. The following are the prerequisites to start the development activities:

1. Create an Azure AI Content service
2. Fetch the endpoint and key of the Azure AI Content Safety service

Once we have these two things in place, we can start building our solution using Visual Studio 2022. Let's get started.

Create an Azure AI Content Safety Service

To create an Azure AI Content Safety service, go to the Azure Portal and type Content Safety in the search box. Click the **Content safety** in the search results as shown in Figure 7-1.

CHAPTER 7   BUILD A CONTENT-FLAGGING APP WITH AZURE AI CONTENT SAFETY

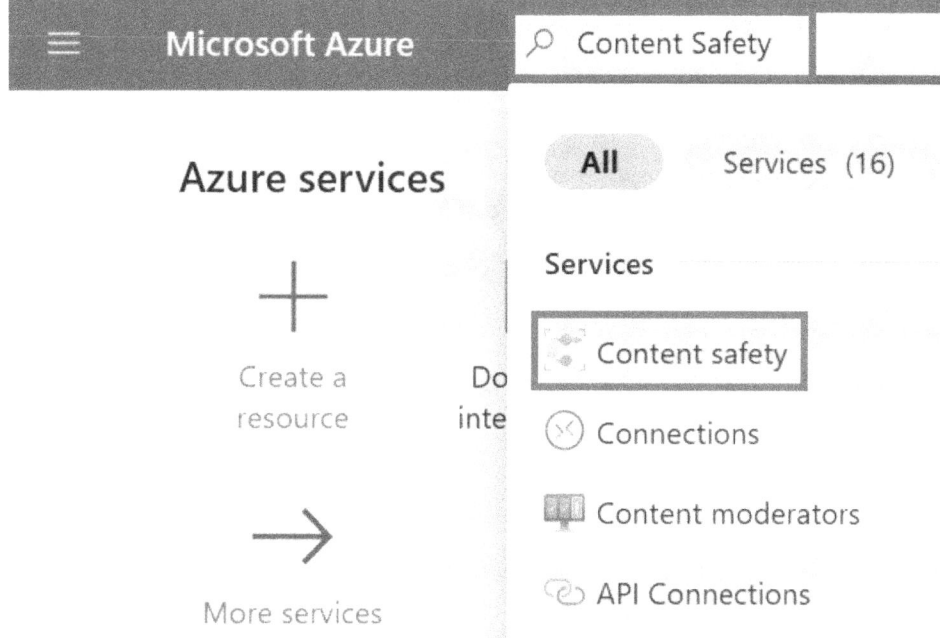

Figure 7-1. *Search for Content Safety*

On the screen shown in Figure 7-2, you can view the list of Content Safety services that you have provisioned. Click **Create** to provision our Content Safety service in Azure.

CHAPTER 7   BUILD A CONTENT-FLAGGING APP WITH AZURE AI CONTENT SAFETY

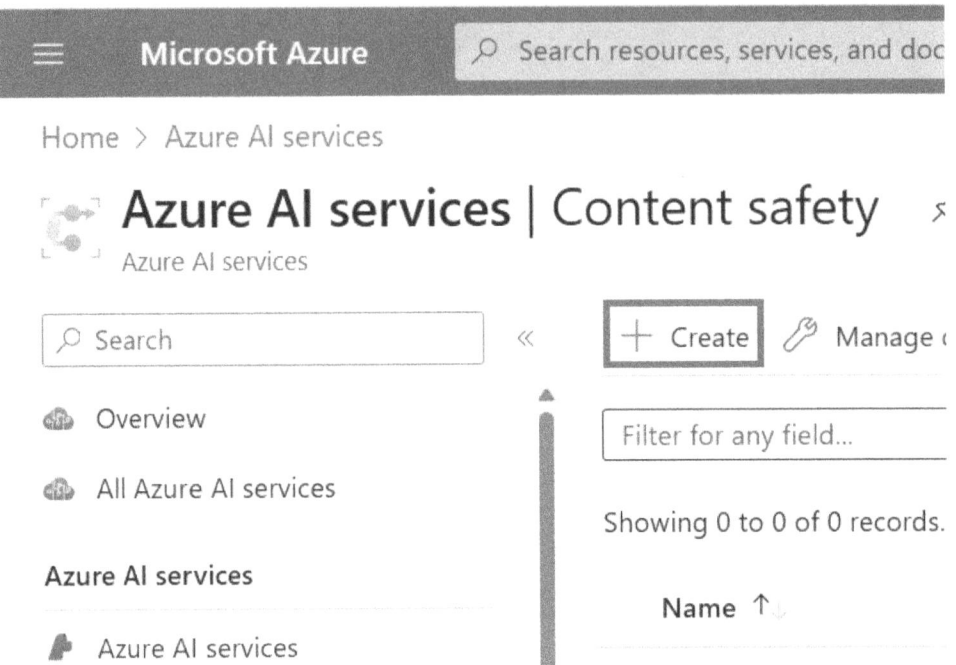

Figure 7-2. Click Create

Next, select your subscription and resource group from the drop-downs available on the screen as can be seen in Figure 7-3. If you don't have a resource group, you can create a new one on this screen. After that, select the region, provide the resource name, and select the pricing tier. The resource name needs to be a unique one. For the purpose of building this solution, we are going to the **Free F0** tier. This tier provides us with the capability to process 5K text records and images per month, which should be enough to build and test our proof of concept (PoC). For workloads running in a production environment, it is advised to use higher tiers. Once you have entered the preceding details, click **Review + create**.

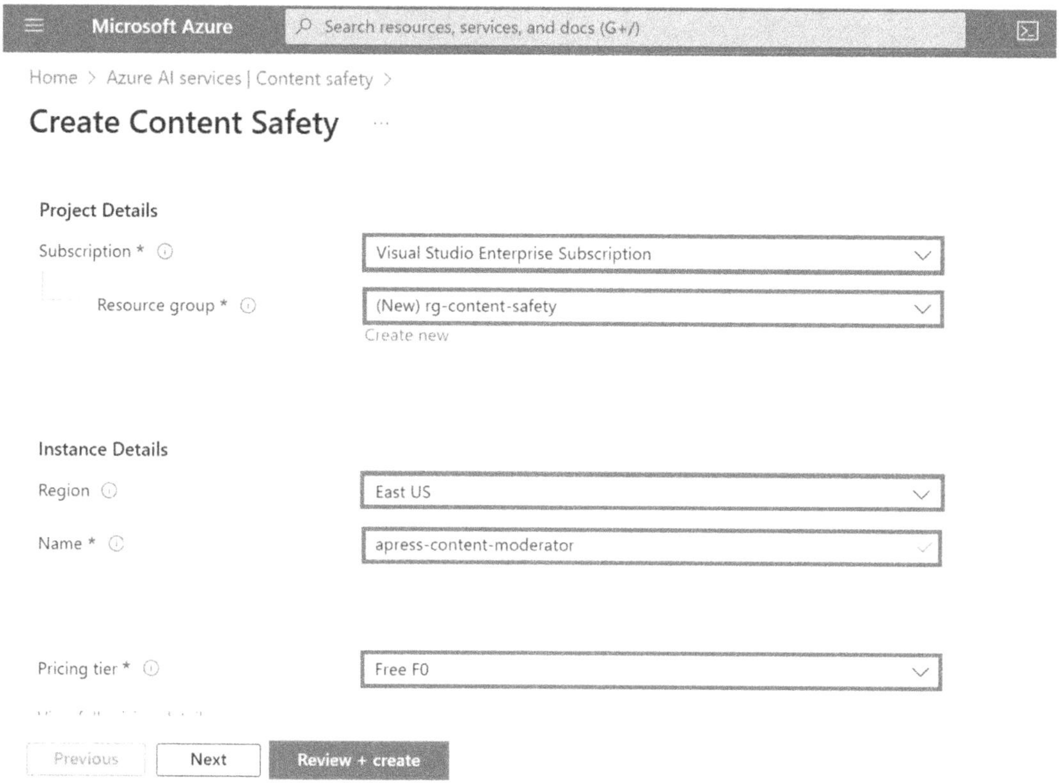

CHAPTER 7   BUILD A CONTENT-FLAGGING APP WITH AZURE AI CONTENT SAFETY

Figure 7-3. Click Review + create

Now you will see a summary of the configuration for the content safety resource that you had entered on the previous screen. A validation check will be done on the configurations. Once the validation of the configuration is done, click **Create**, as shown in Figure 7-4 to provision the resource. If you wanted to make any changes, you could click **Previous** and make the necessary changes for the resource.

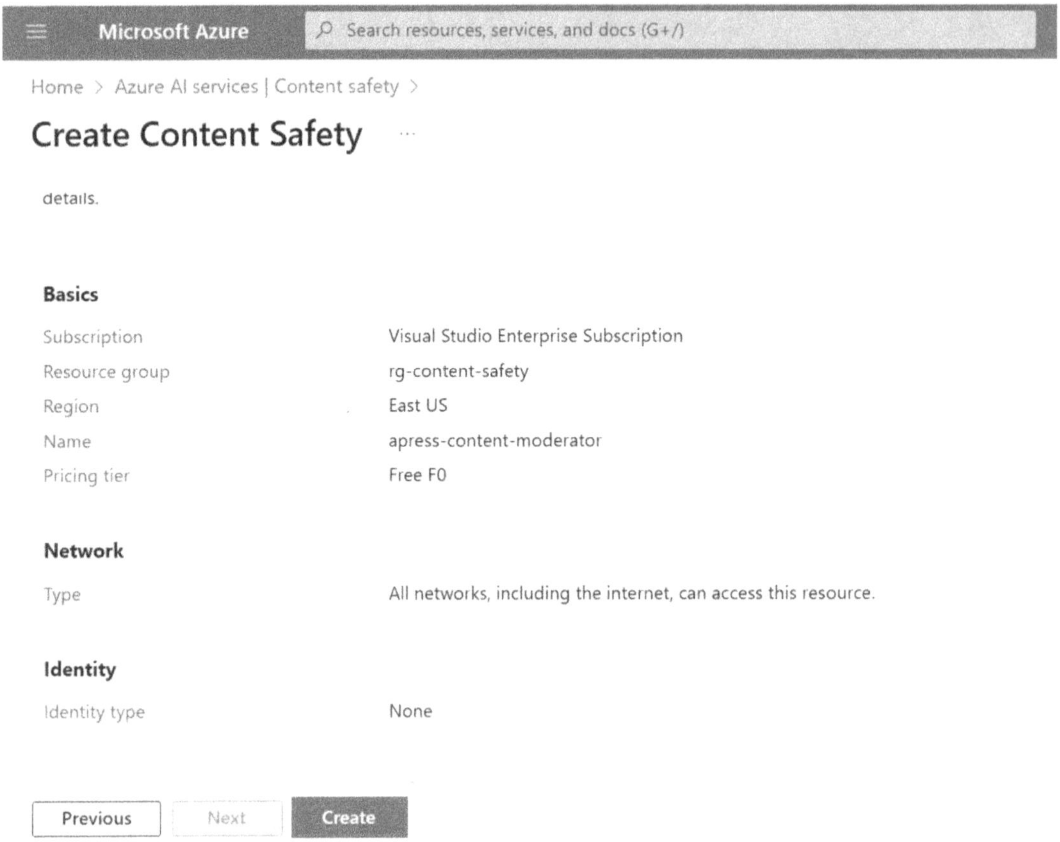

CHAPTER 7   BUILD A CONTENT-FLAGGING APP WITH AZURE AI CONTENT SAFETY

Figure 7-4. Click Create

Once the resource has been created successfully, you will see the message "Your deployment is complete," as shown in Figure 7-5. Once you see that message, click **Go to resource** to view the newly provisioned content safety resource.

CHAPTER 7   BUILD A CONTENT-FLAGGING APP WITH AZURE AI CONTENT SAFETY

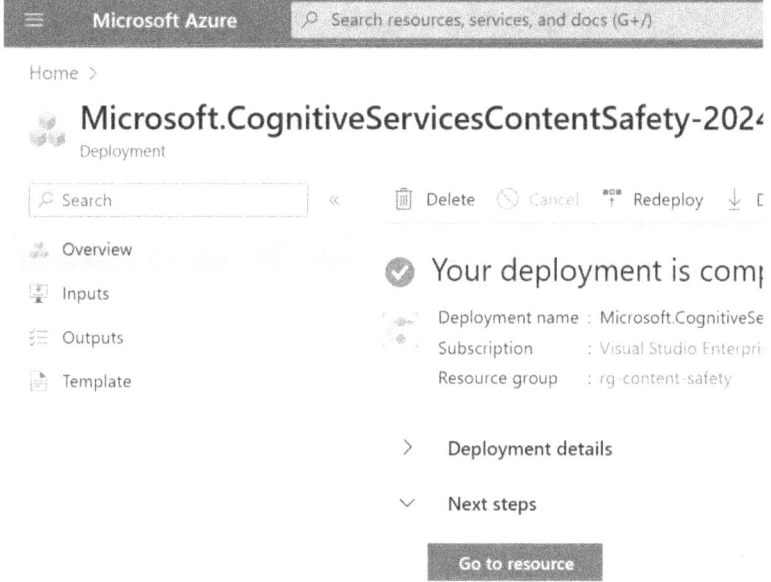

Figure 7-5. *Click Go to resource*

Now that we have provisioned our AI Content Safety service in the Azure Portal, we will need to fetch the access key and endpoint to interact with it from our solution. Access keys are just one way of authenticating our calls to the Content Safety service. We can use other methods like Managed Identity–based authentication which is recommended for production workloads. For the purpose of our PoC, we are going to use key-based authentication.

To fetch the key and endpoint for our Content Safety service, click Keys and Endpoint as shown in Figure 7-6.

153

CHAPTER 7   BUILD A CONTENT-FLAGGING APP WITH AZURE AI CONTENT SAFETY

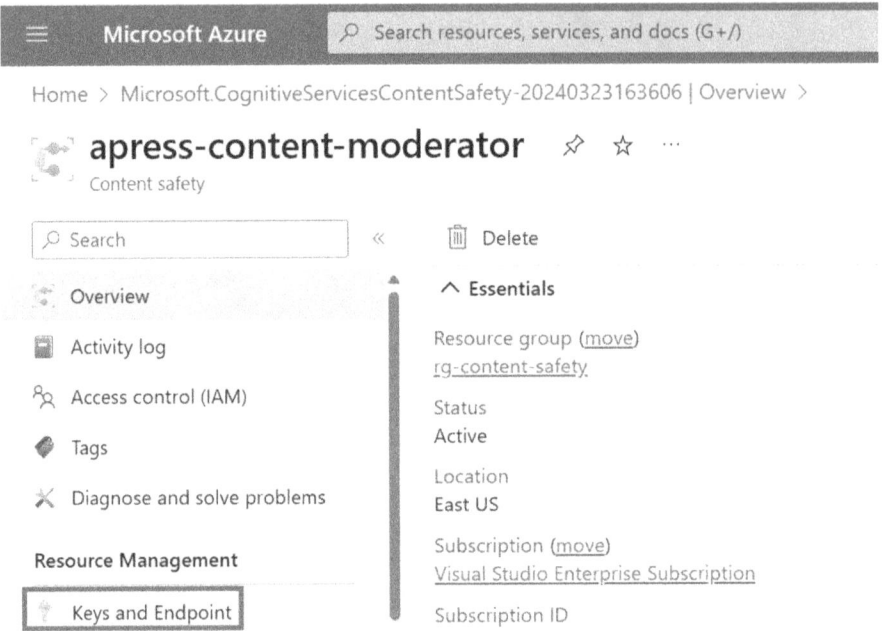

Figure 7-6. *Click Keys and Endpoint*

We will have to fetch either one of the primary or secondary key, the resource endpoint, and the region from the screen shown in Figure 7-7. We will use these values later in our application for authentication purposes.

CHAPTER 7   BUILD A CONTENT-FLAGGING APP WITH AZURE AI CONTENT SAFETY

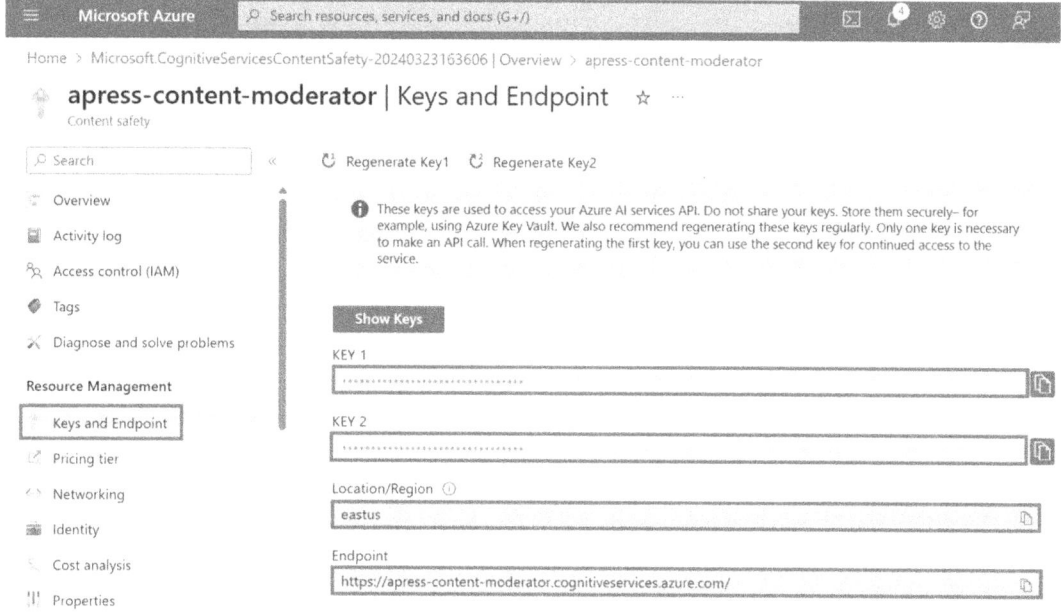

Figure 7-7. *Get the key, endpoint, and region*

Now that we have provisioned the AI Content Safety resource and have the required information to authenticate requests from our application to the Content Safety service, we have completed the prerequisites to build our app. In the next section, we will build a content-flagging app with the Azure AI Content Safety service.

Build a Content-Flagging App with Azure AI Content Safety Service

In this section, we are going to complete the proof of concept for our fictional company to build a feature for our product as briefly discussed in the "Proposed Solution" section.

As we have already discussed the business requirement and provisioned the required resources, let's start building our content-flagging app using the ASP.NET Core Web API template. Open Visual Studio 2022 and click **Create a new project** as shown in Figure 7-8.

155

CHAPTER 7   BUILD A CONTENT-FLAGGING APP WITH AZURE AI CONTENT SAFETY

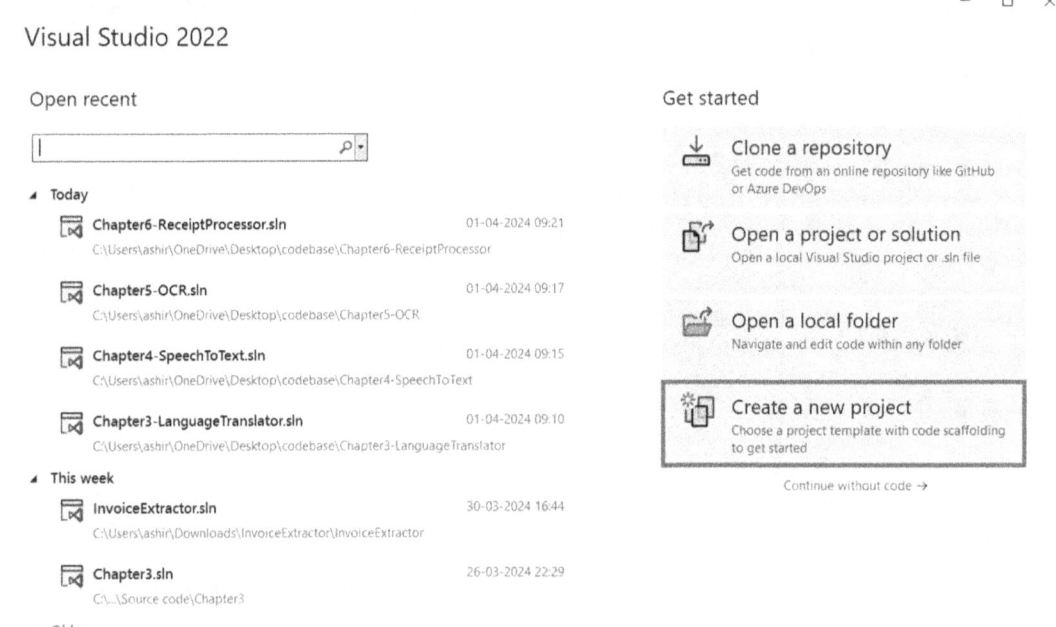

Figure 7-8. *Create a new project*

Select the **ASP.NET Core Web API** project template as shown in Figure 7-9 and click **Next**.

CHAPTER 7   BUILD A CONTENT-FLAGGING APP WITH AZURE AI CONTENT SAFETY

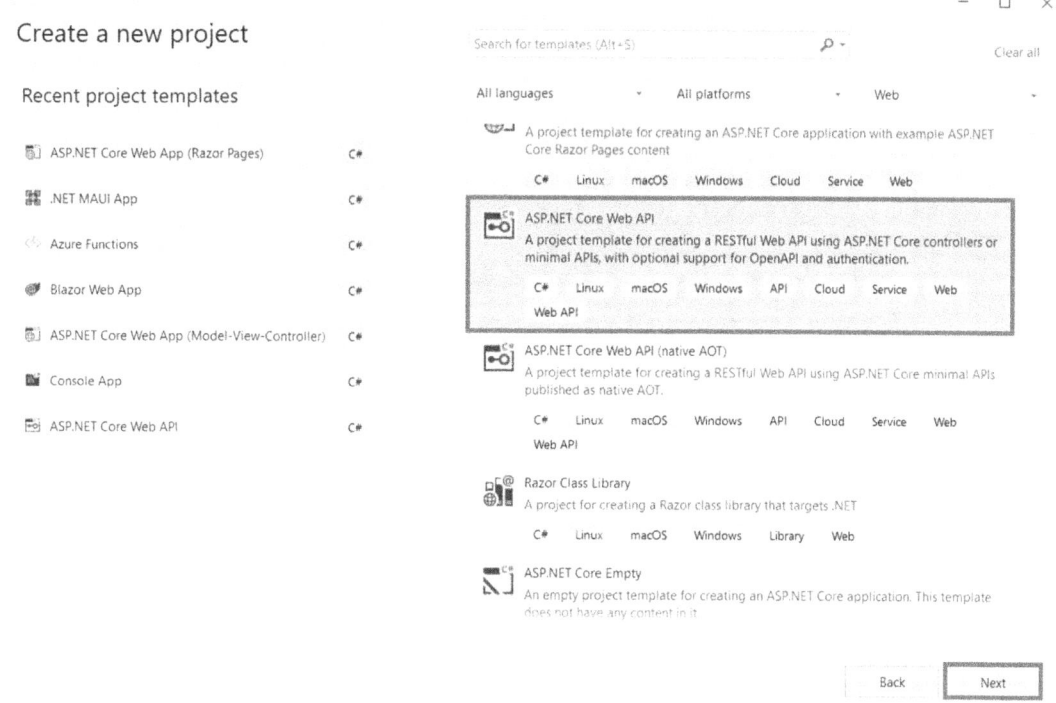

Figure 7-9. *Click Next*

Enter the **project name**, **location**, and **solution name** as shown in Figure 7-10 and click **Next**.

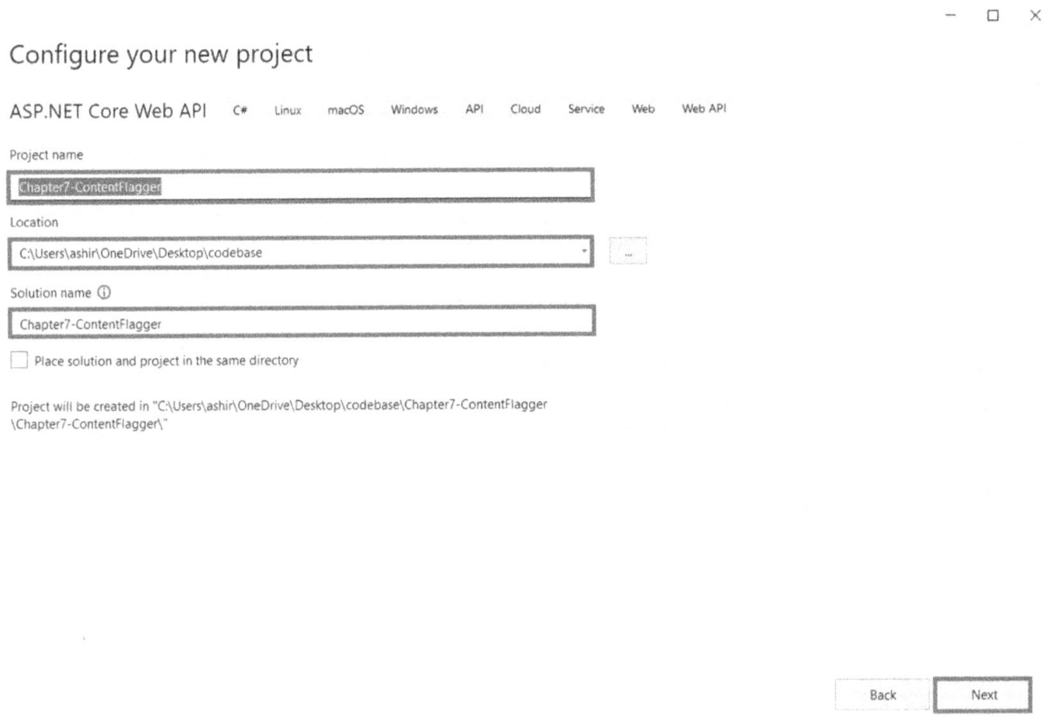

CHAPTER 7   BUILD A CONTENT-FLAGGING APP WITH AZURE AI CONTENT SAFETY

Figure 7-10. Enter the project name, location, and solution name

Now select **.NET 8.0** as the framework and **None** as the authentication type, then check the **Configure for HTTPS**, **Enable OpenAPI support**, **Do not use top-level statements**, and **Use controllers**. Once you are done, click **Create**, as shown in Figure 7-11.

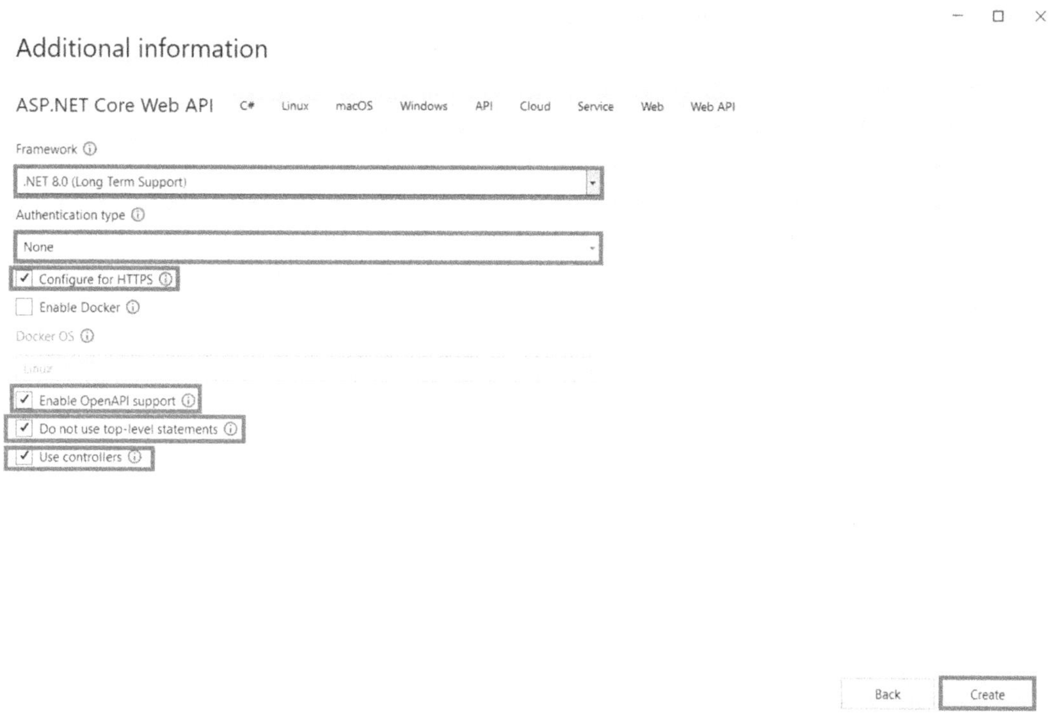

CHAPTER 7 BUILD A CONTENT-FLAGGING APP WITH AZURE AI CONTENT SAFETY

Figure 7-11. Click Create

Now Visual Studio will generate an ASP.NET Core Web API project out of the box. It will contain some boilerplate code for the weatherforecast controller. We can either delete them or ignore them. As a next step, let's add all the packages that we would need to build our solution. To do so, open the NuGet package manager and install the following package:

1. Azure.AI.ContentSafety

Azure.AI.ContentSafety is the official SDK for the Azure AI Content Safety service. We will leverage its power to add text moderation capabilities in our application.

After installing the abovementioned NuGet package, let's open the appsettings.json file and then add the **AzureAiContentSafetyKey** and **AzureAiContentSafetyEndpoint** key-value pairs over there. These values are required to authenticate our requests to the Azure AI Content Safety service. We had fetched these values in the previous section. Let's add these two keys and their values, as demonstrated in Listing 7-1.

Listing 7-1. Add the key-value pairs in appsettings.json

```json
{
  "Logging": {
    "LogLevel": {
      "Default": "Information",
      "Microsoft.AspNetCore": "Warning"
    }
  },
  "AllowedHosts": "*",
  "AzureAiContentSafetyKey": "enter your resource key",
  "AzureAiContentSafetyEndpoint": "enter your resource endpoint"
}
```

Please do note that storing function secrets or sensitive information in the appsettings.json file or hard-coding such information in a variable is not advisable. I recommend using a key vault to store application secrets.

Now that we have added the key and endpoint of our Azure AI Content Safety resource in appsettings.json, let's create a folder called **Model** in our solution. This folder is going to contain our Data Transfer Objects (DTOs). For this project, we will have only one DTO class, that is, ResponseDto. Let's create the ResponseDto class inside the Model folder. This model will be used to share the result with the end user later in the section. The definition for the ResponseDto can be found in Listing 7-2.

Listing 7-2. Code for ResponseDto.cs

```csharp
namespace Chapter7_ContentFlagger.Model
{
    public class ResponseDto
    {
        public int SeverityLevel { get; set; }
        public bool NeedsHumanSupervision { get; set; }
        public bool ShouldBeFlagged { get; set; }
    }
}
```

CHAPTER 7   BUILD A CONTENT-FLAGGING APP WITH AZURE AI CONTENT SAFETY

Now that we have created the ResponseDto class, let's move our focus toward the business implementation of our application. To do so, let's create a folder called **Business** in our solution. As a next step, add an interface called **IAzureAiContentSafetyBusiness** and a class called **AzureAiContentSafetyBusiness**. AzureAiContentSafetyBusiness is going to implement the IAzureAiContentSafetyBusiness. Add the code mentioned in Listing 7-3 in the IAzureAiContentSafetyBusiness interface.

Listing 7-3. Code for IAzureAiContentSafetyBusiness

```
using Chapter7_ContentFlagger.Model;

namespace Chapter7_ContentFlagger.Business
{
    public interface IAzureAiContentSafetyBusiness
    {
        public ResponseDto CheckForHateSpeech(string content);
    }
}
```

The IAzureAiContentSafetyBusiness contains the definition of one method called CheckForHateSpeech. This method will take one parameter – content – which represents the message that the user wants to validate if it contains hate speech or not.

As we have understood the purpose of the CheckForHateSpeech method, let's look at its implementation in the AzureAiContentSafetyBusiness class which is present in Listing 7-4.

Listing 7-4. Code for AzureAiContentSafetyBusiness

```
using Azure;
using Azure.AI.ContentSafety;
using Chapter7_ContentFlagger.Model;
using Microsoft.AspNetCore.DataProtection.KeyManagement;
using static System.Net.Mime.MediaTypeNames;

namespace Chapter7_ContentFlagger.Business
{
```

CHAPTER 7   BUILD A CONTENT-FLAGGING APP WITH AZURE AI CONTENT SAFETY

```
public class AzureAiContentSafetyBusiness : 
IAzureAiContentSafetyBusiness
{
    private readonly IConfiguration _configuration;
    private static ContentSafetyClient client;
    public AzureAiContentSafetyBusiness(IConfiguration configuration)
    {
        _configuration = configuration;
        client = new ContentSafetyClient(new Uri(_configuration["Azure
        AiContentSafetyEndpoint"]),
            new AzureKeyCredential(_configuration["AzureAiContent
            SafetyKey"]));
    }
    public ResponseDto CheckForHateSpeech(string content)
    {
        var request = new AnalyzeTextOptions(content);

        var response = client.AnalyzeText(request);

        var severityLevel = response.Value.CategoriesAnalysis.
        FirstOrDefault(a => a.Category == TextCategory.Hate)?.
        Severity ?? 0;

        ResponseDto responseDto = new ResponseDto();

        if(severityLevel < 4) {
            responseDto.SeverityLevel = severityLevel;
            responseDto.ShouldBeFlagged = false;
            responseDto.NeedsHumanSupervision = false;
        }
        if (severityLevel > 3)
        {
            responseDto.SeverityLevel = severityLevel;
            responseDto.ShouldBeFlagged = true;
            responseDto.NeedsHumanSupervision = true;
        }
```

```
            return responseDto;
        }
    }
}
```

In Listing 7-4, AzureAiContentSafetyBusiness implements the IAzureAiContentSafetyBusiness interface. It utilizes the Azure AI Content Safety service to check for hate speech in text content. In the constructor, it initializes a ContentSafetyClient using the endpoint and key present in appsettings.json. We leverage the AnalyzeText method of the ContentSafetyClient instance to analyze the text. This will return the severity level of the content for different categories like hate, self-harm, sexual, and violence. For the purpose of this PoC, we are only concerned with detecting content promoting hate. Thus, we are fetching the severity level of the **hate** category. The severity level grows from 0 to 7. The higher severity level says that the content is offensive and derogatory in nature and can have server consequences if shown. In our logic, we specify that if the severity level is less than 4, then the content does not need to be flagged, but if the severity level is more than 3, then it requires to be flagged and needs to be verified by a human.

Now that we have written the code for IAzureAiContentSafetyBusiness and AzureAiContentSafetyBusiness, let's go to Program.cs and update the code to register the AzureAiContentSafetyBusiness class as a singleton service for the IAzureAiContentSafetyBusiness interface in the DI container. The updated code for Program.cs is present in Listing 7-5.

Listing 7-5. Updated code for Program.cs

```
using Chapter7_ContentFlagger.Business;

namespace Chapter7_ContentFlagger
{
    public class Program
    {
        public static void Main(string[] args)
        {
            var builder = WebApplication.CreateBuilder(args);

            // Add services to the container.
```

```
        builder.Services.AddControllers();
        // Learn more about configuring Swagger/OpenAPI at https://aka.
        ms/aspnetcore/swashbuckle
        builder.Services.AddEndpointsApiExplorer();
        builder.Services.AddSwaggerGen();

        builder.Services.AddSingleton<IAzureAiContentSafetyBusiness,
        AzureAiContentSafetyBusiness>();

        var app = builder.Build();

        // Configure the HTTP request pipeline.
        if (app.Environment.IsDevelopment())
        {
            app.UseSwagger();
            app.UseSwaggerUI();
        }

        app.UseHttpsRedirection();

        app.UseAuthorization();

        app.MapControllers();

        app.Run();
    }
  }
}
```

Having completed the business implementation, injected the required services into the DI container, configured the key and endpoint in our appsettings.json file, and defined the ResponseDto class, we can now focus on creating our REST endpoint to provide an endpoint to other systems to analyze their content by leveraging the business logic that we have implemented. To do so, let's create an empty API controller inside the Controllers folder of our solution. Let's name it ContentFlaggerController. Inside this controller, add the code shared in Listing 7-6.

Listing 7-6. Code for ContentFlaggerController.cs

```csharp
using Chapter7_ContentFlagger.Business;
using Microsoft.AspNetCore.Http;
using Microsoft.AspNetCore.Mvc;

namespace Chapter7_ContentFlagger.Controllers
{
    [Route("api/[controller]")]
    [ApiController]
    public class ContentFlaggerController : ControllerBase
    {
        private readonly IAzureAiContentSafetyBusiness _
        azureAiContentSafetyBusiness;
        public ContentFlaggerController(IAzureAiContentSafetyBusiness
        azureAiContentSafetyBusines)
        {
            _azureAiContentSafetyBusiness = azureAiContentSafetyBusines;
        }
        [HttpGet]
        public IActionResult Get([FromQuery] string content)
        {
            var result = _azureAiContentSafetyBusiness.
            CheckForHateSpeech(content);

            return Ok(result);
        }
    }
}
```

In Listing 7-6, we are injecting an instance of the IAzureAiContentSafetyBusiness via constructor injection to interact with the business logic for content safety checks. The controller contains an action method, **Get**, which gets invoked every time someone makes a GET request to the endpoint. It accepts a query parameter **content** representing the text content to be checked for hate speech. It then delegates the content analysis to the injected business service and returns the result as an object of type ResponseDto back to the end user.

Now that we have written the code for our solution, in the next section we will test it out.

Test the Content-Flagging App

To test the content-flagging app, we will have to run the Web API project. Once the project runs, it should route you to the swagger page. Over there, we need to expand the API endpoint, **/api/ContentFlagger**, and click **Try it out**. After that, we will add the value to the content field. This goes as a query string to our API. You can add any textual content that you want to analyze for containing hate speech. Once done, click **Execute** as shown in Figure 7-12.

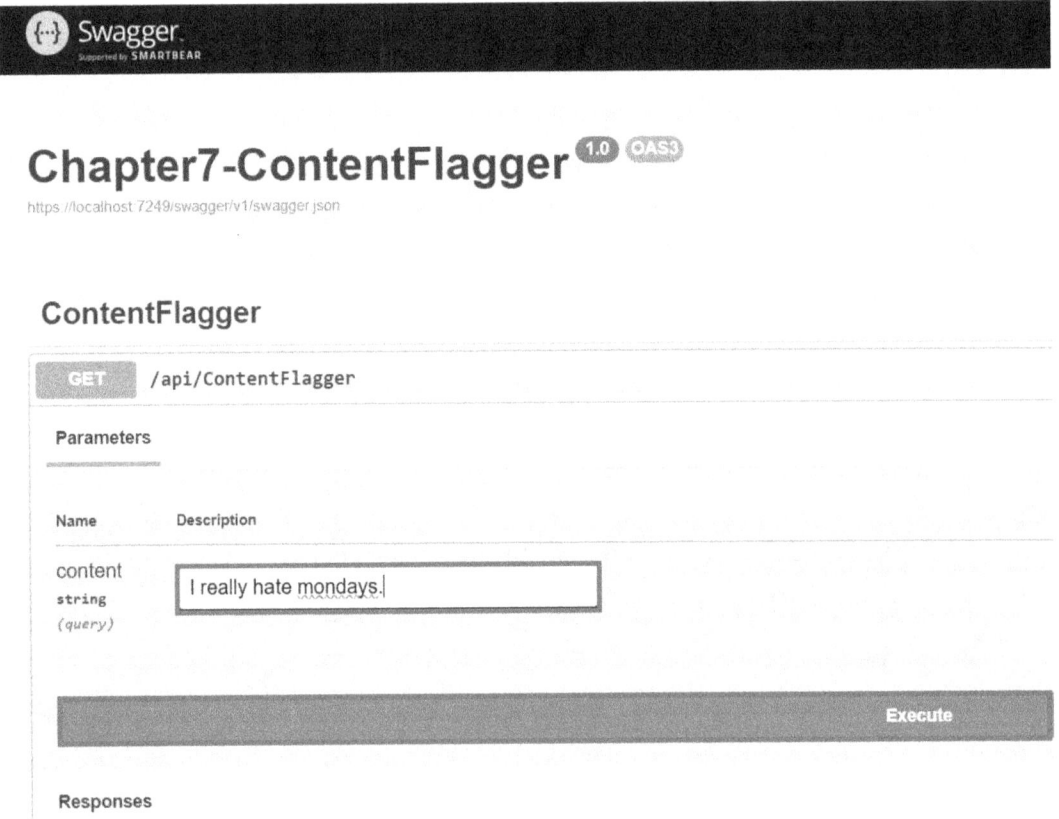

Figure 7-12. Click Execute

Once the API call has been executed, we can view the result in the **Responses** section. The API should return JSON representing the ResponseDto in the response body as shown in Figure 7-13.

Figure 7-13. *View response from the API*

As can be seen from Figure 7-13, our ContentFlagger app was able to accurately identify whether a content needs to be flagged or not.

Summary

In this chapter, you've gained insights into creating intelligent solutions using the ASP. NET Core Web API and the Azure AI Content Safety service through the development of a Web API to flag texts containing harmful content. Our exploration delved into the Azure AI Content Safety service, uncovering its features and applications. Additionally, we navigated through the steps of provisioning an Azure AI Content Safety service within the Azure Portal. Throughout this process, we've acquired knowledge on constructing an intelligent solution by harnessing the capabilities of the Azure AI Content Safety service.

CHAPTER 7　BUILD A CONTENT-FLAGGING APP WITH AZURE AI CONTENT SAFETY

The primary focus of this chapter centered around analyzing the text functionality offered by the Azure AI Content Safety service. In the forthcoming chapter, our attention will shift toward investigating the features provided by the Azure OpenAI service to generate summaries from textual content.

CHAPTER 8

Build a Text Summarizer with Azure OpenAI

With capabilities like text summarization and code generation or the potential to interact with humans in a conversational manner, ChatGPT has amplified the market interest in the field of generative AI. ChatGPT is a flagship product of OpenAI. It is powered by a large language model (LLM), GPT 3.5, which is an iteration of previous series of GPT models. These models were designed on the basis of a transformer architecture that was published by a group of engineers at Google in a research paper called "Attention Is All You Need." But building LLMs from scratch is a resource- and capital-intensive process as it needs a lot of domain expertise and training data. To build GenAI solutions by overcoming these challenges, we can leverage cloud services like Azure OpenAI which provides access to the base models of OpenAI and integrate their capabilities in our applications. In this chapter, we are going to briefly discuss about the Azure OpenAI service and its use cases and build a content summarizer by leveraging its client SDKs.

Structure

In this chapter, we will explore the following aspects of Azure:

- Introduction to the Azure OpenAI service
- Create your first Azure OpenAI service in the Azure Portal
- Create a content summarizer

CHAPTER 8   BUILD A TEXT SUMMARIZER WITH AZURE OPENAI

Objectives

After studying this chapter, you should be able to

- Grasp the essentials of the Azure OpenAI service
- Add the capabilities of the Azure OpenAI service to your applications

Introduction to Azure OpenAI Service

The Azure OpenAI service is a fully managed cloud-based service of Microsoft Azure which enables developers and organizations to leverage the power of the large language models (LLMs) offered by OpenAI to build intelligent applications. With the help of the models offered by the Azure OpenAI service, organizations and developers can build applications with capabilities such as content generation, image understanding, language translation, and code generation. As of now, access to Azure OpenAI is limited due to high demand. It also has first-class integration with other Azure services like Azure AI Search. With the Azure OpenAI service, we get access to the foundation model which can fine-tune our own data. And your data used for fine-tuning your models will stay within the boundary of your resource and will not be used for training purposes by Microsoft.

Azure OpenAI services provide client SDKs in various languages like Python, C#, and Java. It enables developers to easily integrate the Azure OpenAI service in their applications. For the languages for which the SDKs are not available, they can use the REST APIs to integrate the capabilities of the Azure OpenAI service in their applications. We can authenticate our request to Azure OpenAI instances by using key-based authentication or Managed Identity with the help of Microsoft Entra ID. It comes up with a guaranteed SLA of 99.9% like other Azure AI Services.

Some of the key terminologies associated with the Azure OpenAI service are as follows:

1. **Prompts** – A prompt is like a set of instructions or a question that tells the model what to do. It helps the model understand what kind of response is needed. For instance, if you want the model to write a story, you could give it a prompt like "Tell a tale about a detective figuring out a tricky murder in a little town."

CHAPTER 8   BUILD A TEXT SUMMARIZER WITH AZURE OPENAI

2. **Completions** – Completions are what you get back from Azure OpenAI models when you give them something to work on, like a prompt. They're basically the answers or outputs the model comes up with after it thinks about the input you gave it. So, completions are essentially the model's responses to the prompts you provide.

3. **Tokens** – Tokens are the building blocks of text that the model deals with. They could be single words, punctuation marks, or any other parts of a language. When you give a prompt to the model, it chops it up into these tokens to understand and create responses.

Azure OpenAI offers different types of models which are as follows:

1. **GPT 4** – These are a series of models which are enhanced on top of GPT 3.5 models which are capable of comprehending and generating content. By using GPT 4 with Vision, we can also interpret images and derive insights.

2. **GPT 3.5** – These are a series of models which are enhanced versions of GPT 3 which can understand natural language and code. These models have higher token limits than GPT 3 models.

3. **Embeddings** – These are a set of models which convert texts into numerical vectors and compare text similarities between texts.

4. **DALL-E** – These are a series of models which can take a prompt as an input and generate images on the basis of it.

5. **Whisper** – These are a series of models which can perform speech-to-text conversion along with speech translations.

Now that we have explored some of the key features of the Azure OpenAI service, let's explore some of the potential use cases where it can come in handy:

1. **Content Generation** – Models like GPT 4, DALL-E, and GPT 3.5 can be used to generate textual and visual content, such as articles, essays, scripts for dramas, or posters. We can configure the tone, theme, and style of the content by providing effective prompts.

2. **Language Translation** – Some models like GPT 4 and GPT 3.5 can perform language translation. We can provide the content to be translated along with the target language in the prompt, and they will translate it with ease.

As we have explored what Azure OpenAI service is and what its key features and use cases are, let's explore ways to integrate it in our solutions by building a text summarizer app.

Problem Statement

You are working for a fictional company, ANewsTech Corp. With the reduced attention time of readers, the company is focused on providing a short and crisp summary of articles by leveraging the power of generative AI. You are part of the team which is at the helm of building this feature. As part of your work, you are assigned the responsibility to create a proof of concept to build a text summarizer by leveraging the power of generative AI. Your dev lead and architect proposed to use Azure OpenAI for the proof of concept. The proof of concept is important and is necessary to get the work started for the feature. Your team is going to leverage your proof of concept as the base for the further development of the functionality.

Proposed Solution

After going through the requirement, you have broken down the problem into two tasks:

1. Generate a summary from textual content
2. Provide an interface to interact with the solution

To solve both of the abovementioned problems, you have decided to use the ASP. NET Core Web API and the Azure OpenAI service to develop the solution. With the help of the Web API, we are going to provide a REST endpoint to the end users to make requests and receive the desired responses. The API is going to take the textual content from the user's request, then leverage the power of the Azure OpenAI service to generate a summary from the textual content and return back the result as a response.

CHAPTER 8 BUILD A TEXT SUMMARIZER WITH AZURE OPENAI

Before we start building the Web API, we need a couple of things in place. The following are the prerequisites to start the development activities:

1. Create an Azure OpenAI service

2. Deploy the LLM

3. Fetch the endpoint and key of the Azure OpenAI service

Once we have these three things in place, we can start building our solution using Visual Studio 2022. Let's get started.

Create an Azure OpenAI Service

To create an Azure OpenAI service, go to the Azure Portal and type Azure OpenAI in the search box. Click the **Azure OpenAI** in the search results as shown in Figure 8-1.

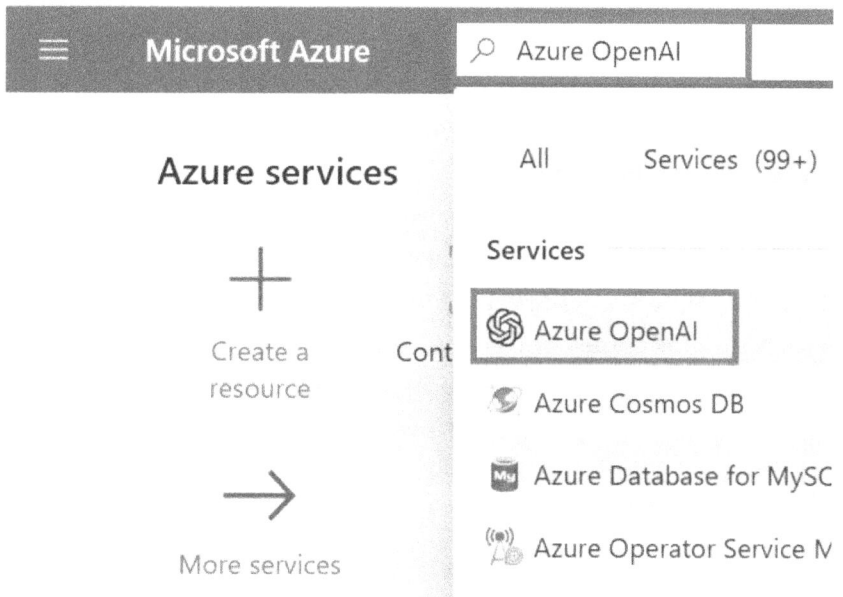

Figure 8-1. *Search for Azure OpenAI*

On the screen shown in Figure 8-2, you can view the list of Azure OpenAI services that you have provisioned. Click **Create** to provision our Azure OpenAI service.

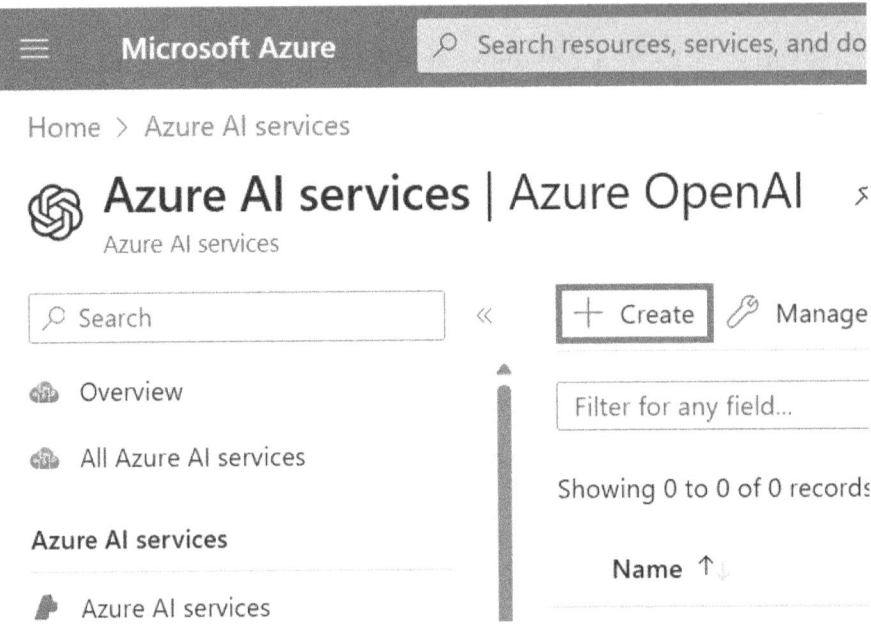

Figure 8-2. *Click Create*

Next, select your subscription and resource group from the drop-downs available on the screen as can be seen in Figure 8-3. If you don't have a resource group, you can create a new one on this screen. After that, select the region, provide the resource name, and select the pricing tier. The resource name needs to be a unique one. For the purpose of building this solution, we are going to the **Standard** tier as it is the only one available at the moment. The pricing comes with pay as you go or with provisioned throughput units (PTUs). With PTUs, you have reserved a certain amount of model processing capacity for your applications. It is ideal to go with PTUs when you have predictable usage patterns. Once you have entered the preceding details, click **Next**.

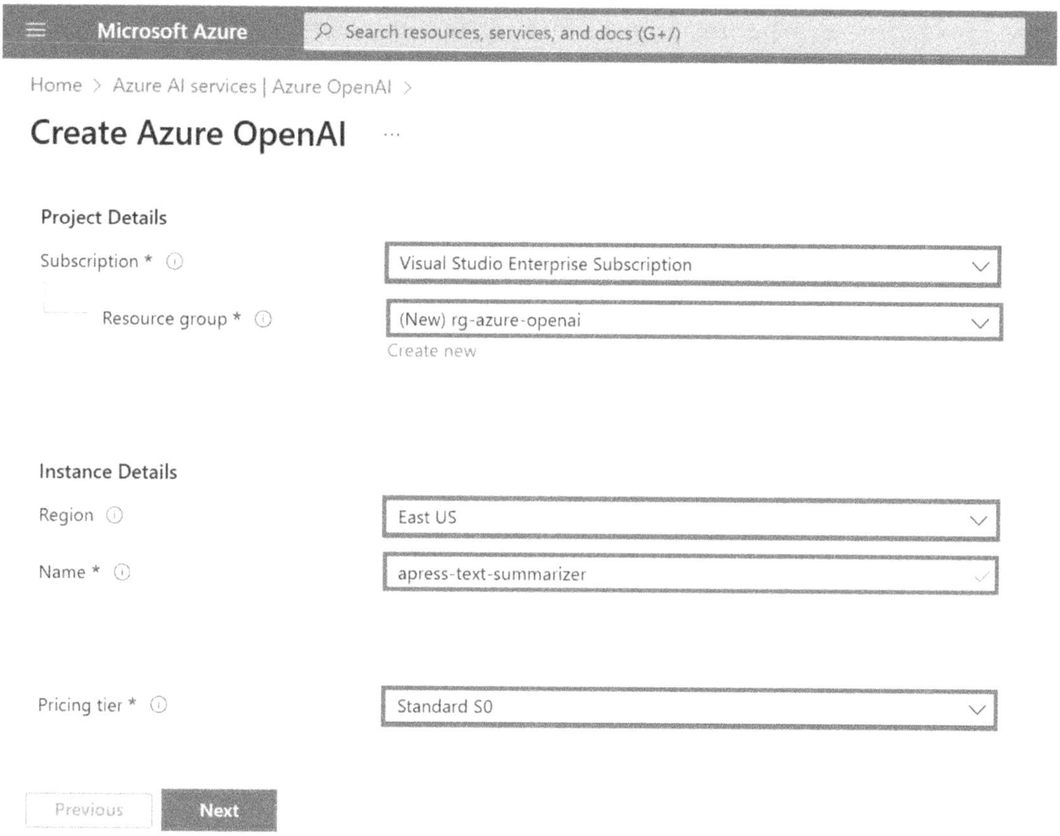

CHAPTER 8 BUILD A TEXT SUMMARIZER WITH AZURE OPENAI

Figure 8-3. Click Next

In the network section, we can configure the network access for our Azure OpenAI resource. For the purpose of our PoC, we are going ahead with **All networks, including the internet, can access the resource** as illustrated in Figure 8-4. For production workloads, you might prefer the later options as you don't want to provide public access to your Azure OpenAI instance.

CHAPTER 8   BUILD A TEXT SUMMARIZER WITH AZURE OPENAI

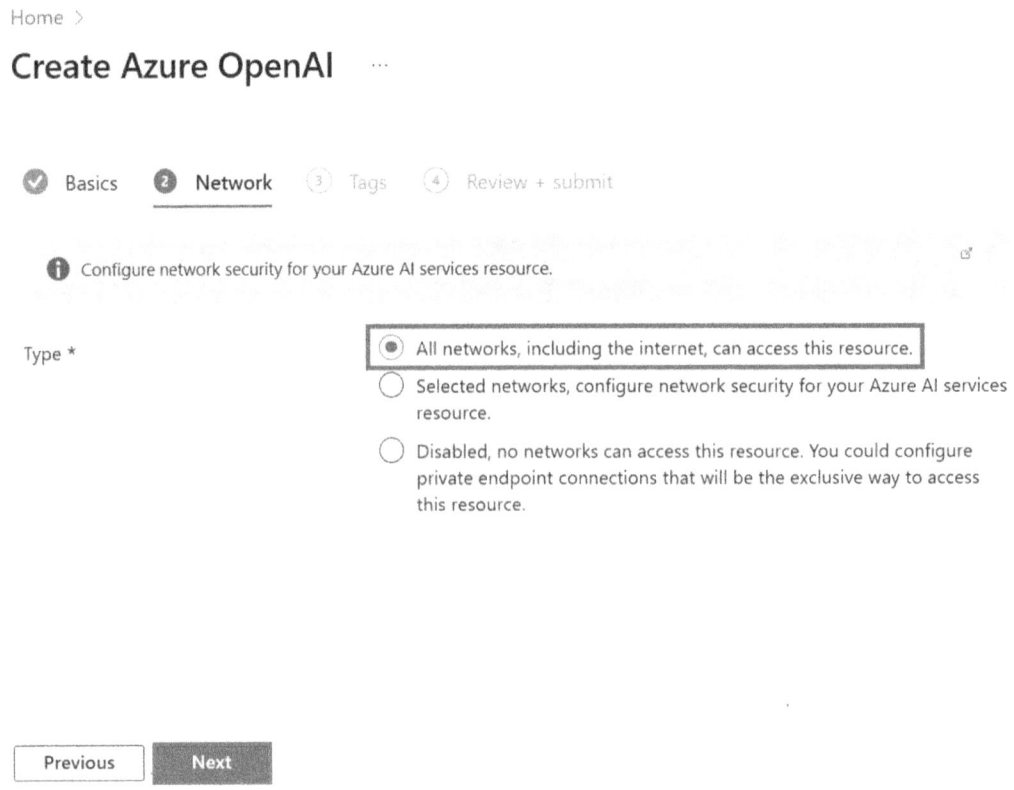

Figure 8-4. Click Next

On the current screen, you can provide the tags for the resource. Tags are useful for resource organization and cost management. It is a best practice to add tags while you provision resources in Azure. For the purpose of our PoC, we are not going to add any tags. Click **Next** as shown in Figure 8-5.

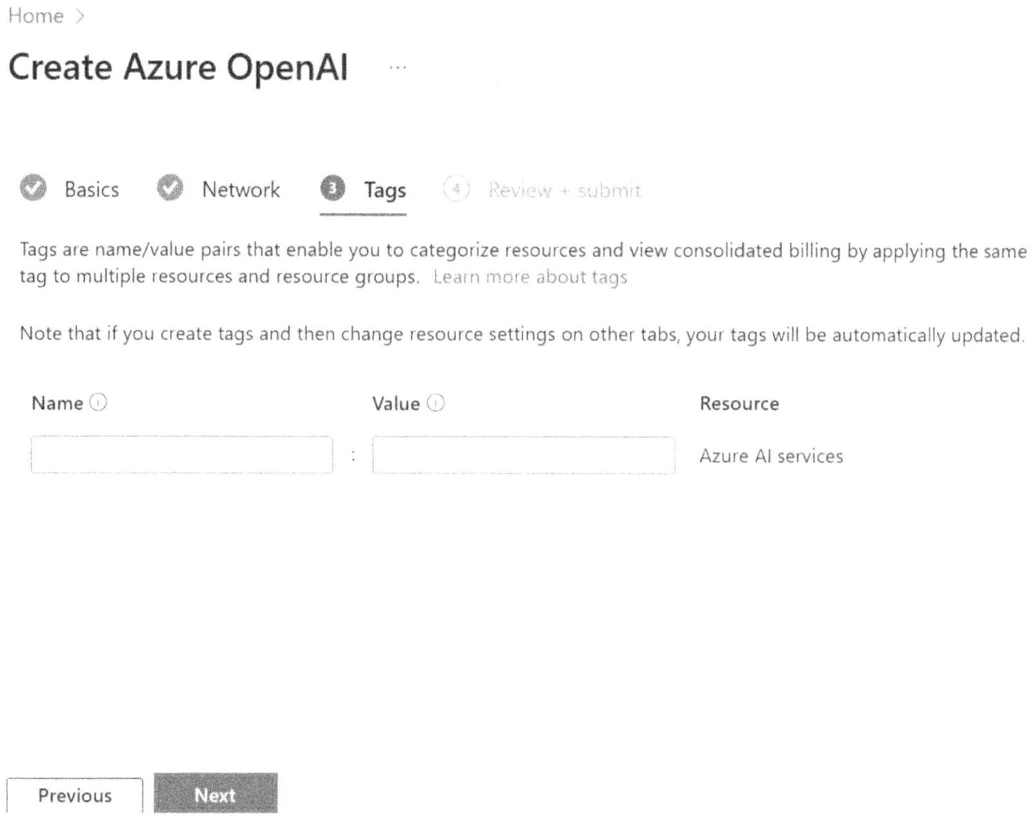

CHAPTER 8   BUILD A TEXT SUMMARIZER WITH AZURE OPENAI

Figure 8-5. Click Next

Now you will see a summary of the configuration for the Azure OpenAI resource that you had entered on the previous screen. A validation check will be done on the configurations. Once the validation of the configuration is done, click **Create** to provision the resource, as highlighted in Figure 8-6. If you wanted to make any changes, you could click **Previous** and make the necessary changes for the resource.

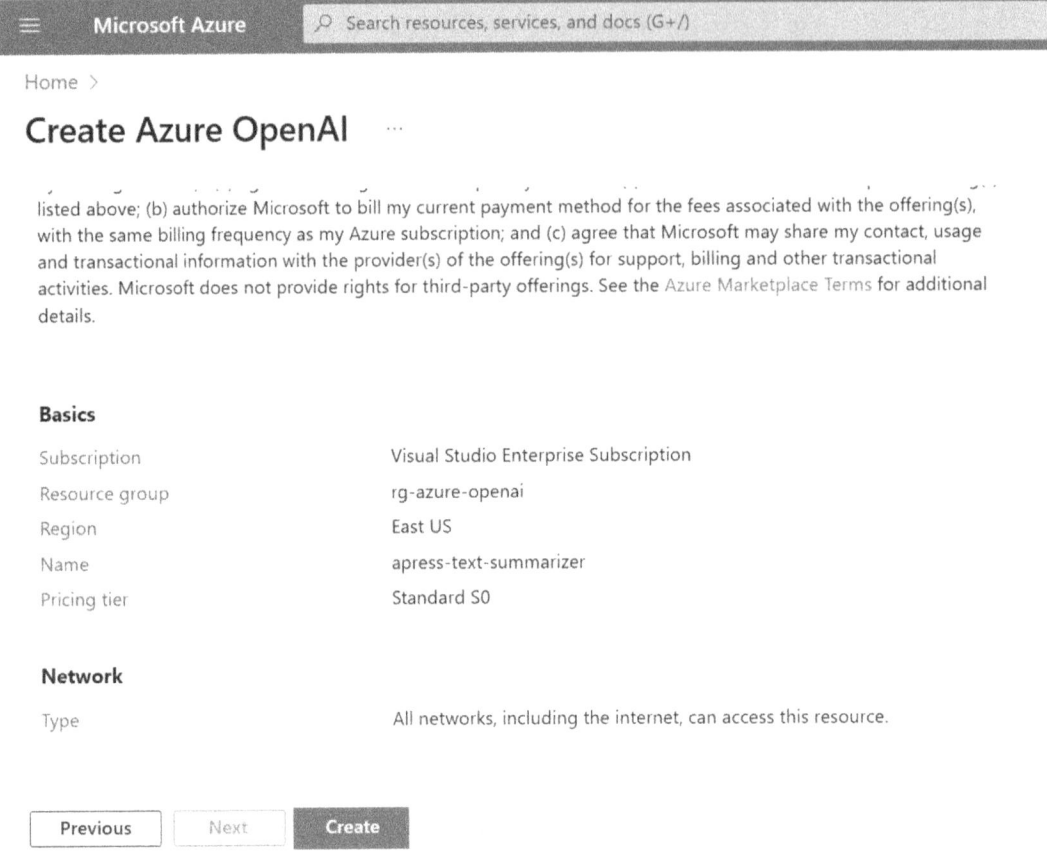

Figure 8-6. Click Create

Once the resource has been created successfully, you will see the message "Your deployment is complete," as shown in Figure 8-7. Once you see that message, click **Go to resource** to view the newly provisioned Azure OpenAI resource.

CHAPTER 8   BUILD A TEXT SUMMARIZER WITH AZURE OPENAI

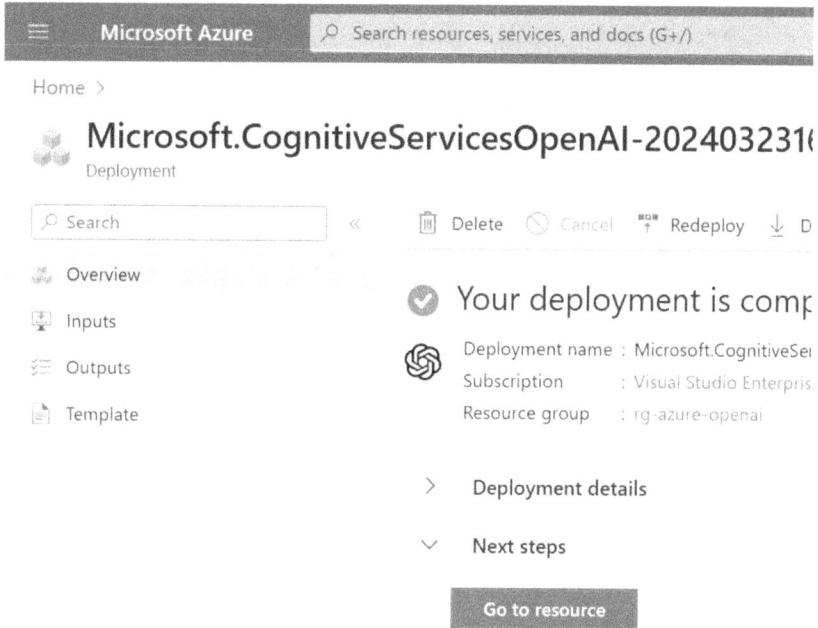

Figure 8-7. *Click Go to resource*

Now that we have provisioned our Azure OpenAI service in the Azure Portal, we will need to fetch the access key and endpoint to interact with it from our solution. Access keys are just one way of authenticating our calls to the Azure OpenAI service. We can use other methods like Managed Identity–based authentication which is recommended for production workloads. For the purpose of our PoC, we are going to use key-based authentication.

To fetch the key and endpoint for our Azure OpenAI instance, click Keys and Endpoint as shown in Figure 8-8. We will have to fetch either one of the primary or secondary key, the resource endpoint, and the region from the screen. We will use these values later in our application for authentication purposes.

CHAPTER 8   BUILD A TEXT SUMMARIZER WITH AZURE OPENAI

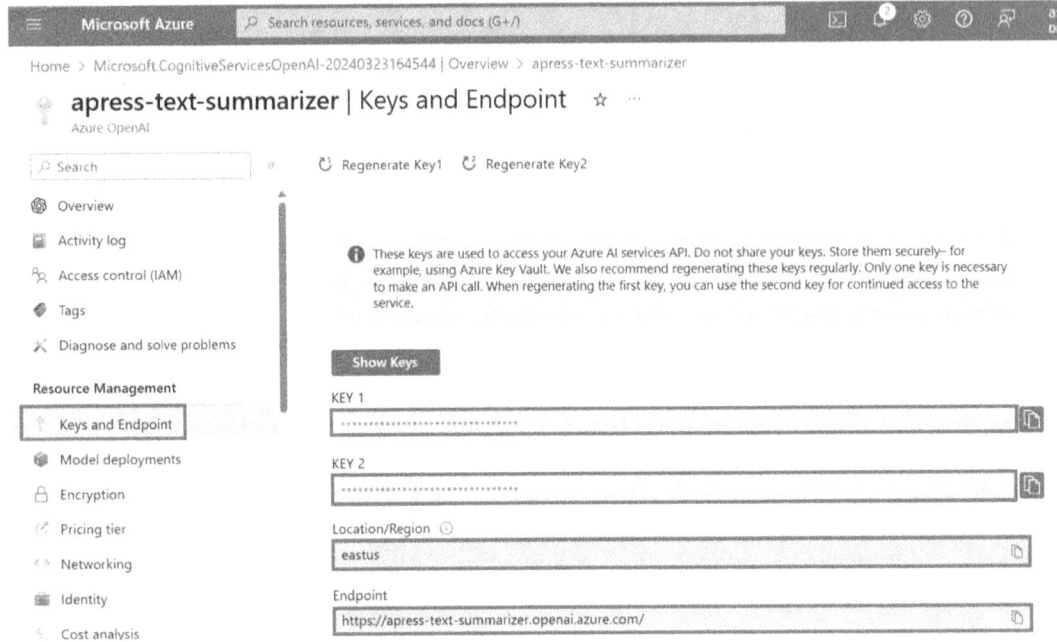

Figure 8-8. *Click Keys and Endpoint*

Now that we have provisioned the resource as well as the keys and endpoint, the next step is to deploy our model. To deploy our first model, click **Model deployments** and then click **Manage Deployments** as shown in Figure 8-9.

CHAPTER 8   BUILD A TEXT SUMMARIZER WITH AZURE OPENAI

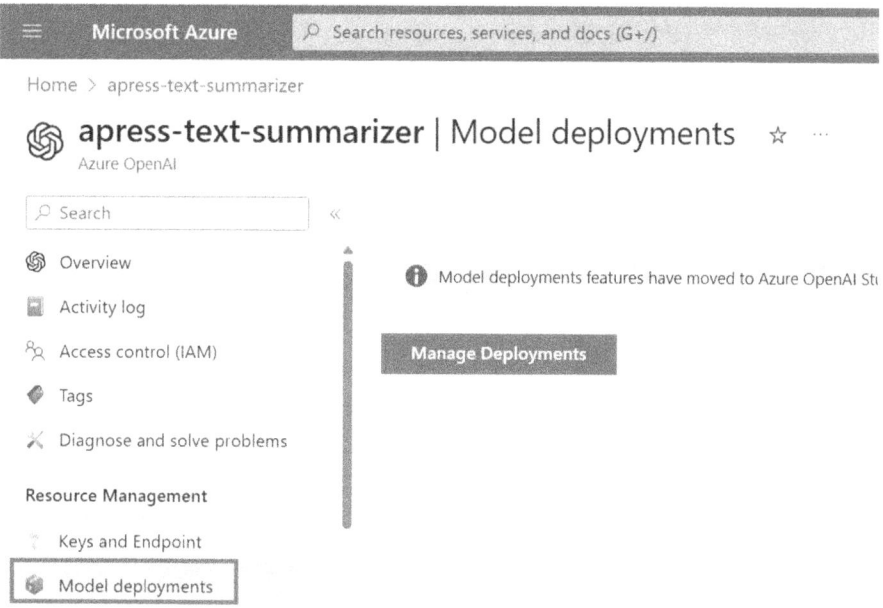

Figure 8-9. *Click Manage Deployments*

Now you will be redirected to the Azure OpenAI Studio. On the current screen, navigate to deployment from the side menu and click **Create new deployment** to provision our very first base model, as illustrated in Figure 8-10.

CHAPTER 8   BUILD A TEXT SUMMARIZER WITH AZURE OPENAI

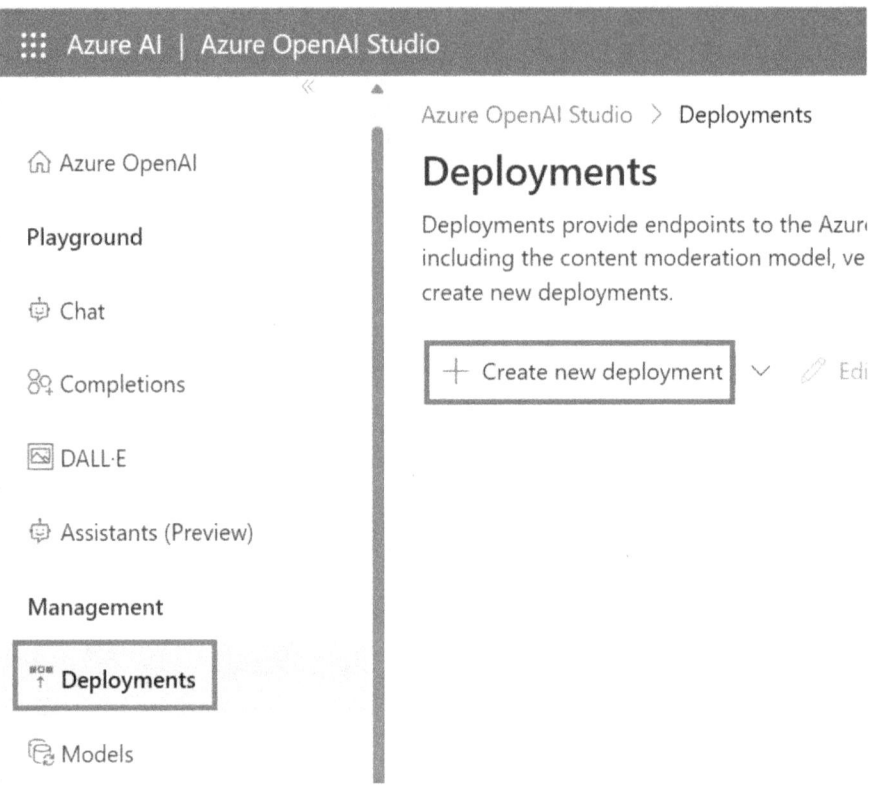

Figure 8-10. *Click Create new deployment*

You will see a pop-up screen which will require us to fill in the information to the deployment. Here, we have to select the model that we want to use and the model version and provide a deployment name. For the purpose of the PoC, we are going to leverage the **gpt-35-turbo** model. Please note that you may not have access to all the models. For certain models like GPT 4, you will have to raise a request to allocate quota to deploy the model. Once you have filled in the required information, click **Create**, as illustrated in Figure 8-11.

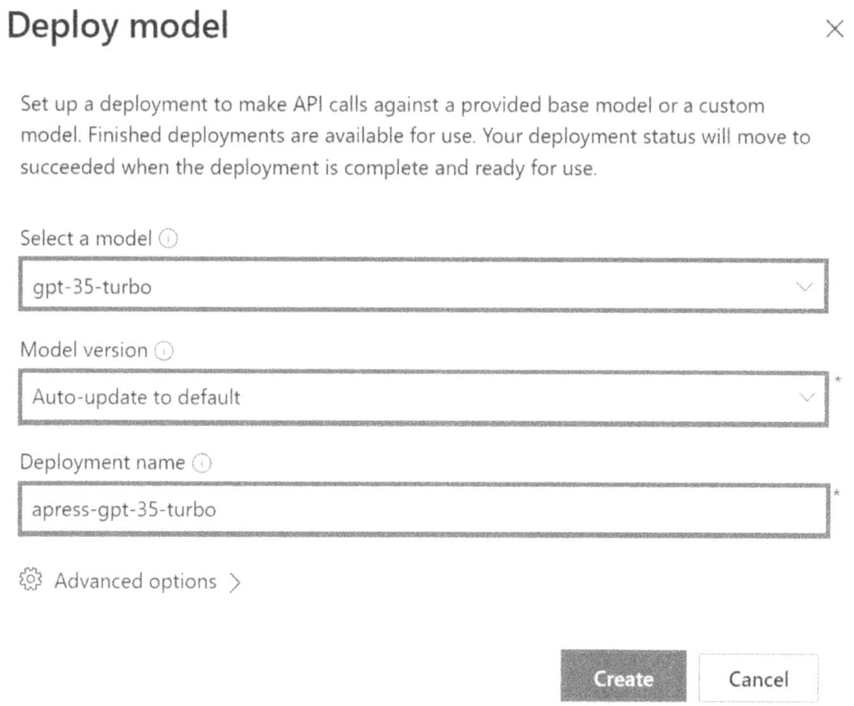

CHAPTER 8 BUILD A TEXT SUMMARIZER WITH AZURE OPENAI

Deploy model

Set up a deployment to make API calls against a provided base model or a custom model. Finished deployments are available for use. Your deployment status will move to succeeded when the deployment is complete and ready for use.

Select a model

    gpt-35-turbo

Model version

    Auto-update to default

Deployment name

    apress-gpt-35-turbo

Advanced options

[Create]   [Cancel]

Figure 8-11. Click Create

The deployment of the model might take some time. Once the deployment of the model is successful, you should be able to view the model in the **Deployment** section as shown in Figure 8-12.

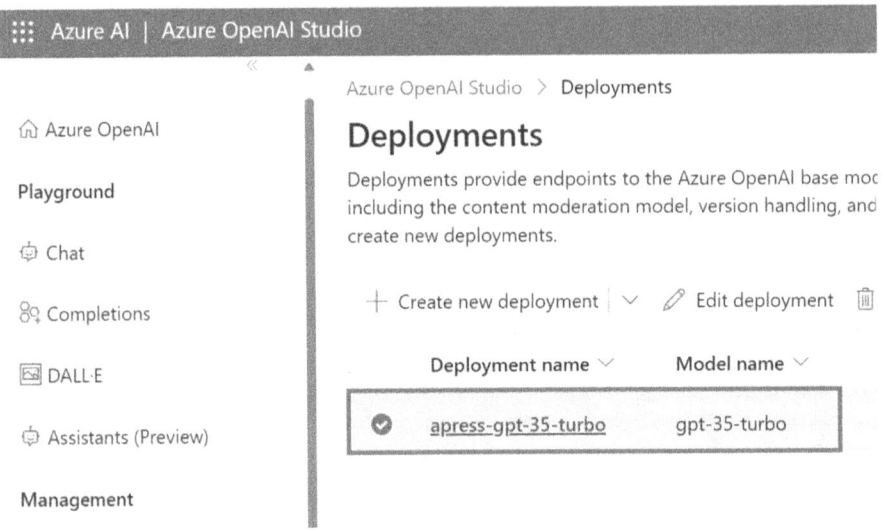

Figure 8-12. Model deployment successful

Now that we have provisioned the Azure OpenAI resource, created a deployment for the gpt-35-turbo model, and have the required information to authenticate requests from our application to the Azure OpenAI service, we have completed all the prerequisites. In the next section, we will learn to build a text summarizer with Azure OpenAI.

Build a Text Summarizer with Azure OpenAI

In this section, we are going to complete the proof of concept for our fictional company to build a feature for our product as briefly discussed in the "Proposed Solution" section.

As we have already discussed the business requirement and provisioned the required resources, let's start building our text summarizer app using the ASP.NET Core Web API template. Open Visual Studio 2022 and click **Create a new project** as shown in Figure 8-13.

CHAPTER 8   BUILD A TEXT SUMMARIZER WITH AZURE OPENAI

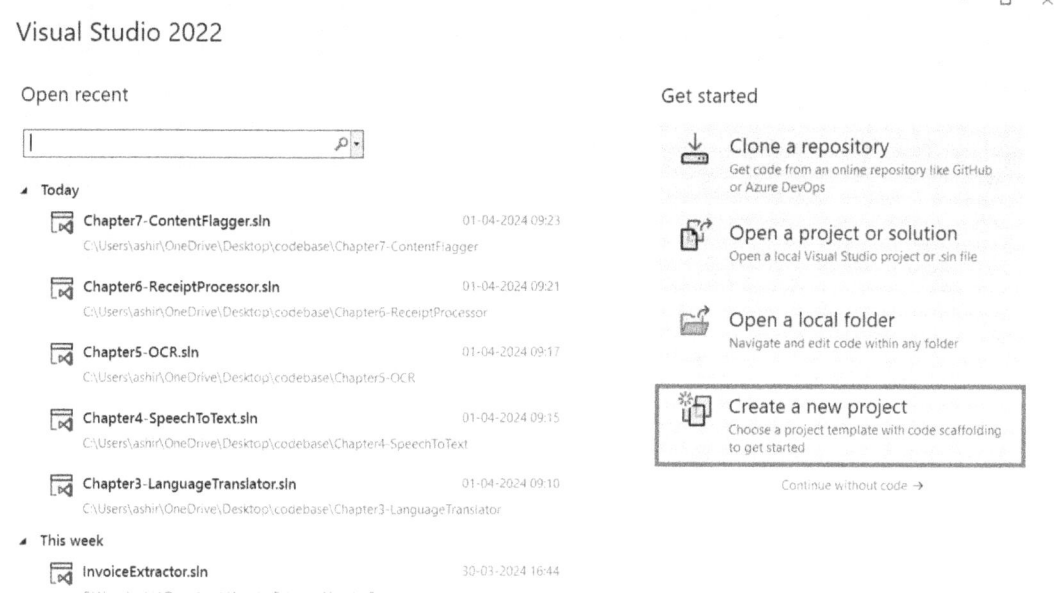

Figure 8-13. *Create a new project*

Select the **ASP.NET Core Web API** project template as shown in Figure 8-14 and click **Next**.

CHAPTER 8   BUILD A TEXT SUMMARIZER WITH AZURE OPENAI

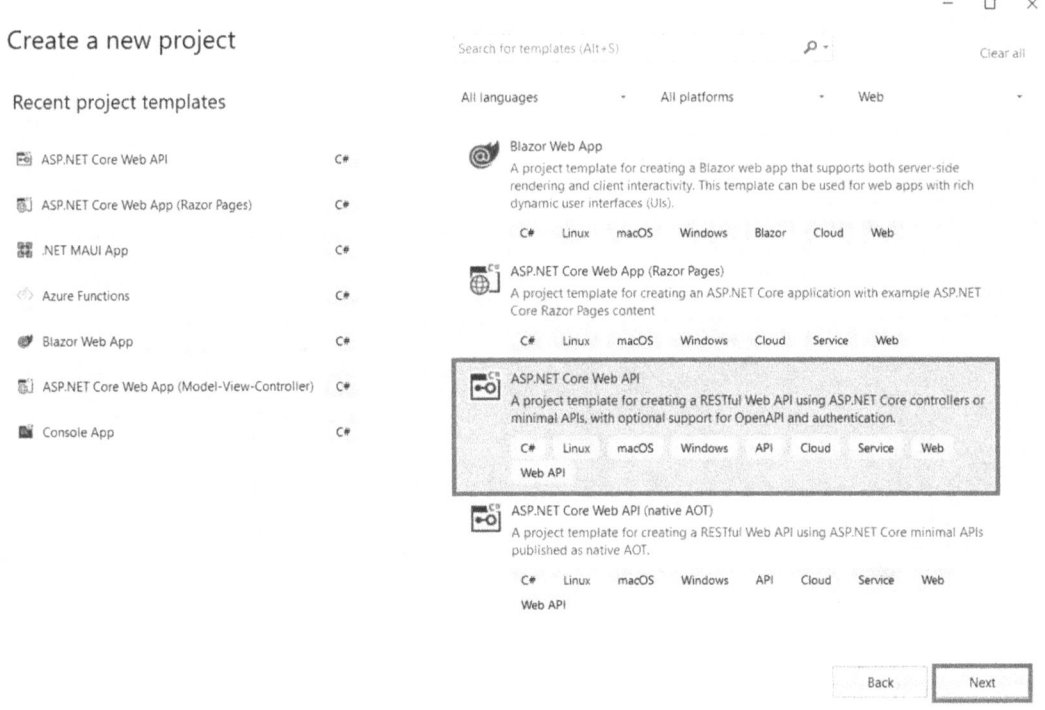

Figure 8-14. *Click Next*

Enter the **project name**, **location**, and **solution name** as shown in Figure 8-15 and click **Next**.

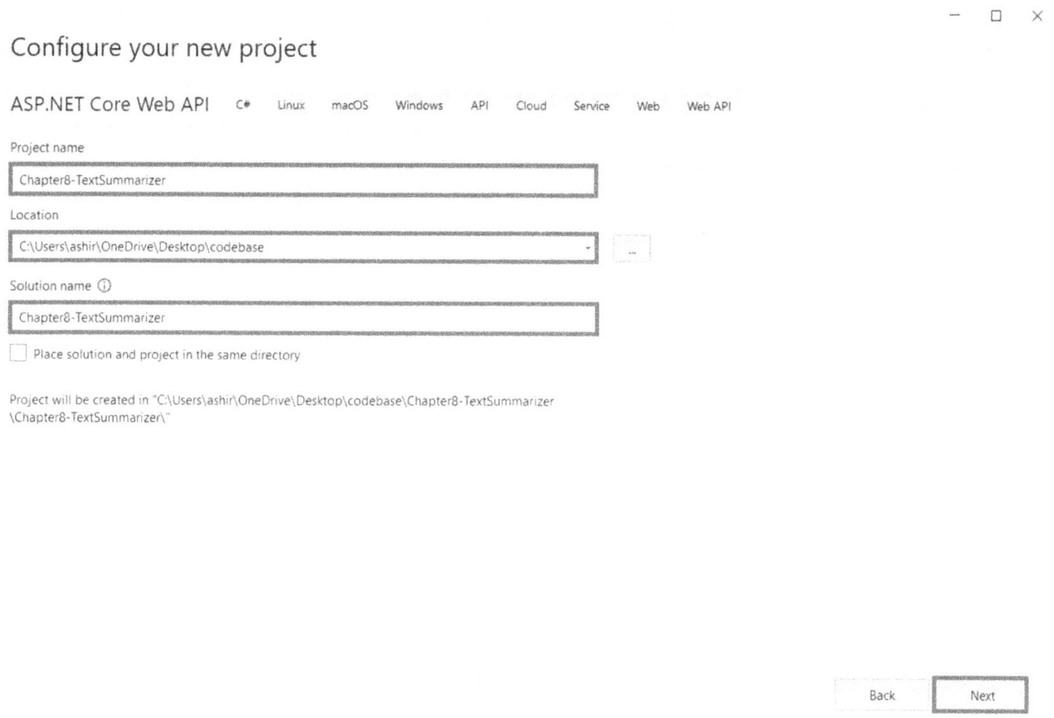

CHAPTER 8　BUILD A TEXT SUMMARIZER WITH AZURE OPENAI

Figure 8-15. Enter the project name, location, and solution name

Now select **.NET 8.0** as the framework and **None** as the authentication type, then check the **Configure for HTTPS**, **Enable OpenAPI support**, **Do not use top-level statements**, and **Use controllers**. Once you are done, click **Create**, as illustrated in Figure 8-16.

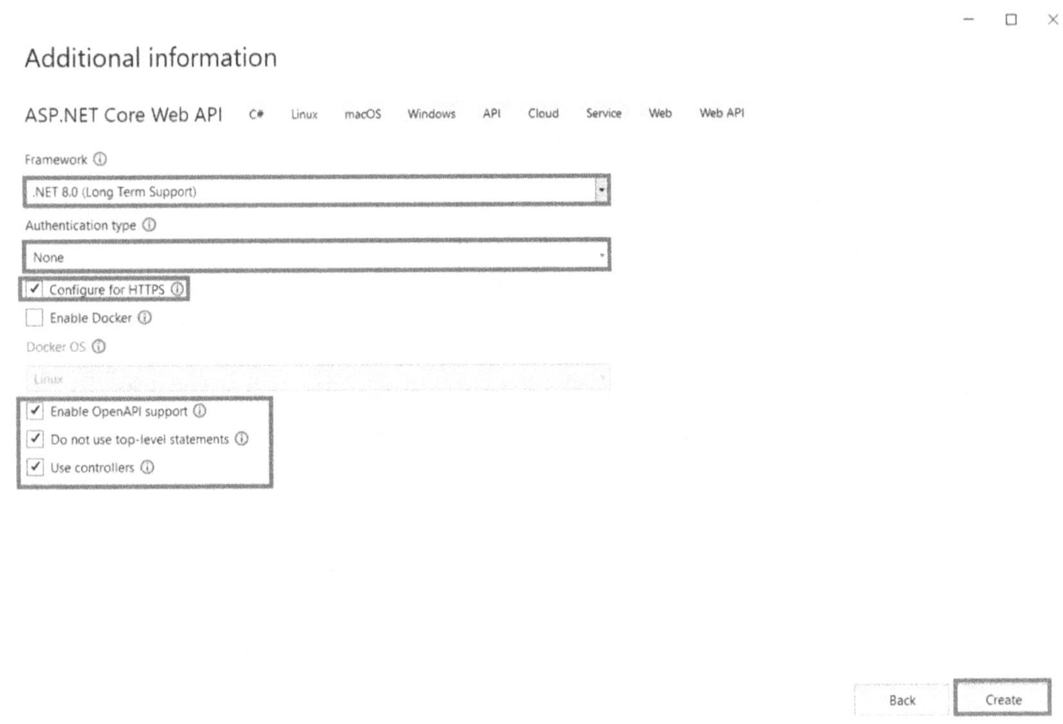

CHAPTER 8   BUILD A TEXT SUMMARIZER WITH AZURE OPENAI

Figure 8-16. Click Create

Now Visual Studio will generate an ASP.NET Core Web API project out of the box. It will contain some boilerplate code for the weatherforecast controller. We can either delete them or ignore them. As a next step, let's add all the packages that we would need to build our solution. To do so, open the NuGet package manager and install the following package:

1. Azure.AI.OpenAI

Azure.AI.OpenAI is the official SDK for the Azure OpenAI service. We will leverage its power to add text summarization capabilities in our application.

After installing the abovementioned NuGet package, let's open the appsettings. json file and then add the AzureOpenAiKey, AzureOpenAiEndpoint, and AzureOpenAiDeploymentName key-value pairs over there. These values are required to authenticate our requests to the Azure OpenAI service. We had fetched these values in the previous section. Let's add these three keys and their values, as demonstrated in Listing 8-1.

Listing 8-1. Add the key-value pairs in appsettings.json

```
{
  "Logging": {
    "LogLevel": {
      "Default": "Information",
      "Microsoft.AspNetCore": "Warning"
    }
  },
  "AllowedHosts": "*",
  "AzureOpenAiKey": "4df090f0a1f84df8baecb39d337511b8",
  "AzureOpenAiEndpoint": "https://apress-text-summarizer.openai.azure.com/",
  "AzureOpenAiDeploymentName": "apress-gpt-35-turbo"
}
```

Please do note that storing function secrets or sensitive information in the appsettings.json file or hard-coding such information in a variable is not advisable. I recommend using a key vault to store application secrets.

Now that we have added the key and endpoint of our Azure OpenAI resource in appsettings.json, let's create a folder called **Model** in our solution. This folder is going to contain our POCO models. For this project, we will have only one POCO class, that is, Payload. Let's create the Payload class inside the Model folder. This model will be used to deserialize the data sent by the user in the request body. The definition for the Payload class can be found in Listing 8-2.

Listing 8-2. Code for Payload.cs

```
namespace Chapter8_TextSummarizer.Model
{
    public class Payload
    {
        public string ArticleData { get; set; }
    }
}
```

Now that we have created the Payload class, let's move our focus toward the business implementation of our application. To do so, let's create a folder called Business in our solution. As a next step, add an interface called IAzureOpenAiBusiness and a class called AzureOpenAiBusiness. AzureOpenAiBusiness is going to implement the IAzureOpenAiBusiness interface. Add the code mentioned in Listing 8-3 in the IAzureOpenAiBusiness interface.

Listing 8-3. Code for IAzureOpenAiBusiness.cs

```
namespace Chapter8_TextSummarizer.Business
{
    public interface IAzureOpenAiBusiness
    {
        public Task<string> GetSummaryAsync(string content);
    }
}
```

The IAzureOpenAiBusiness contains the definition of one method called GetSummaryAsync. This method will take one parameter – content – which represents the article that the user wants to summarize by using our application.

As we have understood the purpose of the GetSummaryAsync method, let's look at its implementation in the AzureOpenAiBusiness class, which is present in Listing 8-4.

Listing 8-4. Code for AzureOpenAiBusiness.cs

```
using Azure;
using Azure.AI.OpenAI;

namespace Chapter8_TextSummarizer.Business
{
    public class AzureOpenAiBusiness : IAzureOpenAiBusiness
    {
        private readonly IConfiguration _configuration;
        private static OpenAIClient openAIClient;
        public AzureOpenAiBusiness(IConfiguration configuration)
        {
            _configuration = configuration;
```

```
            openAIClient = new OpenAIClient(new Uri(_configuration["Azure
            OpenAiEndpoint"]),
                new AzureKeyCredential(_configuration["AzureOpenAiKey"]));
        }
        public async Task<string> GetSummaryAsync(string content)
        {
            var chatCompletionOptions = new ChatCompletionsOptions
            {
                MaxTokens = 400,
                Temperature = 1f,
                FrequencyPenalty = 0.0f,
                PresencePenalty = 0.0f,
                NucleusSamplingFactor = 0.95f,
                DeploymentName = _configuration["AzureOpenAiDeploy
                mentName"]
            };
            string userPrompt = "Please summarize the the following article
            in 60 words or less:\n" + content;
            chatCompletionOptions.Messages.Add(new ChatRequestUserMessage
            (userPrompt));

            ChatCompletions response = await openAIClient.GetChatCompletions
            Async(chatCompletionOptions);
            ChatResponseMessage assistantResponse = response.Choices[0].
            Message;

            return assistantResponse.Content;
        }
    }
}
```

In Listing 8-4, AzureOpenAiBusiness implements the IAzureOpenAiBusiness interface. It utilizes the Azure OpenAI service to generate a summary of articles shared by the end user in textual format. In the constructor, it initializes an OpenAIClient using the endpoint and key present in appsettings.json. We then create a ChatCompletionOption where we define configurations like MaxTokens, Temperature,

FrequencyPenalty, PresencePenalty, NucleusSamplingFactor, and DeploymentName. As per the documentation, a brief definition for each of these configurations is mentioned as follows:

1. **MaxTokens** – This gets the maximum number of tokens to generate.

2. **Temperature** – This sets how creative the answers seem. Higher numbers mean more surprising answers.

3. **FrequencyPenalty** – This gets or sets a value that affects how likely tokens are to appear in generated text based on how often they occur.

4. **NucleusSamplingFactor** – This gets or sets another option called nucleus sampling, which makes the model look at the results of the tokens based on their probability mass.

5. **DeploymentName** – This is the name of the model deployment that we have done in the previous section.

After configuring the ChatCompletionOption, we construct the user prompt and then leverage the GetChatCompletionsAsync method of the OpenAIClient to generate the summary. Once we receive the response, we return it back as the summary for the provided content.

Now that we have written the code for IAzureOpenAiBusiness and AzureOpenAiBusiness, let's go to Program.cs and update the code to register the AzureOpenAiBusiness class as a singleton service for the IAzureOpenAiBusiness interface in the DI container. The updated code for Program.cs is present in Listing 8-5.

Listing 8-5. Updated code for Program.cs

```
using Chapter8_TextSummarizer.Business;

namespace Chapter8_TextSummarizer
{
    public class Program
    {
        public static void Main(string[] args)
        {
```

CHAPTER 8 BUILD A TEXT SUMMARIZER WITH AZURE OPENAI

```
            var builder = WebApplication.CreateBuilder(args);

            // Add services to the container.

            builder.Services.AddControllers();
            builder.Services.AddEndpointsApiExplorer();
            builder.Services.AddSwaggerGen();
            builder.Services.AddSingleton<IAzureOpenAiBusiness,
            AzureOpenAiBusiness>();
            var app = builder.Build();

            // Configure the HTTP request pipeline.
            if (app.Environment.IsDevelopment())
            {
                app.UseSwagger();
                app.UseSwaggerUI();
            }

            app.UseHttpsRedirection();

            app.UseAuthorization();

            app.MapControllers();

            app.Run();
        }
    }
}
```

Having completed the business implementation, injected the required services into the DI container, configured the key and endpoint in our appsettings.json file, and defined the Payload class, we can now focus on creating our REST endpoint to provide an endpoint to other systems to analyze their content by leveraging the business logic that we have implemented. To do so, let's create an empty API controller inside the Controllers folder of our solution. Let's name it SummarizeController. Inside this controller, add the code shared in Listing 8-6.

193

Listing 8-6. Code for SummarizeController.cs

```csharp
using Chapter8_TextSummarizer.Business;
using Chapter8_TextSummarizer.Model;
using Microsoft.AspNetCore.Http;
using Microsoft.AspNetCore.Mvc;

namespace Chapter8_TextSummarizer.Controllers
{
    [Route("api/[controller]")]
    [ApiController]
    public class SummarizeController : ControllerBase
    {
        private readonly IAzureOpenAiBusiness _azureOpenAiBusiness;
        public SummarizeController(IAzureOpenAiBusiness azureOpenAiBusiness)
        {
            _azureOpenAiBusiness = azureOpenAiBusiness;
        }
        [HttpPost(Name = "GetSummary")]
        public async Task<IActionResult> GetSummary([FromBody] Payload requestPayload)
        {
            if (string.IsNullOrEmpty(requestPayload.ArticleData))
            {
                return BadRequest("Article data cannot be empty.");
            }

            var summary = await _azureOpenAiBusiness.GetSummaryAsync(requestPayload.ArticleData);

            return Ok(summary);
        }
    }
}
```

CHAPTER 8   BUILD A TEXT SUMMARIZER WITH AZURE OPENAI

In Listing 8-6, we are injecting an instance of the IAzureOpenAiBusiness via constructor injection to interact with the business logic for content summarization. The controller contains an action method, **GetSummary**, which gets invoked every time someone makes a POST request to the **api/summarize/GetSummary** endpoint. It accepts data from the request body which can be deserialized to the payload type. It represents the text content to be summarized. It then delegates the content summarization to the injected business service and returns the result back to the end user.

Now that we have written the code for our solution, in the next section we will test it out.

Test the Text Summarizer App

To test the content-flagging app, we will have to run the Web API project. Once the project runs, it should route you to the swagger page. Over there, we need to expand the API endpoint, **/api/summarizer/GetSummary**, and click Try it out. After that, we will add the value to the request body field. You can add any textual content that you want to summarize. I have passed the JSON in the request body as shown in Listing 8-7.

Listing 8-7. Request payload for test

```
{
  "articleData": "Boosting productivity doesn't have to be complicated. Start by setting clear goals to provide direction and focus. Prioritize tasks based on their importance and urgency to make the most of your time. Implement time blocking techniques to allocate specific periods for different activities, ensuring you stay on track. Identify and minimize distractions to maintain concentration, and don't forget to take regular breaks to recharge your mind. By incorporating these simple steps into your routine, you can enhance productivity and achieve your goals more efficiently, leading to greater success in both work and life."
}
```

Once done, click Execute as shown in Figure 8-17.

CHAPTER 8   BUILD A TEXT SUMMARIZER WITH AZURE OPENAI

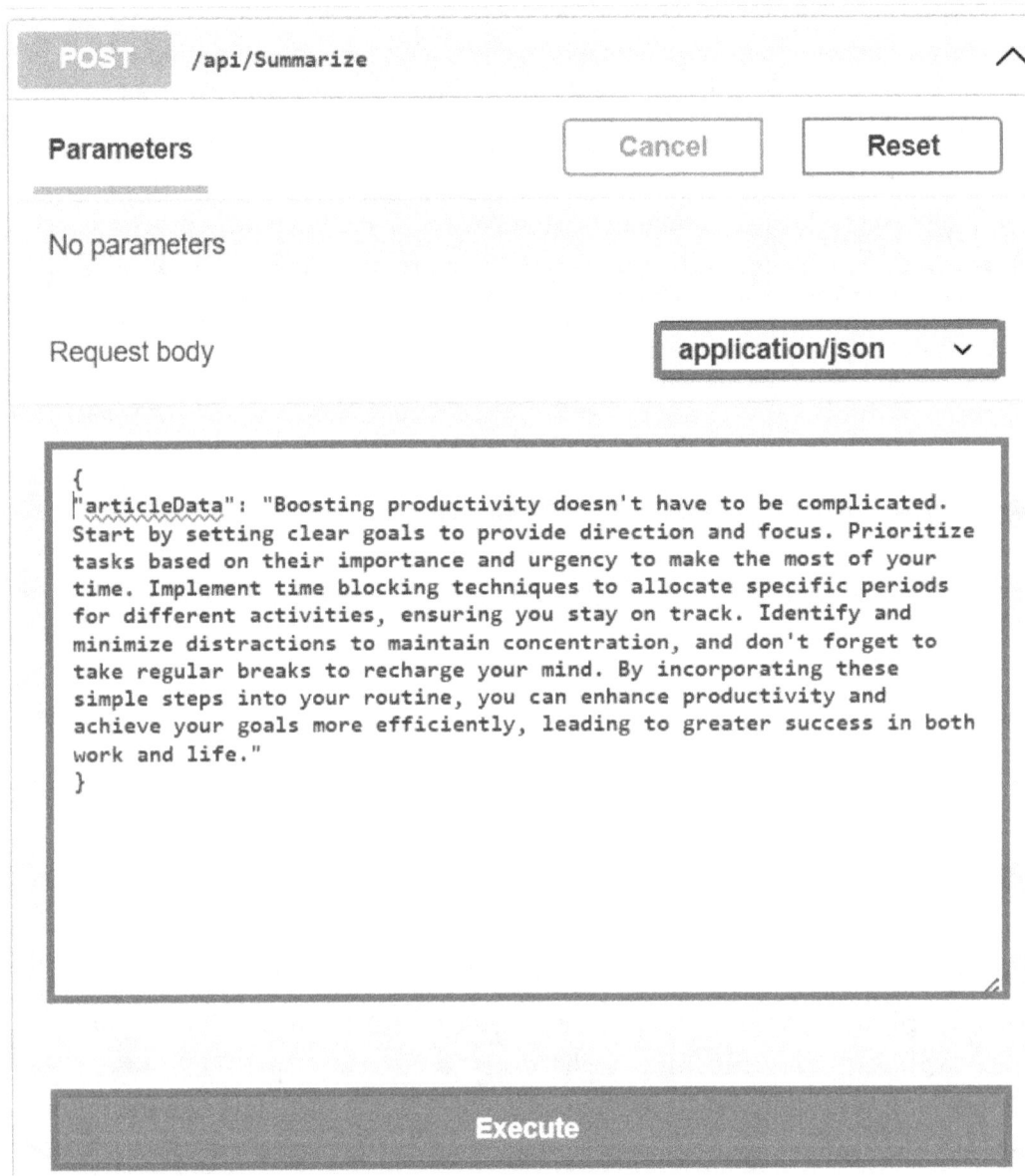

Figure 8-17. Click Execute

Once the API call has been executed, we can view the result in the Responses section. The API should return a string representing the summary of the content we had shared in the request body. We can verify this in the response of the API as shown in Figure 8-18.

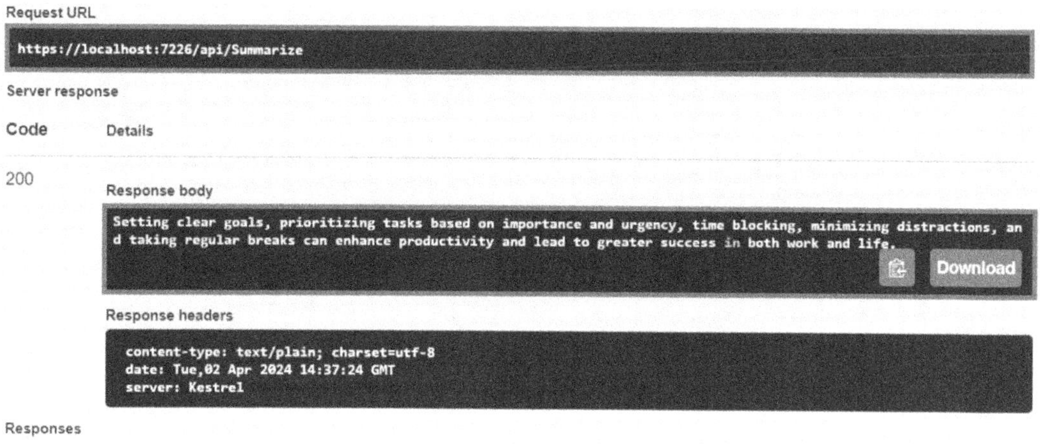

Figure 8-18. View response from the API

As can be seen from Figure 8-18, our text summarizer app was able to creatively summarize the textual content passed by the user in the request body. I hope you enjoyed the chapter.

Summary

In this chapter, you've gained insights into creating intelligent solutions using the ASP. NET Core Web API and the Azure OpenAI service through the development of a Web API to generate summaries from textual content. Our exploration delved into the Azure OpenAI service and the various models offered as part of it, uncovering its features and applications. Additionally, we navigated through the steps of provisioning an Azure OpenAI service within the Azure Portal as well as explored ways to deploy a model using the Azure OpenAI Studio. Throughout this process, we've acquired knowledge on constructing an intelligent solution by harnessing the capabilities of the Azure OpenAI service. The primary focus of this chapter centered around the text summarization functionality offered by the Azure OpenAI service.

Index

A, B

Artificial intelligence (AI)
    aspects, 1
    Azure Cognitive Search, 4
    Azure Services, 3
    Bot Service, 6
    computational systems, 2
    Content Safety (*see* Content Safety service)
    Custom Vision, 8
    Document Intelligence, 7, 111 (*see also* Document Intelligence service)
    Face service, 9
    futuristic concept, 2
    Immersive Reader, 7
    intelligent solutions, 1
    language service, 5, 12 (*see also* Language service)
    objcctives, 2
    OpenAI, 4
    product recognition, 9
    Speech service, 5, 67
    subfields, 2
    Translator (*see* Translator service)
    Video Indexer, 8
    Vision service, 8, 90 (*see also* Vision service)

C

Content Safety service, 6
    aspects, 145
    categories, 146
    cloud-based service, 146
    create button, 149, 150, 152
    development activities, 148
    ecommerce website, 147
    fictional social media, 147
    flagging app
        appsettings.json, 160
        ContentFlaggerController.cs, 165
        create button, 159
        execute button, 166
        IAzureAiContentSafetyBusiness class, 161–163
        name/location/solution name, 158
        packages, 159
        Program.cs, 163, 164
        project creation, 155, 156
        ResponseDto.cs, 160
        template, 156, 157
        testing process, 166, 167
        view response, 167
    key and endpoint, 153–155
    key features, 146, 147
    objectives, 146
    requirement, 148

Content Safety service (*cont.*)
   resource button, 152, 153
   search box, 149
   social media platforms, 147
   subscription/resource group, 150, 151

D, E, F, G, H, I, J, K

Desktop app
   audio files (*see* Speech service)
   create button, 81
   MainPage.xaml, 81–83
   name/location/solution name, 80
   .NET MAUI app, 79
   objectives, 90
   project creation, 78
   structure, 89
   testing process, 85–87
   transcribe button, 86
   UI development workload, 78
   XAML source code, 83–85
Document Intelligence service
   aspects, 111
   create button, 115
   development activities, 114
   financial institution, 113
   Form Recognizer, 112
   healthcare record analysis, 113
   key features, 112, 113
   keys and endpoint, 118–120
   objectives, 112
   requirement, 114
   resource button, 116–118
   resource/time-consuming process, 114
   search bar, 115
   subscription/resource group, 116
   web app (*see* Web app)

L

Language-based document, 12
Language service
   aspects, 12
   creation, 16, 19
   development activities, 14
   document classifier app, 30
      BlobServiceClient/TextAnalytics Client, 35, 36
      create button, 33
      destination container, 40, 41
      DocumentClassifier.cs, 36, 37
      DocumentClassifier function, 41
      local.settings.json, 34
      Next button, 31
      packages, 33
      project creation, 30
      project name/location/solution name, 32
      source container, 39, 42
      testing process, 38–42
   key features, 13, 14
   keys and endpoint, 21, 22
   problem statement, 14
   proof of concept (PoC), 17
   requirement, 14
   resource, 16
   resource group, 17, 20
   search bar, 15
   sentiment analysis, 13
   storage accounts
      access keys, 29
      blob containers, 28
      connection string, 29
      containers, 26
      create button, 23, 25, 28
      destination, 28

INDEX

Go to resource, 26
review button, 24
search box, 22
subscription and resource
    group, 17, 18
Large language models (LLMs), 11,
    169, 170

M

Multi-language text translator app
    create button, 56
    ITranslatorBusiness.cs, 58
    name/location/solution name, 54, 55
    packages, 56
    Payload.cs, 61
    Program.cs file, 57, 58, 60
    project creation, 53
    template, 53, 54
    testing process, 64, 65
    TranslatorBusiness.cs, 59
    Translator.cs, 62, 63
    TranslatorKey and TranslatorRegion
        keys, 57

N

Named entity recognition (NER), 5, 13
Natural language processing (NLP),
    5, 11, 12
.NET Multi-platform app
    create button, 102, 103
    demo image, 109
    extract text button, 108, 109
    MainPage.xaml, 103–105
    name/location/solution name,
        101, 102
    package, 103

project creation, 100
source code, 105–107
template, 101
testing process, 107–109
UI development workload, 99, 100
See also Desktop app
Neural machine translation (NMT), 44

O

OpenAI services
    capabilities, 170
    create button, 173, 174
    deployment creation, 182, 183
    development activities, 173
    features, 171
    keys and endpoint, 179, 180
    key terminologies, 170, 171
    model deployments, 180, 181, 184
    models, 171
    network access, 175, 176
    objectives, 170
    proof of concept, 172
    requirement, 172
    resource tab, 178, 179
    search bar, 173
    structure, 169
    subscription and resource group,
        174, 175
    tags, 176, 177
    text summarizer (*see* Text
        summarizer app)
    validation check, 177, 178

P, Q, R

Personally identifiable information (PII), 13
Provisioned throughput units (PTUs), 174

S

Speech service
  create button, 72, 74
  development activities, 70
  key features, 68, 69
  keys and endpoint, 75–77
  newspapers/magazines, 70
  objectives, 68
  real-time audio translation, 69
  requirement, 70
  resource button, 74, 75
  search bar, 71
  structure, 67
  subscription and resource group, 72, 73
  voice-based biometrics, 69

T, U

Text summarization, 5, 169, 188
Text summarizer app
  appsettings.json, 189
  AzureOpenAiBusiness.cs, 190, 191
  configuration, 186–188
  definition, 192
  IAzureOpenAiBusiness.cs, 190
  packages, 188
  Payload.cs, 189
  Program.cs, 192, 193
  project creation, 184, 185
  SummarizeController.cs, 194
  template, 185, 186
  testing process, 195–197
Translator service, 6
  create button, 48, 50
  development activities, 47
  education/e-learning, 46
  global business communication, 46
  key features, 45
  keys and endpoint, 51, 52
  leveraging information, 46
  multi-language text app (*see* Multi-language text translator app)
  objectives, 44
  requirement, 47
  resource button, 51
  search bar, 47, 48
  structure, 44
  subscription/resource group, 49

V

Vision service
  artifacts/historical documents., 92
  computer vision, 93
  computer vision tasks, 90
  create button, 94, 96
  development activities, 92
  document digitization/processing, 91
  key features, 90, 91
  keys and endpoint, 97–99
  requirement, 92
  resource button, 96, 97
  subscription and resource group, 94, 95
  traffic congestions and safety, 91

W, X, Y, Z

Web app
  appsettings.json, 125, 126
  create button, 124
  DisplayFile.cshtml, 132, 133
  DisplayFile.cshtml.cs, 134, 135
  extract data, 120

FileUpload.cshtml, 136
FileUpload.cshtml.cs, 137, 138
IInvoiceProcessor.cs, 127
Invoice.cs, 127, 128
InvoiceProcessor.cs, 128–130
invoices page, 141, 142
Layout.cshtml class, 139, 141

name/location/solution name, 123
packages, 124
Program.cs, 125, 126, 130, 131
project creation, 121
template, 121, 122
testing process, 141–143
values extraction, 143

GPSR Compliance

The European Union's (EU) General Product Safety Regulation (GPSR) is a set of rules that requires consumer products to be safe and our obligations to ensure this.

If you have any concerns about our products, you can contact us on

ProductSafety@springernature.com

In case Publisher is established outside the EU, the EU authorized representative is:

Springer Nature Customer Service Center GmbH
Europaplatz 3
69115 Heidelberg, Germany